WOMEN AND MUSIC IN IRELAND

Irish Musical Studies

Series Editors:
Lorraine Byrne Bodley (Maynooth University)
Harry White (University College Dublin)

Irish Musical Studies publishes monographs and edited volumes reflecting the plurality and presence of Irish music across history and in the present moment. The series seeks to understand Irish musical practice not only as an expression of Irish, British and North American cultural history, but as an art form whose identity and meaning have been shaped, determined and sometimes silenced by political, religious and social forces from the middle ages to the early twenty-first century.

The series also seeks to enlist biographical, cultural and gender studies, in addition to studies in popular culture, ethnology and film studies in order to deepen the scholarly reception of music as a primary signature and preoccupation of Irish identity in a host of historical and global contexts. Although volumes in the series will clearly be addressed to a wide academic constituency of music history and musicology, the series will also publish monographs and collections which speak to a more general readership in Irish studies. Books in the series embrace art, popular and traditional/folk music.

Proposals or queries should be sent in the first instance to Professors Lorraine Byrne Bodley and Harry White or Boydell & Brewer at the addresses shown below.

Professor Lorraine Byrne Bodley
Department of Music, Maynooth University, Co Kildare,
Republic of Ireland
email: lorraine.byrnebodley@mu.ie

Professor Harry White
University College Dublin, School of Music, Newman Building, Belfield,
Dublin 4, Republic of Ireland
email: harry.white@ucd.ie

Michael Middeke, Editorial Director, Boydell & Brewer Ltd, Bridge
Farm Business Park, Top Street, Martlesham IP12 4RB, UK
email: mmiddeke@boydell.co.uk

Previously published volumes in this series are listed at the back of this volume.

Women and Music in Ireland

Edited by
Jennifer O'Connor-Madsen, Laura Watson and Ita Beausang

SMI society for musicology in ireland
aontas ceoleolaíochta na héireann

THE BOYDELL PRESS

First published 2022
The Boydell Press, Woodbridge

ISBN 978 1 78327 755 1

The Boydell Press is an imprint of Boydell & Brewer Ltd
PO Box 9, Woodbridge, Suffolk IP12 3DF, UK
and of Boydell & Brewer Inc.
668 Mt Hope Avenue, Rochester, NY 14620–2731, USA
website: www.boydellandbrewer.com

A CIP catalogue record for this book is available
from the British Library

CONTENTS

LIST OF FIGURES

LIST OF TABLES

ACKNOWLEDGEMENTS

The successful undertaking of a large collaborative project such as an edited volume depends upon the input and support of many individuals and organisations over an extended period. This is especially true in the case of this book, which came to fruition over the course of a few years following a three-part conference series that originated over a decade ago. Thank you to everyone who contributed to the success of the conferences. In Maynooth University, thanks to Barra Boydell and Fiona Palmer who supported and encouraged the conference and this project from the very beginning. In the RIAM, thank you to Deborah Kelleher for her belief and interest. In Dublin City University, thank you to John O'Flynn and Rhona Clarke for their encouragement and contributions. The conferences would not have been what they were without the many performances that brought the music to life – in this regard, special thank you to Una Hunt, Jane O'Leary and Concorde, Tony Byrne and the late Elizabeth Pink.

The editors wish to express their gratitude to Lorraine Byrne Bodley and Harry White, the series editors of Irish Musical Studies, for their invaluable support, advice, and championing of the book. It is a deep honour to see *Women and Music in Ireland* published as the inaugural book in the 'new' Irish Musical Studies series. We are very grateful to all at Boydell & Brewer who have played a part in steering this book to completion – especially Michael Middeke, commissioning editor, and Elizabeth Howard, assistant editor, who patiently offered guidance and assistance with various queries. We extend further thanks to the anonymous readers of the manuscript for their thoughtful and constructive feedback.

Publication would not be possible without the generosity of key academic institutions and societies in this country. Grants in support of publication costs were kindly awarded by the National University of Ireland Publication Scheme and the Society for Musicology in Ireland (SMI). We are indebted to the SMI, particularly the President John O'Flynn and his predecessor Lorraine Byrne Bodley, for supporting the development of the book and series.

Antonio Cascelli, Head of the Music Department at Maynooth University, and colleagues in the Music Department encouraged and facilitated the development of this book in many ways. Many thanks to

Laoise Doherty in the RIAM, Lisa Fitzpatrick in Maynooth University and colleagues in Sing Ireland for their positivity and encouragement.

Many colleagues in libraries, archives, educational settings, and arts and media organisations around the country generously shared their time and expertise. We are grateful to staff in the following institutions for facilitating access to manuscripts, scores, catalogues, and images: RTÉ Archives; National Gallery of Ireland; Royal Irish Academy of Music Library; Manuscripts and Archives Research Library at Trinity College, Dublin; National Library of Ireland. Further support for research which informed the book was provided by the Diana Ambache Charitable Trust and the Arts Council of Ireland. As well as the organisations mentioned above, numerous individuals generously gave of their time and expertise, including Claire Cunningham, Úna Hunt, Roy Stanley, Jane Maxwell, Philip Shields, Katie Rowan, Iain Burnside, Ronald Corp, the ConTempo Quartet, David Byers, David Rhodes, and David Scott. Thanks to Michael Lydon for his work on the index.

The editors are indebted to family and friends for their love and support throughout this project. Jenny: for Declan, Conor, and Amelia: thank you for everything. Thanks to my family the O'Connors and the Madsens. Laura: thanks, as ever, to my parents Brenda and Richard; to my siblings Nicola, Miriam, and Adam; and special thanks to Mark. Ita: thanks to my siblings Edmund, James, Patrick, and Mary Hogan; and my children Mary, Patrick, Anne, Nora, Edmund, David, and Clare.

September 2022

CONTRIBUTORS

Ita Beausang is a PhD graduate of University College Cork and emeritus lecturer at Technological University Dublin. Her main research interests are concentrated on contextual studies of music in Ireland in the eighteenth and nineteenth centuries. Her book *Anglo-Irish Music 1780–1830* is the standard work on the period. She acted as research assistant to Aloys Fleischmann for his chapter in the *New History of Ireland* vol. 6 and has contributed articles to *Irish Musical Studies* vols 5, 9 and 12. She was an advisory editor for the *Encyclopaedia of Music in Ireland*. Her book *Ina Boyle (1889–1967): A Composer's Life*, with co-author Séamas de Barra, was published by Cork University Press in 2018. In 2010 she was awarded honorary life membership of the Society for Musicology in Ireland.

Rhona Clarke was born in Dublin. She studied music at University College, Dublin and has a PhD from Queen's University, Belfast. Her output includes choral, chamber, orchestral and electronic works. She has received commissions from the RTÉ National Symphony Orchestra, the Sydney Philharmonia Chorus, Chamber Choir Ireland, the Choir of the Chapels Royal, the Cork International Choral Festival, Hard Rain Soloists, Concorde, Music Network, and the National Concert Hall, among others. Her work has been performed and broadcast throughout Ireland and worldwide. Since 2009 she has been collaborating with visual artist Marie Hanlon on short experimental films with music, live music with visual projections and joint exhibitions. A portrait CD of her chamber music, *A Different Game* (Fidelio Trio), was released in March 2017. In February 2022, a new CD of Clarke's choral music performed by the State Choir Latvija was released. Rhona Clarke is a member of Aosdána, Ireland's affiliation of creative artists.

Barbara Jillian Dignam is Assistant Professor in Music in the School of Theology, Philosophy and Music at Dublin City University (DCU). She holds a PhD in musicology from Maynooth University. Her research explores twentieth- and twenty-first-century musics that intersect music, language and digital technologies in her investigation of, among other things, human interactions with cultural output and the relationships and processes underpinning them. She contributed to *The Encyclopaedia of Music in Ireland* (2013) and has published on contemporary music in

Ireland in *TEMPO* and in *Irish Musical Studies 11: Irish Musical Analysis* (Dublin, 2014). Barbara is principal editor of *Creative Impulses, Cultural Accents: Brian Boydell's Music, Advocacy, Painting and Legacy* (Dublin, 2021). Barbara sits on the Council of the Society for Musicology in Ireland and is chair of the SMI Grants committee (2021–24).

Margarethe Engelhardt-Krajanek is a cultural scientist. She studied at the University of Music and Performing Arts in Vienna and communication and aesthetics at Bergische Universität Wuppertal/ Germany. Since 1993 she has been a science journalist at the Cultural Program Ö1 of the Austrian Broadcasting Cooperation ORF. She has published a number of works on the sociology of music and other music-related topics. She has received national and international prizes for her radio programmes. In 2000 she published a biography of the Irish composer Mary Dickenson-Auner, *A Life with the Violin*.

Daithí Kearney is an ethnomusicologist, geographer and performer. He is lecturer in music and co-director of the Centre for Creative Arts Research at Dundalk Institute of Technology. His research is primarily focused on Irish traditional music but extends to performance studies, community music, music education and the connection between music and place. Recent publications include contributions to the *Companion to Irish Traditional Music* (2012), *Ancestral Imprints* (2012), the *Encyclopaedia of Music in Ireland* (2013), *Spacing Ireland* (2013) and *New Crops Old Fields* (2016). He has also contributed to the *Journal of the Society for Musicology in Ireland, Ethnomusicology Ireland, The Yearbook for Traditional Music, Popular Music* and *Estudios Irlandeses*.

Axel Klein is an independent researcher. He is the author of the monographs *Swan Hennessy: Bird of Time* (Mainz, 2019) and *O'Kelly: An Irish Musical Family in Nineteenth-Century France* (Norderstedt, 2014); co-editor of *Irish Music in the Twentieth Century (Irish Musical Studies 7)* (Dublin, 2003); and has contributed many more articles to encyclopaedias and edited collections. Klein was elected a Corresponding Member of the Society for Musicology in Ireland in 2015. In May 2022 he was awarded a DMus *honoris causa* by the National University of Ireland.

Helen Lawlor (neé Lyons) lectures in music at the Technological University Dublin Conservatory of Music and Drama. She has previously lectured in ethnomusicology, Irish music and music education at Dundalk Institute of Technology. Helen is author of *Irish Harping 1900–2010* (2012), and co-editor of *Harp Studies: Perspectives on the Irish Harp* (2016) and *Harp Studies II: World Harp Traditions* (forthcoming). She has contributed articles to *The Encyclopaedia of Music in Ireland, Ancestral Imprints, Sonus,*

American Harp Journal, *JSMI* and *JMI*. She is the executive editor of the *Journal of the Society for Musicology in Ireland* and is an advisory board member of *Irish Musical Studies*. She was chairperson of ICTM (Ireland) from 2019 to 2021. Helen holds a BMusEd (TCD), MMus (UCD), and a PhD in music from UCD for which she was awarded an *Ad astra* research scholarship. Helen plays Irish harp, specialising in traditional Irish music.

Nicola LeFanu has composed over a hundred works, which have been widely played, broadcasted and recorded; her music is published by Novello and by Edition Peters. She has been commissioned by the BBC, by festivals in the UK and beyond, and by leading orchestras, ensembles and soloists. Her catalogue includes a number of works for string ensemble, and chamber music for a wide variety of mediums, often including voice. She has a particular affinity for vocal music and has composed eight operas. Her mother was the composer Elizabeth Maconchy. LeFanu studied at Oxford, RCM and, as a Harkness Fellow, at Harvard.

Karol Mullaney-Dignam is a lecturer in the Department of History at the University of Limerick. She is Course Director of the MA in Public History and Cultural Heritage. Her research interests lie in the cultural and social history of Irish music in the long nineteenth and twentieth centuries, as well as contemporary public history narratives and practices. Her work has been supported by the Irish Research Council and Royal Irish Academy. Recent publications include chapters in *Sound Heritage: Making Music Matter in Historic Houses* (2021); *Irish Musical Studies 12: Documents of Irish Music History in the Long Nineteenth Century* (2019); and *Music Preferred: Essays in Musicology, Cultural History and Analysis in Honour of Harry White* (2018).

Jennifer O'Connor-Madsen holds a BA, an MA and a PhD in musicology from Maynooth University. Her doctoral thesis, completed in 2010, explores the role of women and music in nineteenth-century Dublin. She is the founder and organiser of the Women and Music in Ireland conference series and has contributed to numerous RTÉ Lyric FM documentaries on the subject. She has spoken at conferences both nationally and internationally and has contributed articles to the *Journal of the IAWM* (2010), the *Lexikon Europäische Instrumentalistinnen des 18. und 19. Jahrhunderts* (2012) as well as multiple articles for the *Encyclopaedia of Music in Ireland* (2013). She is currently artistic and operations manager with Sing Ireland.

Mary Louise O'Donnell is a musician and musicologist who has performed extensively as a soloist and with various ensembles. Her first book, *Ireland's Harp: The Shaping of Irish Identity c. 1770–1880*, was published in 2014. Mary Louise has received awards and grants to further her research, including an Irish Research Council Postdoctoral Fellowship, Fulbright Scholarship, Centre Culturel Irlandais Fellowship and a Dobbin Scholarship (Ireland Canada University Foundation). In 2019, she was appointed Musician-in-Residence with Fingal County Council. Mary Louise frequently performs with her sister Teresa; their album *Heavenly Harps, Heavenly Cloths: Contemporary Music for the Irish Harp by Brian Boydell* was released in 2020.

Teresa O'Donnell is a harpist and musicologist. She has performed with the Irish Chamber Orchestra. She has previously lectured at Dublin City University. Her research is published in the *Journal of the Society for Musicology in Ireland*, the *Journal of Music Research Onli*ne and the *American Harp Journal*. She co-authored with her sister, Mary Louise O'Donnell, *Sisters of the Revolutionaries: The Story of Margaret and Mary Brigid Pearse* (2017). In 2021, Teresa was awarded a PhD scholarship from the Irish Institute of Catholic Studies, Mary Immaculate College, Limerick.

Tes Slominski is an avid fiddle player and the founder of the Blue Ridge Irish Music School in Charlottesville, Virginia. She completed her PhD, entitled 'Music, Gender, and the Public Sphere in Twentieth-Century Ireland' at New York University in 2010. Her dissertation investigates the social and political forces that allowed or denied Irish women instrumentalists access to public traditional music performance opportunities in the early and mid-twentieth century. Tes was awarded an ACLS Recent Doctoral Recipients Fellowship in 2011 and her book, *Trad Nation: Gender, Sexuality, and Race in Irish Traditional Music*, was published in 2020.

Ruth Stanley has lectured at the Department of Keyboard Studies at MTU Cork School of Music. She served on the Council of the Society for Musicology in Ireland from 2015 to 2018. In 2011 she was conferred with a PhD from Queen's University, Belfast, where she received a DEL postgraduate scholarship, Lamor-University Scholarship and Harrison Bursary. She holds a Master's degree from Mary Immaculate College, Limerick, BMus degree from CIT Cork School of Music, and LRSM diploma in piano performance. Ruth's research focuses on the history of classical, popular and traditional musics in Ireland and Northern Ireland in the twentieth century, especially pertaining to broadcasting and issues of identity. Her published work includes contributions to the *Encyclopaedia of Music in Ireland* (2013) and *Music and Identity in Ireland* (2014).

Laura Watson is Associate Professor of Music at Maynooth University. She is the author of *Paul Dukas: Composer and Critic* (Woodbridge, 2019) and co-editor of *Paul Dukas: Legacies of a French Musician* (Abingdon, 2019). Her current research focuses on women, gender and music in the twentieth and twenty-first centuries and on popular musicians' memoirs. Her research is published in journals such as *Popular Music and Society, Twentieth-Century Music* and *Journal of the Society for Musicology in Ireland*. Recent book chapters feature in *Made in Ireland: Studies in Popular Music* (2020) and *Music, Memory and Memoir* (2019). Laura is a member of the editorial board for the *Journal of the Society for Musicology in Ireland* and has twice been elected to the Council of the Society for Musicology in Ireland. She is a co-founder of Sounding the Feminists, a volunteer group that campaigns for gender equality in music in Ireland.

PREFACE

Women and Music in Ireland is the inaugural volume of the new series of *Irish Musical Studies*, published by Boydell & Brewer. The original series, published initially by Irish Academic Press (from 1990 until 1995) and subsequently by Four Courts Press (from 1996 until 2019) comprised twelve volumes, making this new volume the thirteenth in all to appear. Each volume of the original series was designed to explore specific themes within the general domain of Irish musical scholarship, including the development of musicology as an Irish discipline, music and Irish cultural history, documents and sources of Irish musical history, the growth of theory and analysis in Ireland, as well as period-based collections devoted to Irish art music in the seventeenth, nineteenth and twentieth centuries. Two volumes of conference proceedings also appeared, one to mark the first international musicological conference in the history of the state in 1995 and the other to publish selected papers in Bach scholarship originally presented at the Ninth Biennial Conference on Baroque Music held at Trinity College Dublin in 2000. The series also featured an anthology of Irish church music, preceded by a companion volume of essays on the same subject.

The distinguishing feature of these volumes was that all of them, with the exception of the Bach volume, addressed topics that had hitherto received little or no previous scholarly attention, and certainly not to the extent of a collected volume of essays exclusively concerned with the topic in question. In this specific regard, *Women and Music in Ireland* is likewise a pioneering collection, and it thereby reflects the pervasive ambition of the series as a whole to open out and indeed to deepen our scholarly comprehension of Irish musical life. As the chapters in this new volume individually and collectively attest, the general discourse of women and music here attains not only to an Irish inflection of purpose and scholarly enquiry, but a decisive retrieval of the role of women in shaping the complexion of Irish musical life from the eighteenth century to the present day.

In this enterprise, many of the essays published here skilfully interrogate or deconstruct historical, social and cultural assumptions that have either eclipsed or distorted – often through the agency of gender politics

– the originality and significance of women to the profession and practice of music in Ireland. But this book transcends the prejudices and retrievals it so strikingly comprehends. It situates Irish music and music in Ireland within the domain of feminist theory and critique, and thereby both reconfigures and enlarges the meaning of Irish music itself. The singular nature of this intellectual originality enriches in turn *Irish Musical Studies* as a whole. There could scarcely be a more opportune or timely volume with which to inaugurate this new series, for which Jennifer O'Connor-Madsen, Laura Watson, Ita Beausang and their contributors have our ardent thanks.

Lorraine Byrne Bodley and Harry White
Series Editors, Irish Musical Studies

Introduction

Laura Watson, Jennifer O'Connor-Madsen and Ita Beausang

Women and Music in Ireland portrays an ever-changing kaleidoscope of women's musical work and leisure activities in Ireland over the course of several centuries, from the sixteenth century to the present day. Such a long trajectory naturally encompasses many shifts in Ireland's political formation, social structures, economic fortunes, cultural values and practices, and demographics. Centuries of British colonialism, until independence was achieved (for twenty-six counties) in the early twentieth century, and entrenched patterns of emigration further shaped the country's identity and positioning in the global consciousness. The enacting of partition in 1921 led to the formation of Northern Ireland as a British jurisdiction, distinct from the independent Republic of Ireland. Regardless of politically constructed borders in Ireland, this book is concerned with women and music across the island. As part of this it is attentive to figures such as Alicia Needham and Joan Trimble, who spent much of their lives in what is now Northern Ireland and in Great Britain. The peripherality of Ireland as an island nation prompted many musicians to develop their careers internationally. Mary Dickenson-Auner, for example, cultivated a reputation as a violinist and composer across continental Europe, with only occasional visits back to the country of her birth where she was less well-known.

While some Irish musicians made an impact on music education and concert life abroad, others, such as Annie Patterson, remained in the country and committed to building infrastructures here. Some of these were formal entities, such as annual festivals, and therefore highly visible; the most famous example is the Feis Ceoil, which Patterson co-founded. Other infrastructures were less formal, however, and sustained by networks of women whose names have largely been forgotten today. Examples of these include 'schools' or 'academies' of music run from the home by women for whom teaching was one of their many domestic roles. A handful of women held official teaching posts at the prestigious Royal Irish Academy of Music (RIAM), while a few others contributed to the institution in a less recognised way in their capacity as assistants to male professors.

Social expectations of most women confining their musical pursuits to a private setting permeated traditional music as much as it did classical/ art music, with the result that women's contributions to that genre were often rendered invisible. This is despite the reality that women played a central role in sustaining the tradition, by teaching and passing the torch from one generation to the next. A notable exception to the tendency to minimise the role of women and girls in traditional music can be seen in attitudes towards the Irish harp. The instrument long celebrated as emblematic of the nation underwent a revival in the twentieth century. Harping became recast as a highly gendered, hyper-visible feminised activity. The instrument, its practitioners and the associated repertoire therefore vividly represent one way in which the concepts of women, music and Ireland intersect.

As the chapters in this collection demonstrate, however, the relationships between women and music in Ireland (including those pertaining to the harp) are multifaceted; they may be experienced and understood in multiple ways. Far from simply reinforcing assumptions about the nation's musical identity and history, these accounts bring fresh insights and perspectives to this subject and its complexities. While the study of women, gender and music had been established elsewhere in anglophone musicology by the mid-1990s, this volume is the first book to appraise the field as it pertains to Ireland. This research, therefore, advances knowledge and understanding of Irish art music and traditional music; it also situates existing narratives in new contexts.

Women and Music in Ireland Conferences

The Women and Music in Ireland conferences began as a means of addressing the neglect of women in the existing research on music in Ireland in the early twenty-first century. The concept of conferences dedicated to the work of women and gender studies in music in the UK had been gaining momentum and the conference series organiser and founder, Jennifer O'Connor-Madsen, believed there was a need for a similar approach in Ireland to address the imbalance. Early discussions on the conference were met with enthusiasm from Fiona Palmer, the head of the Music Department at Maynooth University in 2009, but with hesitation from some male peers – there was a question around the need for an event focused on women.

The first conference attracted interest from national and international speakers on a wide range of areas. The sessions included papers on women from the eighteenth century to contemporary composers, some of whom were in attendance, and the keynote address was given by Ita Beausang. Despite disruption caused by the cancellation of flights due to the eruption of the Eyjafjallajökull volcano, the conference was a success.

Concerts performed by Deborah Kelleher, Elizabeth Pink, Una Hunt and the Concorde ensemble brought the papers to life, showcasing the works and compositions of several of the women discussed during the conference sessions. The second conference, in 2012, took place at the Royal Irish Academy of Music. It was financed in part by a crowdfunding campaign on Fund:It with rewards including attendance at the conference or mentions in the booklet. As before, sessions addressed a range of topics, including one concerning resources on women and music, which featured presentations from the music librarians in the RIAM, Dublin Institute of Technology (now TU Dublin: Technological University Dublin), and the Contemporary Music Centre (CMC), as well as a roundtable discussion with composers Ailís Ní Ríain and Evangelia Rigaki. Further highlights were a lunchtime recital of nineteenth-century music, performed by Elizabeth Pink and Anthony Byrne, and an evening concert by Concorde. Rhona Clarke delivered the keynote address on her work as a composer in Ireland. The third and final conference in the series took place in 2014 in the Music Department of St Patrick's College, Drumcondra (now part of DCU: Dublin City University) and was co-organised by Jennifer O'Connor-Madsen and Rhona Clarke. Themed sessions centred on the Irish harp, contemporary composers, and a panel discussion with traditional musician practitioners – Aoife Granville, Michelle Mulcahy and Síle Denvir. The lunchtime concert was performed by the Fidelio Trio and there was a lecture recital by Lisa Lutter on the songs of Adela Maddison. The keynote address was given by Nicola LeFanu, who also spoke at a CMC-led panel discussion with Rhona Clarke, mezzo-soprano Aylish Kerrigan and Lisa Lutter, entitled 'Do Labels Matter?' The consistent thread throughout all three conferences was the organiser, Jennifer O'Connor-Madsen, the support of the Society for Musicology in Ireland (SMI) and the CMC. The conference was met with enthusiasm in each host institution through the support and encouragement of Fiona Palmer at Maynooth University, Deborah Kelleher, the director of the RIAM, and John O'Flynn, the head of the Music Department at DCU. The conferences provided space for conversations on gender, autonomy, equality and exclusion; they encouraged students to consider topics for research centred on the women highlighted; and they illustrated the significant role that women had played in so many facets of music in Ireland.

Developments since the Women and Music in Ireland Conferences

Since the final Women and Music in Ireland conference in 2014, much has happened in the field – and by 'the field' we refer to the activities of women in music in (and outside of) Ireland, which encompass but are not limited to scholarship. Social and political transformations specific to

Ireland during the 2010s drove and defined some of these developments, while others can be attributed to and understood as responses to an international shift in how the world listened to women. Developments can be classed into three broad categories: the national and global impact that women in Ireland/Irish women have made in areas of creative practice; the proliferation of academic research on women and music in Ireland; and the emergence of a feminist movement in the country's music sector.

Creative practice covers a spectrum of activity, such as recordings, composition, songwriting, sonic art and performance, but perhaps the most high-profile breakthrough for women and music in Ireland under this banner has been in conducting. On 9 February 2020, Galway-born Eimear Noone became the first woman in history to conduct at the Academy Awards annual ceremony. Noone, who studied music at Trinity College Dublin, had established a successful career in Hollywood by 2020 as a composer and conductor of music for video games, but had flown under the radar of listeners outside the video-game world. The Oscars performance and its 'memeification' at the hands of US blogger Perez Hilton – who posted to his millions of subscribers a shot of the conductor in action with the caption 'Eimear Noone cutting through the patriarchy!' – launched Noone to a global audience and in a manner that highlighted the gendered aspects of her achievement. What is also striking, though, is Noone's role at the fore of a relatively young creative industry – music for video games – and one that has only recently consolidated as a subfield of research, known as ludomusicology. That development exemplifies how the parameters of 'women and music in Ireland' continue to expand. Another musician who steadily built an international profile since the early 2000s and has since rocketed to international prominence is the trailblazing Jennifer Walshe. Arguably celebrated abroad more than in her native country, she was the first Irish composer elected to the Akademie der Künste in Berlin (2019) and the first appointed Professor of Composition at Oxford University (2021). (For more on Walshe, see Dignam (Chapter 14), this volume.)

An additional example of an Irish woman with a dual career as a creative practitioner and academic, albeit with a different, more historical focus, is pianist Una Hunt. As a performer, recording artist, editor and radio broadcaster, Hunt has contributed to preserving the legacy of women such as nineteenth-century composer Fanny Robinson and her twentieth-century counterpart Joan Trimble (see Stanley, this volume). A welcome development of the past decade is the increased availability of commercial recordings of works by historical Irish women composers. Further to the Trimble and Robinson recordings, listeners can now easily access CDs and audio streams of music by Ina Boyle and Rhoda Coghill (see Beausang and Watson, respectively, this volume). There is no shortage of recordings featuring contemporary Irish women musicians, especially in the genre of popular music. Breakthrough acts in the past few years include solo hip-hop artist Denise Chaila and all-female rock band Pillow Queens. In 2021 Pillow Queens made their US debut with a primetime appearance on *The Late Late Show with James Corden* and received airplay in the UK. While Chaila has yet to attract the same level of international interest, she has brought a welcome transnational voice to the domestic popular music scene. On tracks such as 'Duel Citizenship' (2019) and 'Anseo' (2020) she references her dual Irish and Zambian identities. Using her art to speak about and to an increasingly diverse country, Chaila is a beacon for Irish women of colour who are rarely heard in the musical mainstream. Similarly, as a band comprising four openly queer musicians, whose tracks bear titles such as 'Gay Girls' (2020), Pillow Queens represent and powerfully amplify another marginalised cohort of Irish women.

Pillow Queens are not the first 'out' band in the scene. As Hanlon has documented, Maria Walsh and Carole Nelson were openly lesbian when they formed Zrazy in 1991. They were explicitly feminist, too: their 1992 track '6794700' protested the country's abortion ban by repeating the contact details for a crisis pregnancy helpline.[1] Recent research, such as Hanlon's, illuminates the gendered dimensions of Ireland's popular music history. Further studies in this field include Dillane's analysis of Sinéad O'Connor; she persuasively argues that the singer's life and work 'provide a kaleidoscopic insight into different registers and experiences of Irish womanhood'.[2] McLaughlin and Braniff are similarly attentive to the influences, career and legacy of Ottilie Patterson, a woman born in rural Northern Ireland in 1932 who became a popular blues singer in Britain.[3] Scholarship on women and music in Ireland has extended in other directions too. The 2021 special issue of *Ethnomusicology Ireland* aimed to 'document, expand and reflect on the experience of women in the world(s) of folk and traditional music'.[4] The twelve featured articles take major strides in developing this research field. Here and elsewhere, Slominski has recently explored intersections of Irish traditional music,

1 Ann-Marie Hanlon, '"Missing from the Record": Zrazy and Women's Music in Ireland', in Áine Mangaoang, John O'Flynn and Lonán Ó Briain (eds), *Made in Ireland: Studies in Popular Music* (New York and Abingdon, 2021), pp. 67–78.

2 Aileen Dillane, 'Raging Mother Ireland: Faith, Fury and Feminism in the Voice and Songs of Sinéad O'Connor', in Mangaoang, O'Flynn and Ó Briain (eds), *Made in Ireland: Studies in Popular Music*, pp. 54–66, at p. 55.

3 Noel McLaughlin and Joanna Braniff, 'Irish Lady Sings the Blues: History, Identity, and Ottilie Patterson', in Mangaoang, O'Flynn and Ó Briain (eds), *Made in Ireland: Studies in Popular Music*, pp. 97–108.

4 Verena Commins, Síle Denvir, Úna Monaghan and Méabh Ní Fhuartháin, 'Editors' Preface', *Ethnomusicology Ireland*, 7 (2021), 1–2, at p. 1. See <https://www.ictm.ie/journal/issue-7/> for the full issue [accessed 6 October 2021].

gender and sexuality, paying particular attention to marginalised figures.[5] A concern with restoring such figures to their rightful places in narratives of Irish music is evident in scholarship across popular, traditional/folk and classical/art music genres. A revisionist, feminist approach to classical/art music history is a driving force in this edited collection, as it was in a handful of other studies from the preceding decade: the Beausang and de Barra book on Ina Boyle (2018), Watson's article on Coghill (2016) and O'Connor's doctoral thesis (2010).

The proliferation of research on women and music in Ireland since the 2014 conference, especially in the last few years, must be situated in an international context that includes scholarly enquiry but also a general resurgence of feminist discourse in the public sphere. Allegations in October 2017 that US film producer Harvey Weinstein had sexually assaulted multiple women prompted the viral #MeToo movement. Countless women across the globe used the #MeToo hashtag to disclose their experiences of sexual assault and harassment, thereby laying bare the staggering, endemic scale of violence against women. In 2020, women in Irish traditional music used the #MiseFosta hashtag to highlight that this scourge was pervasive in their performance scene. Although the #MeToo movement was primarily a form of social media activism, feminist campaigners in Ireland were organising on the ground too. As the Repeal movement gathered momentum, so, too, women and allies in the arts industries felt empowered to protest other forms of gender-based injustices.[6] Collectives such as Sounding the Feminists, FairPlé, and Why Not Her?, established between 2017 and 2020, act to address various types of gender inequalities in the music sector. The presence of scholars in the activist movement has supported the study of women and music in Ireland.[7]

The emergence of this field resonates with international academic developments. Echoing the three-part Women and Music in Ireland conference series, Bangor University in Wales hosted conferences on Women's Work in Music in 2017, 2019 and 2021, which developed into an edited book.[8] A separate forthcoming book on women's musical leadership and the related Arts and Humanities Research Council (AHRC)-funded Women's Musical Leadership Online Network (WMLON) confirm that feminist

5 Tes Slominski, *Trad Nation: Gender, Sexuality, and Race in Irish Traditional Music* (Middletown, 2020).

6 See Laura Watson, 'Sounding the Feminists: Campaigning for Institutional Change to Support Women in Music in Contemporary Ireland', in Laura Hamer and Helen J Minors (eds), *The Routledge Companion to Women and Musical Leadership: The Nineteenth Century and Beyond* (New York, 2023).

7 See Laura Watson, 'Feminist Musical Activism in Ireland (2016–21) and Feminist Musicology', *Ethnomusicology Ireland*, 8 (forthcoming, 2022).

8 Rhiannon Mathias (ed.), *The Routledge Handbook of Women's Work in Music* (Abingdon, 2022).

research remains on the agenda for musicologists in the twenty-first century.[9] Recent publications such as *The Cambridge Companion to Women in Music since 1900* indicate new ways forward for scholars, with feminist musicology reaching beyond its 'traditional' themes such as women composers and gendered readings of works to incorporate matters such as working conditions for women in a range of music careers.[10]

Overview of the Book

This book is primarily a record of the conferences; its focus on classical/art music and Irish traditional music reflects the main themes of the research presented at those events. As discussed above, the study of women and music in Ireland has evolved widely and rapidly since then. Scholars have broken new ground in the fields of popular music and traditional/folk music. Increasingly porous boundaries between academia and activism have generated new research questions and methodologies, such as those used by Monaghan to investigate how gender shapes participation in the Irish traditional music scene.[11] Alongside these developments there remains the need to pursue historical, musicological research on women in the traditional and classical/art music worlds, to recover the identities and activities of those who were marginalised or excluded from the established narratives. The editors hope that this volume will take an important step in addressing that lacuna in Irish music history and open the door to further research on what is a vast subject.

The volume contributes to the fields of musicology, Irish studies and gender studies. Fifteen chapters shed new light on how women have been a force in Irish musical life for centuries. The authors discuss a diverse range of historical and contemporary individuals and their activities: composers, concert performers, amateur players, broadcasters, pedagogues and festival curators. They situate the creative practices and values of these women in a broader social and cultural landscape, exploring conditions such as educational infrastructures, gendered associations with instruments and repertoires, and how music making has been socially classed. Contributors, who are based in Ireland and abroad, encompass scholars, traditional performers, classical performers, composers, educators and activists. They bring a rich variety of perspectives and experiences to bear on the subject. The book is organised thematically in four parts.

9 See <https://gtr.ukri.org/projects?ref=AH%2FW000369%2F1> [accessed 5 October 2021].

10 Laura Hamer (ed.), *The Cambridge Companion to Women in Music since 1900* (Cambridge, 2021).

11 Úna Monaghan, '121 Stories: The Impact of Gender on Participation in Irish Traditional Music', *Ethnomusicology Ireland*, 7 (2021), 17–32.

Part I begins by establishing a 'Place for Women Musicians in Irish Society of the Eighteenth and Nineteenth Centuries' by exploring the position they carved out within society of that time. Ita Beausang argues that in spite of the romantic concept of Hibernia with her harp, women and music in Ireland have received much less attention from the public than Irish women writers, poets and activists. She advocates for their importance and highlights their contributions from the eighteenth century. In Chapter 2, Karol Mullaney-Dignam explores music as an accomplishment for fashionable ladies in elite Irish households. She examines the integral role it had in both social and cultural life, and music as a necessary accomplishment for women of, or aspiring to, social rank and fortune.

In Chapter 3, a consideration of the changing role of women in music in Dublin in the eighteenth and nineteenth centuries, Jennifer O'Connor-Madsen charts their involvement in the development of the music profession in the capital city where their contributions to pedagogy and concert life helped shape the cultural developments of Dublin at that time. In the final chapter of Part I, Mary Louise O'Donnell remains in nineteenth-century Dublin to highlight the careers of the Glover Sisters, leading figures in the city's musical life as harpists, singers and teachers. This chapter records their lifelong musical collaboration with their father, John William Glover, as well as their contributions to music.

In Part II, 'Women and Practice in Irish Traditional Music', the role of women and their work in the traditional music sphere are examined. The harp occupies a unique place both as a symbol of Ireland and a musical instrument throughout history, and in Chapter 5 Helen Lawlor traces the association of the harp since the ninth century with mythology and gender to the twentieth and twenty-first centuries, where it has become predominantly a female pursuit. The chapter considers the changing gender trajectory and considers the implications of the modern-day gender imbalance for the development of the tradition into the future.

In Chapter 6 Daithí Kearney restores due recognition to Irish traditional musician Josephine Keegan, who challenged the male dominance of the tradition. Highlighting her multiple achievements as piano accompanist to male soloists, fiddle soloist of note in her own right, collector and composer of Irish traditional music and pedagogue, this chapter reconsiders her importance to the genre along with her male contemporaries that she accompanied. The final chapter in Part II, by Teresa O'Donnell, relates the subsequent history of harp playing in Dublin and evaluates the legacy of Sheila Larchet Cuthbert, Mercedes Garvey and Gráinne Yeats. As friends, teaching colleagues and lifelong members of Cairde na Cruite (Friends of the Harp), they transformed harp performance and pedagogy in Ireland for the remainder of the twentieth century.

Part III considers the 'Gaps and Gender Politics in the History of Twentieth-Century Women Composers and Performers' through the prism of four case studies. Axel Klein reconstructs the life of Alicia Adélaïde Needham using her autobiographical notes and diaries. Needham was a popular composer of small-scale works and occasional conductor, whose music was performed on both sides of the Irish Sea from the 1890s to the 1920s. Despite these achievements she was neglected by music historians. The same fate awaited Mary Dickenson-Auner, a virtuoso violinist and prolific composer, following her death in 1965 – and in Chapter 9 Margarethe Engelhardt-Krajanek combs through the archives to reveal the history of a musician whose career took her from Dublin to London, Vienna and elsewhere, and featured performances with Bartók and Schoenberg. At the age of sixty she turned to composition, producing multiple large-scale works, and securing some public performances in Ireland and on the continent. The final two chapters in Part III focus on Joan Trimble and Rhoda Coghill, whose lives spanned most of the twentieth century and whose careers encompassed piano performance and composition. Trimble was by far the more prolific composer. As Ruth Stanley shows, however, her work was relentlessly critiqued through a gendered lens. This, as Stanley details, is striking in the reception of her 1957 opera *Blind Raftery*, which was commissioned by the BBC. In Rhoda Coghill's case, her work as a pianist shone a light on gendered attitudes to women performers. Laura Watson gives an account of Coghill's decades-long performance career, highlights of which included a prestigious appointment as Station Accompanist at Radio Éireann in 1939 and a string of solo concert appearances. Despite these accomplishments, her work was minimised in the historical narrative and subjected to gender-coded commentary.

Part IV, 'Situating Discourses of Women, Gender and Music in the Twenty-First Century', proposes new strategies for thinking about creative practices, women's musical participation, and scenes such as electroacoustic music and Irish traditional performance. Drawing on her fifty years of experience, composer Nicola LeFanu asks what lessons may be learnt from the past to promote the status of women in the composition profession. She points out that progress and gains so far in gender equality cannot be taken for granted. In Chapter 13 composer Rhona Clarke discusses her recent collaborations with visual artist Marie Hanlon, reflecting on how the joint creative process has impacted her approach to other compositions for concert audiences. Clarke's practitioner perspective brings a new, subjective angle to the discourse around women and music in Ireland. Barbara Jillian Dignam also brings practitioner experiences to the fore in Chapter 14, which evaluates women and the electroacoustic scene in contemporary Ireland. Findings from two surveys she conducted almost a decade apart inform her analysis. Like

Clarke, she is attentive to the value of collaborative efforts for the careers of women in music. Finally, in Chapter 15 Tes Slominski offers an intersectional critical account of how the Irish traditional music scene maintains heteropatriarchal oppression. She uses feminist texts by Adrienne Rich and Gayle Rubin to theorise the marginalisation of LGBTQ+ people in this setting. Subsequently, she recommends strategies communities can use to support women and other marginalised individuals.

Part I

Establishing a Place for Women Musicians in Irish Society of the Eighteenth and Nineteenth Centuries

1

Daughters of Hibernia: Seen and Not Heard?

Ita Beausang

In the past fifty years the area of women's studies in Ireland has yielded an impressive harvest of academic endeavour. Irish women's social, political and literary history has been thoroughly investigated, and many scholarly works have been published. In 1987 the third International Interdisciplinary Congress on Women was held in Dublin, at which an imposing array of topics was presented.[1] However, women and music in Ireland were neither mentioned at this event nor included in any subsequent bibliography of women's studies. Despite the romantic concept of Hibernia with her harp it seemed that, unlike Irish women writers, poets and activists, Hibernia's musical daughters were neither visible nor audible.

Before evaluating the status of women in the Irish musical landscape today it is essential to consider their role in the past, although sources of information are rare.[2] Edmund Spenser, who lived in Kilcolman Castle, Co. Cork, for ten years from 1587, wrote an account of the 'wandering women called *Mona-Shull*' (trans. Mná Siubhail, travelling women), who were also ballad singers.

The Musical Academy, 1757

Almost two centuries after Spenser's account of the 'wandering women', in 1757 a Musical Academy 'composed of ladies, patronesses, and of ladies and gentlemen' was founded in Dublin by playwright Kane O'Hara and Lord Mornington. In 1764 Mornington was elected first Professor of Music at the University of Dublin (more commonly known as Trinity College Dublin or TCD). The Musical Academy was the

1 Carol Schreier Rupprecht, 'Third International Congress on Women', *Signs*, 104 (1988), 235–42.

2 This chapter was presented by the author in an earlier form at the first Women and Music in Ireland conference, Maynooth University, 15 April 2010.

first musical institution in the British Isles to admit women members. Patronesses included the Countess of Tyrone, Countess of Charleville and Countess of Mornington. Lady Freke, Miss Cavendish and Miss Nichols were listed as harpsichord players, and there were five aristocratic female vocal performers.[3] The Musical Academy was an exclusive organisation. It was governed by nineteen statutes, enacted in 1758, some of which applied to women. According to statute no. 2:

> The male academics only shall have a right of suffrage in the Academy.

Statute no. 4:

> No public mercenary performer, professor, or teacher of music shall ever be admitted into any rank of the Academy on any account whatsoever.

Statute no. 16:

> Married male academics shall have the privilege of introducing their wives at every musical performance.

An annual benefit concert was held at which:

> all rank [was] obliterated, profession disregarded and female timidity overcome in the cause of charity while noblemen, statesmen, lawyers, divines and ladies exerted their best abilities like mercenary performers to amuse the public.[4]

Unlike the woman-friendly policy of the Musical Academy, the catch and glee clubs very popular in eighteenth-century Dublin and Cork did not admit ladies as members. There was one notable exception, the Beefsteak Club, founded in Dublin *c.*1752 by Thomas Brinsley Sheridan, manager of Smock Alley Theatre. Although the membership was all male, the Irish actress Peg Woffington, one of the most famous actresses in London, was permitted to attend their meetings and was elected its first president.

Music Societies

In 1831 a Grand Dublin Musical Festival was held between 29 August and 5 September. The chorus numbered 159 singers selected from the Dublin Festival Choral Society, the Liverpool Festival Choral Society, and the cathedral choirs of Armagh, Limerick, Cashel and Lismore. The sopranos

3 John T. Gilbert, *A History of the City of Dublin (1854–9)* (Shannon, 1972), vol. 1, p. 79.

4 Gilbert, *A History*, pp. 77–8.

included twenty-two women from Dublin, Liverpool, Rochdale and Preston; the altos were boy choristers from the cathedrals.[5]

Most of the music societies in Dublin in the first half of the nineteenth century were exclusively male.[6] The Anacreontic Society (*c.*1740–1850) did not admit women as members, but allowed them to attend 'ladies' concerts' or 'open concerts'.[7] The rules of the Antient Concerts Society Dublin, founded in 1834, precluded women from attending weekly meetings. Boy choristers were employed to sing treble parts, and professional female singers were engaged as soloists. However, 'on occasions when it is desirable to produce an increased effect the committee have found it necessary to engage the assistance of female voices'.[8] For the first Dublin performance of Mendelssohn's *Elijah* in 1847, the choir included twenty-five sopranos and sixteen altos.

In 1837 the Dublin Choral was the only music society in Dublin to admit women members.[9] However, the Dublin Sacred Harmonic Society (1841–47), founded 'for the improvement of Psalmody and the Cultivation of Sacred Vocal Music',[10] did not confine membership to social status or class and was open to both sexes.[11] The Metropolitan Choral Society (1842–47), which specialised in oratorio, had a well-trained mixed chorus of over fifty voices. Soloists for their concerts included Clara Novello and Adelaide Kemble, who appeared in English opera at the Theatre Royal, Hawkins Street, and four local singers, the Misses Searle and the Misses La Vega.

In 1838, when women were forbidden inside the walls of Trinity College, the college board granted permission for ladies to attend a concert by the University of Dublin Choral Society (founded 1837) 'in bonnet, not in evening dress'. Permission was extended subsequently, with one 'ladies' concert' scheduled each season.[12] From 1850 the society held concerts in the Antient Concert Rooms, Great Brunswick Street [now Pearse Street], at which women members of the Antient Concerts Society

5 Michael Murphy, 'The Musical Press in Nineteenth-Century Ireland', in Michael Murphy and Jan Smaczny (eds), *Music in Nineteenth-Century Ireland, Irish Musical Studies*, 9 (Dublin, 2007), pp. 257–60.

6 I am indebted to Catherine Ferris for information on Dublin music societies in 'The Use of Newspapers as a Source for Musicological Research: A Case Study of Dublin Musical Life 1840–1844' (Unpublished PhD dissertation, Maynooth University, 2011).

7 Ferris, 'The Use of Newspapers as a Source for Musicological Research', p. 93.

8 Dublin, 'The Ancient Concerts', *The Musical World*, 22 March 1838, p. 202.

9 *Dublin Almanac and General Register of Ireland* (Dublin, 1838).

10 *Saunders Newsletter*, 11 May 1843.

11 *Dublin Almanac* (Dublin, 1841) p. 178.

12 Gerald Fitzgibbon, 'College Choral 1837–1987', *Hermathema: A Trinity College Dublin Review*, p. 48, cited by Ferris, 'The Use of Newspapers as a Source for Musicological Research', p. 157.

performed.[13] In 1869 female singers performed at a concert within the college walls.[14] A year later, after a long struggle with Trinity College Board, women were admitted as associate members of the society. They were finally granted full membership in 1904, the same year TCD first admitted women as students.

Visiting Singers

Throughout the nineteenth century female singers travelled from London to perform in Dublin and provincial centres.[15] They ranged from Angelica Catalani, 'the Queen of Song', in 1807 to Clara Butt in 1899 (the year that she gave the first performance of Elgar's *Sea Pictures* dressed as a mermaid). In 1848 Jenny Lind, 'the Swedish Nightingale', had spectacular success in a season of Italian opera at the Theatre Royal, Hawkins Street. She retired a year later from opera to concentrate on a concert career. In 1859 she returned to Ireland for a tour lasting almost a month, during which she gave a total of sixteen concerts in Dublin, Cork, Killarney, Limerick, Waterford, Kilkenny, Belfast, Londonderry and Ballymena. A week later she returned to Dublin for a performance of *Messiah*, to benefit Mercer's Hospital and the Irish Musical Fund.

Some years earlier another concert tour took place when Franz Liszt and an intrepid troupe of performers gave a series of concerts from 17 December 1840 to 16 January 1841 in Dublin, Kilkenny, Cork, Clonmel, Limerick and Belfast. The female singers were Miss [Mary Sarah] Steele soprano, and Louisa Bassano contralto; the latter had the distinction of singing the mezzo recitatives in the first English performance of *Elijah*, at Birmingham Town Hall in 1846.

In November 1741 Handel engaged soprano Christina Maria Avolio for his 'Musical Entertainments' in Dublin. On 13 April 1742 she sang in the *Messiah* premiere together with two other female singers from London, alto Susannah Cibber, sister of Thomas Arne, and soprano Mrs Maclaine, whose husband, Charles, from Aberdeen, was Handel's

13 Caitríona Doran, 'The Robinsons: A Nineteenth-Century Dublin Family of Musicians and their Contribution Towards Musical Life in Dublin' (Unpublished MA dissertation, Maynooth University, 1998), p. 34.

14 Olinthus J. Vignoles, *Memoir of Sir Robert P. Stewart* (Dublin, 1898), p. 94.v, cited by Ferris, 'The Use of Newspapers as a Source for Musicological Research', p. 170.

15 Ita Beausang, 'Echoes of the Lied: Women's Vocal Repertoire in Nineteenth-Century Ireland', in Aisling Kenny and Susan Wollenberg (eds), *Women and the Nineteenth-Century Lied* (Farnham, 2015), pp. 251–8.

organist assistant.[16] It is not known whether the top soprano line was sung by local sopranos or by choirboys.[17]

Music and Society

Outside Dublin, music was an intrinsic part in the social life of the landed gentry. Keyboard instruments, harps and guitars were essential in their homes. Music sellers and instrument makers flourished in the main urban centres, while music masters travelled to country houses to teach their aristocratic pupils. Composers published sets of variations and sonatas, which they dedicated to their patrons.[18] Music was considered a desirable accomplishment for young ladies to enhance their marriage prospects. The diarist and letter writer Mrs Delany, friend of Dean Swift, and godmother of Lord Mornington, held convivial musical evenings in her house, Delville, in Glasnevin, but in 1753 she expressed some reservations in a letter to her sister, Mrs Dewes:

> an immoderate love to [*sic*] music may draw young people into many inconveniences: I would therefore confine it as much as I could to an amusement, and never allow it to be their business. Painting has fewer objections, and generally leads people into much better company.[19]

Women seeking employment as teachers and governesses placed advertisements in newspapers, some of which underlined their aptitude in music as a key selling point:

> A lady who has taught the pianoforte and singing in families of distinction, by whom she can be recommended, and whose capability is vouched by some of the first professors, wishes for a similar situation in Dublin or the country. If required she will also instruct in English, Geography, and works to save unnecessary trouble. However, she does not understand French.[20]

Some women worked as music sellers and publishers. When her husband Samuel died in 1776 Anne Lee took over the family music business at 2 Dame Street until 1788.[21] Elizabeth Rhames was listed at 16 Exchange

16 Jonathan Bardon, *Hallelujah: The Story of a Musical Genius and the City that Brought His Masterpiece to Life* (Dublin, 2015), p. 127.

17 Bardon, *Hallelujah*, p. 168, fn 3.

18 Philip Cogan dedicated keyboard music to the Duchess of Leinster, Lady Earlsfort, Lady Clonmel, the Hon. Mrs Walpole, Mrs John Latouche.

19 *The Autobiography and Correspondence of Mary Granville, Mrs Delany*, ed. Lady Llanover (London, 1861), vol. 3, p. 207.

20 *Freeman's Journal*, 31 May 1811.

21 Charles Humphries and William Smith, *Music Publishing in the British Isles* (Oxford, 1970).

Street as a music seller and haberdasher from 1777 until 1806.[22] When she died in 1795 her son Benjamin continued the business in her name.[23]

Sydney Owenson, later Lady Morgan, first earned her living as a governess. When her mother died, the girl was sent to a boarding school in Clontarf, where her father Robert Owenson, an impoverished actor, paid for extra music lessons. She and her sister also studied with John Field's teacher, the Italian musician Tommaso Giordani. In a letter to her father, she quoted her future employer, Mrs Featherstonehaugh of Bracklyn Castle, who interviewed her for a governess post on the recommendation of M. Fontaine, *maître de ballet*:

> I assure you, my dear, I am much prepossessed in your favour by all that our good Fontaine has told me of you, and your being so merry and musical, as he tells me you are, is very much in your favour with us for we are rather dull and mopy [*sic*].[24]

Sydney Owenson's interest in music continued when she became a successful novelist. (For more on Owenson see Mullaney-Dignam, Chapter 2, this volume.) The first purchases she made from her literary earnings were an Irish harp by Egan and a fashionable black cloak. In 1805 she published *Twelve Original Hibernian Melodies*, three years before Thomas Moore's first volume of *Irish Melodies*. After marrying the physician Sir Charles Morgan, she often entertained Moore to dinner in her house at 35 Kildare Street where 'he sang some of his most beautiful songs in his most delightful manner'.[25] In 1831 she invited the violinist Paganini, who was performing at the Grand Dublin Musical Festival, to dinner and a soirée.[26]

Music Education

Many Irish women chose convent life during the nineteenth century. In 1800 there were six religious orders in Ireland, with 120 nuns living in eleven houses. By 1901 there were eight thousand nuns with a total of thirty-five religious orders or congregations. Where nuns were involved in education, music was an important part of the curriculum. According to the prospectus of the boarding school at the Ursuline Convent in Cork, prior to 1850, the yearly fees were thirty guineas, with music fees an additional £11 7s 6d.[27] Women also taught music privately in their own

22 *The Gentleman's and Citizen's Almanack* (Dublin, 1777), p. 67.

23 *The Gentleman's Almanack* (1806), p. 82.

24 *Lady Morgan's Memoirs: Autobiography Diaries and Correspondence*, ed. W.H. Dixon (London, 1862), vol. 1, pp. 156–7.

25 *Lady Morgan's Memoirs*, vol. 2, p. 321.

26 *Lady Morgan's Memoirs*, vol. 2, p. 327.

27 Maria Luddy, *Women in Ireland, 1800–1918: A Documentary History* (Cork, 1995), p. 106.

homes or travelled to schools and pupils' homes. In 1833, a Mrs Allen, a daughter of Johann Bernhard Logier, was widowed with ten children to support. Her academy at 56 Rutland Square (now Parnell Square), under the patronage of Her Excellency the Duchess of Clarendon, wife of the Viceroy, the Earl of Clarendon, had fourteen pianos on the premises.[28] Other families whose wives and daughters taught music were the Ashes, Corris, Elsners, Glovers, Wilkinsons and Willis's.[29] Piano teachers Elizabeth Meeke and Henrietta Flynn (with whom Charles Stanford took his first lessons) studied with Ignaz Moscheles before returning to establish private teaching practices in Dublin.[30]

When the Irish Academy of Music was founded in 1848 the committee was exclusively male, as was the new committee in January 1856 when the academy was reconstituted. In 1856 Fanny Robinson (née Arthur) became the institutions's first female professor of pianoforte. Later that year a class was advertised by the academy 'for the instruction of female pupils in singing, harmony and composition, under the direction of Professor Smith Mus.Doc. T.C.D. and Mr Joseph Robinson assisted by Miss Julia Cruise'.[31] Groups of aristocratic ladies joined fundraising committees and organised charity concerts and opera performances, but no woman was appointed to the Board of Governors until 1915.[32] The study of music in the academy was a serious business, not merely perceived as an accomplishment for young ladies or a frivolous activity. In 1857 female pupils were required to sign a declaration before they were admitted to vocal or pianoforte classes:

> I, the undersigned, request admission as a pupil in the Irish Academy of Music, and I undertake to observe all rules which shall from time to time be prescribed by the Committee respecting the management of the Classes; and I do hereby declare that in applying for admission to the Academy it is my intention to adopt Music as my profession, either alone, or as part of the general Profession of Teaching.[33]

28 Derek Collins, 'Music in Dublin', in Richard Pine and Charles Acton (eds), *To Talent Alone: The Royal Irish Academy of Music 1848–1998* (Dublin, 1998), pp. 24–6.

29 Jennifer O'Connor, 'The Role of Women in Music in Nineteenth-Century Dublin', (Unpublished PhD dissertation, Maynooth University, 2010), pp. 33–46.

30 Pine and Acton, *To Talent Alone*, pp. 497–8.

31 *Freeman's Journal*, 17 October 1856. Julia Cruise was the second wife of Richard Michael Levey (O'Shaughnessy), professor of violin at the RIAM and leader of the Theatre Royal orchestra from 1834 to 1880.

32 Sarah Harrison (1863–1941), artist, suffragette and first woman elected to Dublin City Council.

33 Pine and Acton, *To Talent Alone*, p. 71.

In 1862 female classes were advertised by the academy, 'confined to Ladies who purpose making Music their Profession either as Governesses or otherwise'.[34] In 1875 the post of Lady Superintendent was established to keep the books, control the housekeeping and arrange the teaching schedule.[35] Women gradually outnumbered men as teachers and enjoyed progressive rates of pay.[36] When the Cork Municipal School of Music was opened in 1878, a Resident Lady Superintendent was appointed at £20 a year to begin with, together with 'coal and gas, four rooms in the main house, a kitchen and a servant's bedroom'.[37] The Dublin Municipal School of Music, founded in 1890 under the aegis of the Royal Irish Academy of Music (which had been granted the title 'Royal' by Queen Victoria in 1872) employed a substantial number of women teachers for strings and piano, but the administration and management committees consisted entirely of men.

Notable Women

Many remarkable women made significant contributions to the annals of music in nineteenth-century Ireland. Catherine Hayes (1818–61), the Limerick prima donna, toured fifteen countries on four continents,[38] and sang with the Italian Opera Company at a Command Performance in Buckingham Palace for Queen Victoria.[39] Fanny Robinson (1831–79), pianist, teacher and composer, pupil of distinguished pianist Sigismond Thalberg, came to Dublin from England in 1849 to play at a concert in the Antient Concert Rooms, and married the conductor Joseph Robinson five months later. She gave the first solo piano recital in Ireland in 1856,[40] performed concertos in London and Paris, and composed; her output included piano music and the much-performed oratorio *God is Love*.[41] (For more on Robinson see O'Connor-Madsen, Chapter 3, this volume.)

In 1883, Edith Oldham (1865–1950) was one of three students of the Royal Irish Academy of Music (RIAM) who won scholarships to the Royal College of Music in London, where she enjoyed a close friendship with

34 *Freeman's Journal*, 20 May 1862.

35 Pine and Acton, *To Talent Alone*, p. 165.

36 See O'Connor, 'The Role of Women', pp. 80–2.

37 Bernard Curtis, *Centenary of the Cork School of Music: Progress of the School, 1878–1978* (Cork, 1978), p. 25.

38 Basil Walsh, *Catherine Hayes: The Hibernian Prima Donna* (Dublin, 2000), pp. 166–79.

39 Walsh, *Catherine Hayes*, pp. 113–14.

40 *Saunders Newsletter*, 10 April 1856.

41 See 'A Piano Portrait: Fanny Robinson', presented by Una Hunt on *The Lyric Feature*, RTÉ Lyric FM, 22 February 2013; Jennifer O'Connor, 'Robinson [née Arthur], Fanny', in Harry White and Barra Boydell (eds), *The Encyclopaedia of Music in Ireland*, vol. 2 (Dublin, 2013), p. 888.

the director of the college, Sir George Grove.[42] On her return to Dublin in 1888 she became Professor of Piano at the RIAM, the only female teacher there to hold a diploma in music. In 1895 she was one of the founders of Feis Ceoil, of which her future husband, the scholar Richard Irvine Best, was the first registrar.[43] The four O'Hea sisters Margaret, Alice, Mary and Ellen (whose pseudonym as a composer was Elena Norton), contralto Elizabeth Scott-Fennell, piano pedagogue Annie Curwen, Charlotte Milligan Fox (author of *Annals of the Irish Harpers*), and composers Lady Helen Dufferin and Alicia Adélaïde Needham (see Klein, Chapter 8, this volume) were other notable women in the chronology of music in Ireland at the time.[44]

In his short story 'The Dead' James Joyce immortalises three fictional Dublin women in whose lives music was central – Aunt Julia, Aunt Kate and their niece, Mary Jane Morkan, who:

> was the main prop of the household for she had the organ at Haddington Road. She had been through the Academy and gave a pupils' concert every year in the upper room of the Antient Concert Rooms. Many of her pupils belonged to the better-class families on the Kingstown and Dalkey line. Old as they were, her aunts also did their share. Julia, though she was quite grey, was still the leading soprano in Adam and Eve's, and Kate, being too feeble to go about much, gave music lessons to beginners on the old square piano in the back room.[45]

Another woman who made an outstanding contribution to Ireland's musical infrastructure as an author, prolific journalist, composer and arranger, lecturer and tireless advocate of Irish music was Annie Patterson (1868–1934). Born in Lurgan, Co. Down, she studied piano, organ, singing and composition at the RIAM. By 1889 she was awarded the degree of MusD of the Royal University of Ireland, becoming the first woman in Ireland and the UK to earn a doctorate in music. Patterson was also the first woman conductor in Ireland. In 1891 she founded the Dublin Choral Union, which aimed 'to encourage Irish talent, only local artists engaged', and conducted her own choral and orchestral works at public concerts.[46]

Patterson was a member of the Gaelic League and the National Literary Society, and in 1897 a co-founder of Feis Ceoil. She was an organiser of the first Oireachtas, for which she composed a 'Song of the Movement', *Go mairidh ár nGaedhilg slán* [*Long Live Our Irish Language*], the rallying song

42 'A Tale of Two Siblings', *The Lyric Feature*, presented by Claire Cunningham, RTÉ Lyric FM, 8 March 2013.

43 Pine and Acton, *To Talent Alone*, pp. 166–79.

44 See O'Connor, 'The Role of Women'.

45 James Joyce, 'The Dead', *Dubliners* (London, 1956), p. 199.

46 *Freeman's Journal*, 9, 12, 25 March 1892, 23 February 1893.

of the Gaelic League, performed in Irish by a choir and harpists.[47] From October 1899 to December 1901 she contributed 115 articles on a range of musical topics to the *Weekly Irish Times* and published seven books on music and musicians between 1902 and 1926.[48] In 1909 Patterson called for the establishment of a Free National Conservatoire of Music in Ireland, and prophesied that, in fifty years, 'Erin would then hold her own, not alone in Folk Song but in orchestral music and operatic music as well'.[49]

For someone who was so firmly rooted in the Dublin musical scene it is surprising that in 1909 Patterson moved to Cork to a post as organist of St Anne's, Shandon, where she remained until her death twenty-five years later. As lecturer in Irish music at University College Cork from 1924 she gave a public lecture or recital once a term and taught composition to an occasional music student, including Aloys Fleischmann. She also served as a council member of the Society of Women Musicians, founded in London in 1911, which supported women composers and was connected to the women's suffrage movement.[50] Patterson's life spanned many social changes for women. The male-dominated society was slowly beginning to be challenged. By 1931 a woman, Maud Davin, had been appointed Director of the Municipal School of Music in Dublin. But three years later she had to resign her post prior to her marriage to Frank Aiken, a government minister. Under the marriage bar women who worked in the public and civil service had to resign on marriage. The bar was officially lifted in 1973.

Professional Women

In *Music and Broadcasting in Ireland,* Richard Pine gives an account of working conditions for women musicians in the early days of the Irish radio station 2RN. Rates of pay were less for women than for their male counterparts, and the standard civil service ban on married women was in place. In 1932 when the orchestra was being expanded, newspaper advertisements for the posts advised: 'Women on marriage may be required to resign'.[51]

47 'The Oireachtas', *Gaelic Journal,* May 1897, p. 1, cited by D.A.J. MacPherson, *Women of the Irish Nation: Gender, Culture, and Irish Identity, 1890–1914* (London, 2012), Ch. 4, n. 114.

48 O'Connor, 'The Role of Women', pp. 130–64.

49 Annie Patterson, 'The Interpretation of Irish Music', *Journal of the Ivernian Society,* 2 (1909), pp, 31–42, at p. 42.

50 Paula Gillett, *Musical Women in England, 1870–1914: Encroaching on All Man's Privileges* (London, 2000), p. 222. Ruth Stanley, 'Crusades for "Musical Home Rule" and an "Irish Bayreuth": Remembering Irish Composer and Campaigner Annie W. Patterson (1868–1934)', presented at UCC Research Seminar Series, 29 September 2016.

51 Richard Pine, *Music and Broadcasting in Ireland* (Dublin, 2005) pp. 66–7.

An appointments board consisting of Patterson, John F. Larchet, professor of music at University College Dublin, and Vincent O'Brien, musical director of the radio station 2RN, recommended that the leader of the orchestra, Terry O'Connor, and station accompanist, Kitty O'Doherty, both married women, should be confirmed in their existing posts despite the ruling. The Minister for Posts and Telegraphs, Senator Joseph Connolly, refused to accept the recommendation, until the Secretary of the Department assured him of the board's opinion that 'these ladies are so essential as to outweigh the objections to the employment of married women'. The minister finally accepted this with a stringent condition:

> That it be definitely understood that if and when there is available a sufficiently qualified musician to take the place of either a married woman member of the orchestra whose husband is in a position to provide adequately for her, or a woman member of the orchestra who might be termed a 'Pin-Money' earner, the replacement will take place.[52]

Midway through the twentieth century, Aloys Fleischmann's volume *Music in Ireland* (of which only four of its thirty-seven contributors were women) provided a road map of the music profession in the thirty-two counties of Ireland. There were no women music inspectors in the Department of Education nor any women on the official teaching staff of university music departments, except for UCD where there were two female assistants, Rita Broderick and Máiréad Ní Phiogóid. Apart from Patricia Read, founder of the Read School of Pianoforte Playing (1915), and May Cosgrave of the Leinster School of Music (1904), both private music schools, women did not occupy positions such as principals or directors.[53] However, the teacher-training colleges were populated by women staff, including nuns, and the Register of Music Teachers, i.e. teachers in private practice, listed in *Music in Ireland*, consisted almost entirely of women.[54]

Professional organisations, such as the Irish Federation of Musicians and the Leinster Society of Organists and Choirmasters, were male dominated. Olive Smith, honorary treasurer of the Music Association of Ireland (MAI), was the only woman officer of the association.[55] Only two works by women composers, Ina Boyle and Joan Trimble, were included

52 Pine, *Music and Broadcasting*, p. 67.

53 Aloys Fleischmann (ed.), *Music in Ireland: A Symposium* (Cork, 1952), pp. 127–8.

54 Fleischmann, *Music in Ireland*, pp. 339–60.

55 Olive Smith's groundbreaking musical initiatives for young people in Ireland include the founding in 1970 of the Irish Youth Orchestra (Irish National Youth Orchestra, INYO, since 1987). See Gillian Smith, *Olive Smith: A Musical Visionary* (Bantry, 2019).

in the list of first performances of works by Irish composers 1935–51.[56] From 1938 to 1998 orchestral works by 129 Irish composers performed by the RTÉ Symphony Orchestra (SO)/National Symphony Orchestra (NSO) and RTÉ Concert Orchestra (CO) included 18 works by nine women.[57] Twenty years later *The Binding of the Years* by Deirdre Gribbin was performed in 2018 at the 70th anniversary concert of the RTÉ NSO.

Change for the Better

Unlike in the 1950s, women in Ireland today are heads of music departments in universities and institutes of technology and comprise many of the lecturers in various music disciplines. Women are active as performers, composers, choral directors, conductors, educationalists, community musicians, promoters and arts administrators. They hold key posts in the Arts Council of Ireland, Culture Ireland, the Irish Traditional Music Archive, Music Network, the Contemporary Music Centre, Chamber Choir Ireland, Crash Ensemble and Music Generation, and are the driving forces in arts centres and music festivals all over the country. During the 1990s Chamber Choir Ireland celebrated International Women's Day with concerts of music by women composers. In 2017 Nathalie Stutzmann was appointed principal guest conductor of the RTÉ NSO, the first woman to hold this post. Women have influential positions in RTÉ's Music Department, the Music Inspectorate of the Department of Education and Skills and the music section of the Teaching Council. The revival and development of interest in the Irish harp in Ireland is a result of the efforts of many women who have supported Cairde na Cruite since it was founded in 1960.

The Encyclopaedia of Music in Ireland contains short accounts of many women who played significant roles in Irish musical life in the twentieth century, including pianist and composer Rhoda Coghill, composer Joan Trimble, and renowned singers and recording artists Bernadette Greevy and Ann Murray, piano teacher Mabel Swainson, choir director Ethna Barror, and the legendary singer and teacher Veronica Dunne.[58] (For more on Coghill, see Watson, Chapter 11, this volume; for more on Trimble, see Stanley, Chapter 10.) In the twenty-first century, among those who have achieved international renown include a host of singers such as Patricia Bardon, Orla Boylan, Tara Erraught and Paula Murrihy,

56 Fleischmann, *Music in Ireland*, pp. 170–5.

57 Pine, *Music and Broadcasting in Ireland*, pp. 82–4, 144, 458–9, 570–1. The composers in question and numbers of works they had performed were: Ina Boyle (4), Elizabeth Maconchy (5), Joan Trimble (1), Antoinette Kirkwood (1), Alicia Needham (2), Rhona Clarke (1), Marian Ingoldsby (1), Gráinne Mulvey (1), Jane O'Leary (2).

58 Veronica Dunne (1927–2021) had an international singing career and was a gifted teacher. She launched every major Irish singer.

while leading choral conductors include Blanaid Murphy, Ite O'Donovan and Bernie Sherlock.[59]

The American-born composer and pianist Jane O'Leary settled in Galway in 1972. She founded the chamber music ensemble Concorde in 1976, which has commissioned and premiered over one hundred compositions by Irish composers. O'Leary was Artistic Director of Music for Galway from 1981 to 2013, a member of the Arts Council from 1998 to 2003, and chairperson of the Contemporary Music Centre from 1989 to 1995. Her compositions have been premiered by leading performing groups at home and abroad. In 1985 Concorde decided to programme more music by women composers. In 2001 O'Leary wrote: 'It would now appear ridiculous to advertise a concert as "devoted to the works of female composers" as we did in June 1987 at the Royal Hospital Kilmainham. If such a thing happens now, it is certainly unworthy of observation.'[60] In 1996 she stated that no music by Irish women composers was yet available on commercial CD.[61]

Since then, the situation has improved substantially. Music by Irish women composers has featured on Marco Polo, Capstone, Navona, Black Box, Métier, Ergodos, Dutton Epoch, and RTÉ Lyric FM labels and on promotional CDs from the Contemporary Music Centre (CMC).[62] Women composers have been commissioned by national organisations such as Concorde, Crash Ensemble and RTÉ; the gendered distribution of public funds, however, has yet to be measured.[63] Women composers

59 Blanaid Murphy: Palestrina Choir, Dublin Bach Singers, Carlow Choral Society, RIAM Chorale; Ite O'Donovan: Lassus Scholars, Piccolo Lasso; Bernie Sherlock: Culwick Choral Society, Young Dublin Singers, TU Dublin Chamber Choir, Irish Youth Choir, New Dublin Voices.

60 Jane O'Leary, '25 Years of Concorde', *Journal of Music in Ireland*, 1 September 2001, <https://journalofmusic.com/focus/25-years-concorde> [accessed 18 March 2021].

61 Jane O'Leary, 'Women Composers in Ireland: A Changing Profile', *International Alliance for Women in Music Journal*, October 1996, pp. 16–17.

62 Elaine Agnew, 'Strings A-Stray' (1998); Ina Boyle, Orchestral Works (2018); Rhona Clarke, 'Dancing in Daylight' (2016), 'A Different Game' (2017); Concorde, 'Celtic Connections' (1997), 'Rational Option Insanity' (1999), 'Reflections' (2010); Cliona Doris, 'A Pale Yellow Sky' (2008); Deirdre Gribbin, 'Venus Blazing' (2010), 'Island People' (2013); Elizabeth Hilliard, 'Sea to the West (2017); Una Hunt, 'Joan Trimble: Two Pianos – Songs and Chamber Music (1999), 'Piano Portraits, the Music of Fanny Robinson' (2018); Aylish Kerrigan, 'I am Wind on Sea' (2016); Gráinne Mulvey, 'Akanos' (2014); Jane O'Leary, 'The Passing Sound of Forever'(2017),'Celtic Connections' (1997), 'In the Stillness of Time' (2007); Judith Ring, 'What Was'; Jennifer Walshe, 'Grúpat'(2009), 'Nature Data' (2010).

63 Sounding the Feminists and the Contemporary Music Centre are currently engaged in a gender audit project to determine how public funds are distributed among composers of different genders.

have also featured as RTÉ Lyric FM composers-in-residence and in the RTÉ/CMC Composer Lab initiative.[64] In 2019 Jennifer Walshe became the first Irish-born composer elected to Germany's Akademie der Künste, the Berlin-based academy of arts founded in 1696, which has an international membership.

In the area of music education Laura Watson has demonstrated that the representation of women composers on the Leaving Certificate music syllabus is nonexistent and has called for revision.[65] There have been major developments in the provision of university music courses and postgraduate opportunities in the past thirty years. In 2015 Lorraine Byrne Bodley was elected the first woman president of the Society for Musicology in Ireland (SMI). The SMI Music Theses Register lists a high proportion of women contributors at both MA and PhD level. Similarly, there is a significant number of female contributors and subject editors in *The Encyclopaedia of Music in Ireland*. The revival of interest by publishers of books and articles on music by Irish women authors marks a milestone in the history of musicology in Ireland. In 2018, *Ina Boyle 1889–1967: A Composer's Life*, co-authored by Ita Beausang and Séamas de Barra, was the first book published about the life and music of a female Irish composer.

The first Women and Music in Ireland conference was hosted by the Department of Music at Maynooth University, in association with the Society for Musicology in Ireland. Fourteen papers were presented together with three concerts of music by 10 Irish women composers. Two further conferences on this theme were held in 2012 and 2014. The six-part series *Women of Note* and other *Lyric Feature* programmes on RTÉ Lyric FM, produced by Claire Cunningham and musicologist Una Hunt, added an important dimension to the history of women and music in Ireland, by profiling the lives and works of forgotten female musicians in the nineteenth and twentieth centuries.[66]

There is one significant area where women musicians in Ireland are still noticeably in the minority. Jane O'Leary was the only woman composer member of Aosdána until 1996, when Eibhlís Farrell was elected.[67] Today

64 RTÉ Lyric FM: Elaine Agnew (2008–09); Linda Buckley (2011–12). Composer Lab: Anne-Marie O'Farrell (2015); Amanda Feery (2016); Maria Minguella (2018); Kerry Hagan (2019).

65 Laura Watson, 'Sexism and the Leaving Certificate Music Syllabus', *Journal of Music*, 24 August 2015, <https://journalofmusic.com/focus/sexism-and-leaving-cert-music-syllabus> [accessed 18 March 2021].

66 Composers featured on *Women of Note*: Augusta Holmès, Adela Madison, Hope Temple, Annie Patterson, Dorothy Parke, Ellen O'Hea (Elena Norton), Mary Dickenson-Auner, Alicia Adelaide Needham, Charlotte Milligan-Fox, Helen Dufferin, Rhoda Coghill, Ina Boyle.

67 Founded by the Arts Council of Ireland in 1981 to provide financial support to Irish artists.

there are eight women members out of a total of thirty-one musicians,[68] whereas the proportion of women in the literature and art sections is much higher. Elsewhere, in a different effort to redress the gender gap, a ten-month Female Conductor Programme supported by Grant Thornton and RTÉ NSO was first presented by the National Concert Hall (NCH) in 2017–18.

Bridging the Gap

For Irish women composers, performance of their works remains as difficult in the twenty-first century as it was for Ina Boyle a hundred years ago. In September 2016 *Composing the Island*, a festival of music in Ireland for a hundred years, was presented by RTÉ and the National Concert Hall at which there was a conspicuous absence of music by women composers. Gender balance is noticeably absent in programmes of public concerts and music festivals.[69] In response to this exclusion a new movement, 'Composing the Feminists', was launched, modelled on 'Waking the Feminists', the campaign organised in response to the neglect of women playwrights in the Abbey Theatre's centenary programme. In 2017, renamed 'Sounding the Feminists', a six-woman working group, chaired by composer Karen Power, was established as 'an Irish-based collective of composers, sound artists, performers, musicologists, educators, students, critics, promoters, industry professionals, organisations and individuals committed to promoting and publicising the creative work of female musicians'.[70] On behalf of the Contemporary Music Centre, composer Amanda Feery curated a two-part mixtape of music by Irish women artists.[71]

On International Women's Day 2018 Josepha Madigan TD, Minister for Culture, announced a five-year programme to promote and commission work by female artists together with the NCH and Sounding the Feminists. That day also marked the launch in Clonmel, Co. Tipperary, of 'Finding a Voice', a festival celebrating women composers; it is now an annual event curated by Róisín Maher. In April 2018, two 'Musical Tales' were held in Dublin to coincide with the Dublin City Council 'One City One

68 Elaine Agnew, Rhona Clarke, Siobhán Cleary, Eibhlís Farrell, Gráinne Mulvey, Jane O'Leary, Jennifer Walshe and Linda Buckley.

69 Michael Dervan, 'Gender Balance Not Being Taken Seriously by Irish Music Organisations', *Irish Times*, 18 July 2018, <https://www.irishtimes.com/culture/music/gender-balance-not-being-taken-seriously-by-irish-music-organisations-1.356 7760> [accessed 18 March 2021]. See also Mark Fitzgerald, 'Composing Equality', *Enclave Review*, 16, 2018 <http://enclavereview.org/composing-equality/> [accessed 18 March 2021].

70 See <www.soundingthefeminists.com> [accessed 18 March 2021].

71 <https://www.mixcloud.com/cmcireland/amanda-feery-mixtape/> [accessed 10 May 2021].

Book' initiative. Paralleling the scope of the book *The Long Gaze Back*, an anthology of short stories by Irish women writers, Mark Fitzgerald curated recitals consisting of music by Irish women.[72]

After more than four hundred years the struggle for Hibernia's musical daughters to bridge that gap continues, confirming that women in Ireland and their music will be seen and heard in the future.

72 Sinéad Gleeson (ed.), *The Long Gaze Back* (Dublin, 2016). For more on the concerts, see <https://www.cmc.ie/events/2018/apr/musical-tales-2018-lunch-timeconcert> [accessed 10 May 2021].

2

'No Accomplishment So Great for a Lady': Women and Music in the Eighteenth- and Nineteenth-Century Elite Irish Household

Karol Mullaney-Dignam

Historical aspects of the country house in Ireland beyond the architectural have received increased scholarly attention over the past decade,[1] and recently the women of these houses have been the focus of dedicated studies.[2] For the most part, though, the sounds of elite daily life have eluded historical investigation, despite the fact that material traces and documentary evidence – specifically of music – survive.[3] Music making was integral to social and cultural life both within and beyond the country house and one of the necessary 'accomplishments' for women of, or aspiring to, social rank and fortune. Contemporary conduct books such as *The Young Ladies' Conduct, or, Rules for Education*, published in London in 1722, promoted the idea that 'music refines the taste, polishes the mind; and is an entertainment, without other views, that preserves

1 Examples include: Terence Dooley and Christopher Ridgway (eds), *The Irish Country House: Its Past, Present and Future* (Dublin, 2011); Patricia McCarthy, *Life in the Country House in Georgian Ireland* (Yale, 2016); Terence Dooley and Christopher Ridgway (eds), *The Country House and the Great War: Irish and British Experiences* (Dublin, 2016).

2 See, for example: Ruth Thorpe, *Women, Architecture and Building in the East of Ireland, c.1790–1840* (Dublin, 2013); Terence Dooley, Maeve O'Riordan and Christopher Ridgway (eds), *Women and the Country House in Ireland and Britain* (Dublin, 2018); Maeve O'Riordan, *Women of the Country House in Ireland, 1860–1914* (Liverpool, 2018).

3 See: Karol Mullaney-Dignam, 'Useless and Extravagant? The Consumption of Music in the Irish Country House', in Andrew Hann and Jon Stobart (eds), *The Country House: Material Culture and Consumption* (Swindon, 2016), pp. 156–65. Information about recent research on music in country houses across the Anglophone world can be found at the Sound Heritage project website: <https://sound-heritage.soton.ac.uk/music-resources-guide>.

[young ladies] from the rust of idleness, that most pernicious enemy to virtue'.[4] The concept of music as a suitable female diversion was also propagated by women themselves in Britain and Ireland in the Georgian, and later the Victorian, eras. There was, according to Grace, Countess Granville and Viscountess Carteret (1654–1744), 'no accomplishment so great for a lady as music, for it tunes the mind'.[5] The majority of women were not as prominent as Lady Granville – whose titles were granted *suo jure* (in her own right rather than through marriage) in January 1714/15 – and have been relegated to obscurity.[6] However, historical evidence of music and related activities can be used to create narratives of these women's lives, homes and surroundings, restoring them to the social and cultural historiography of the Irish country house.

The Irish country house – the residence of a landowner at the centre of a landed estate held in freehold or owned outright and leased in smaller parcels to tenants – had its heyday with the Protestant Ascendancy in the eighteenth and nineteenth centuries. Prior to this, as the British crown confiscated and regranted land, the country residences of landowners typically took the form of defensive castles or fortified tower-houses. Political stability and greater economic growth following the accession of the House of Hanover to the kingdoms of Great Britain and Ireland, in 1714, encouraged Protestant landowners to become more settled and more prosperous; several built new, fashionable, unfortified homes. By this time, the majority of land in Ireland was owned by those who professed the established state religion (Anglicanism), which was only practised by a minority of the Irish population. So it was that throughout the eighteenth and nineteenth centuries, when wealth was typically underpinned by land, the associated political, social and economic power was held almost entirely by a minority landowning elite. It is important to note that the Irish landowners were not a homogenous socio-economic grouping: some possessed far more resources, and much bigger houses and estates, than others.[7]

One of the first significant (and largest surviving) country houses constructed in Ireland was Castletown House, near Celbridge in Co. Kildare. It was built in the classical Palladian style by the Conollys in the 1720s.[8] While this family held thousands of acres of land in

4 John Essex, *The Young Ladies' Conduct, or, Rules for Education* (London, 1722), p. 85.

5 Letter from Countess Granville to Mrs Pendarves [afterwards, Mrs Delany], 14 March 1733/4, in Lady Llanover (ed.), *The Autobiography and Correspondence of Mary Granville, Mrs Delany*, 3 vols (London, 1861), vol. 1, p. 435.

6 This was the date prior to the introduction of the new Gregorian calendar.

7 Terence Dooley, *The Big Houses and Landed Estates of Ireland: A Research Guide* (Dublin, 2007).

8 Patrick Walsh, *Castletown, Co. Kildare* (Dublin, 2007).

ten different counties, as well as property in England, some of their contemporaries held just a few hundred acres of land and earned their livings as clergymen or military men; these were acceptable occupations too for cadet branches of large landowning families. Extant personal correspondence and financial records indicate that some members of the Irish landed class spent sizeable sums of money on urban musical experiences, including attendance at operas and concerts of instrumental music. Their country houses were manifestations of political, social and economic power but they were also family homes and sites of material acquisition and display – what Thorstein Veblen labelled 'conspicuous consumption'.[9] Thus, historical records that detail expenditure on music-related goods and services provide some of the best evidence of musical activity.

The Consumption of Music

The attainment of musical knowledge allowed women in particular to 'perform' publicly as consumers of music but this did not mean that they necessarily understood or enjoyed the music in question. Despite being a patron of what she termed 'Italian music' concerts and publications, Lady Louisa Augusta Conolly née Lennox (1743–1821), for example, preferred the less 'serious' musical offerings of the theatre or playhouse. While visiting her ancestral home at Goodwood in England in 1772, she wrote to her husband Thomas that the 'musical men' there were 'all very obliging and let themselves down to songs not worthy of them to please my bad taste in music'.[10] Clearly self-conscious about her musical preferences, she also wrote to her sister Sarah:

> I wonder if it is possible for me ever to acquire such a taste … Though I have often tried, I never found that I could like Italian music. I have a notion that it is owing to some fault in the formation of my ear that sounds strike me differently from what they do other people.[11]

It is significant that although Lady Louisa was troubled by her inclination towards popular theatre songs, she dutifully attended operas and instrumental concerts in Ireland and England. Motivated more by social and philanthropic concerns than enthusiasm for the music, she brought the young ladies in her care to hear music at churches such as St Werburgh's in Dublin and attended subscription concerts in the city, at the Rotunda

9 Thorstein Veblen, *The Theory of the Leisure Class: An Economic Study in the Evolution of Institutions* (London, 1899).

10 Louisa Conolly to Thomas Conolly, 3 April 1772 (Irish Architectural Archive, Conolly Letters, 94/136/1).

11 Louisa Conolly to Sarah Bunbury, 29 January 1772 (Irish Architectural Archive, Conolly Letters, 94/136/1).

Assembly Rooms and the William Street Exhibition Rooms. Being 'seen' to appreciate music of quality was evidently an important aspect of elite female social behaviour in the eighteenth century.

The Georgian era was what Christopher Wright has termed 'an age of musical princes'.[12] Elite musical culture in Ireland reflected that of much of continental Europe, sustaining both native and foreign suppliers of musical goods and services. In his examination of what was written, printed, published, owned, and sometimes read in Ireland between 1680 and 1784, Toby Barnard has demonstrated that Ireland was caught up in the cultural currents of the eighteenth-century cosmopolitan rather than more introverted and insular concerns.[13] Ita Hogan has estimated that there were more than sixty music sellers and publishers in Dublin during the period from 1780 to 1830, with comparative numbers in the provincial towns.[14] Italian instrumentalists, singers and composers proliferated, and Italian vocal and instrumental musical styles dominated; the lingua franca of music spoken by almost every European composer had developed in Italy.[15] That country emerged largely unscathed by the territorial power struggles that afflicted much of the rest of the continent, which allowed for greater mobility of musical artists both in and out of the major musical cities of Venice, Rome, Naples and Bologna. It also facilitated developments in a variety of musical forms, many of which were encountered by wealthy British and Irish people on the Grand Tour.[16]

Origins notwithstanding, most of the leading continental musicians, singers and actors of the day included Ireland in their itineraries and, as Brian Boydell observed, 'a great many celebrities braved the hazardous and unreliable sea conditions to pay extended visits ... some settling there permanently'.[17] Second only to London in terms of population, Dublin city was a cultural hub of significant social and intellectual stature, on account of the independent Irish parliament and the vice-regal court at Dublin Castle. Apart from the cathedrals and larger churches, which served as concert venues throughout the eighteenth century, the castle was among the few non-domestic sites capable of accommodating sizeable audiences in the early decades, although much of the music performed there would have occurred in connection with social dancing at formal balls. Still, an official 'master of the state music' – a position

12 Christopher Wright, *George III* (London, 2005), p. 100.

13 Toby Barnard, *Brought to Book: Print in Ireland, 1680–1784* (Dublin, 2017).

14 Ita Hogan, *Anglo-Irish Music, 1780–1830* (Cork, 1966), pp. 101–12.

15 H. Diack Johnstone and Roger Fiske (eds), *The Blackwell History of Music in Britain*, vol. 4: *The Eighteenth Century* (Oxford, 1990), p. xiv.

16 See, for example, Elizabeth Fitzgerald, *Lord Kildare's Grand Tour: The Letters of William Fitzgerald, 1766–1769* (Cork, 2000).

17 Brian Boydell, *Rotunda Music in Eighteenth-Century Dublin* (Dublin, 1992), p. 15.

held by a succession of immigrant musicians – oversaw musical functions and composed pieces for 'state' ceremonial occasions.[18] The arrival of the viceroy (or Lord Lieutenant) to live 'in state' at the castle marked the beginning of the Dublin social season. This usually coincided with the sitting of the Irish parliament at College Green, until its abolition by the Acts of Union, which came into effect in 1801.

Long after the 1801 unification of the kingdoms of Great Britain and Ireland, the Dublin Season continued to see an influx of courtiers and parliamentarians from their country seats to attend social events at Dublin Castle. This provided a seasonal boost to the city's economy.[19] Suppliers of all types of goods and services – music masters, musicians and music tradesmen among them – used targeted newspaper advertisements to attract the custom and patronage of the so-called 'nobility and gentry'. While this grouping of hereditary titleholders, politicians, military officers, entrepreneurs and ecclesiastics was bound largely by religion and landownership, there was substantial variation in the rank and fortune of individuals. This meant that although Dublin operated as the cultural capital for many, those who could afford to sought new practices and materials in London and further afield. For less affluent landowners, a trip to a provincial urban centre such as Limerick or Cork was often a more affordable option. In any case, time spent 'in town' meant purchasing fashionable fabrics and accessories, experiencing the latest entertainments, socialising with peers and, where relevant, finding suitable marriage partners. Members of the landowning class were regarded as the animators and arbiters of 'fashionable' society and culture. They were patrons of the performance arts and visual arts, and their patronage was a vital element in the success of any public venue or event.

Music in the Life Cycle of Girls and Women

Amanda Vickery has contended in the English context that 'consumption of urban culture and fashionable leisure among genteel women was patterned on the life cycle' with 'children expected to be innocent of [urban culture and fashionable leisure], those of a marriageable age at the centre of it and those with family responsibilities above it'.[20] The

18 Brian Boydell, 'Music, 1700–1850', in T.W. Moody and W.E. Vaughan (eds), *A New History of Ireland*, vol. 4: *Eighteenth-Century Ireland, 1691–1800* (Oxford, 1986), pp. 568–628, at p. 569 and pp. 574–6.

19 Elizabeth (Daisy) Burke Plunkett, Lady Fingall, *Seventy Years Young: Memories of Elizabeth, Countess of Fingall*, first published in London, 1937 (Dublin, 1991), pp. 58–76.

20 Amanda Vickery, *The Gentleman's Daughter: Women's Lives in Georgian England* (New Haven and London, 1999), p. 265.

evidence shows that the lives of women of the Irish country house were also moulded in this way and unfolded against a backdrop of musical activity both outside and within the home. Informal music education began as early as children were exposed to the proclivities and practices of relatives. As Ursula M. Rempel has noted, subjects like 'needlework, penmanship, drawing, dancing and music' were usually 'more important in the female curriculum' than 'arithmetic, geography, religion, literature and languages, botany/natural history'.[21] Dancing masters provided lessons in social courtesy and deportment as well as the fashionable dance steps, while it was not uncommon for a proficient governess or female relative to teach performance basics in music. In later years, formal instruction was provided by specialist teachers outside the home, but the frequency and quality depended on the resources and social mobility of a landlord and his family.

Women and girls exposed to music from a young age evidently understood its different social contexts as each stage of their lives was marked by musical practices that cultivated different familial and social relationships. In 1785, at the aforementioned Castletown House, Lady Louisa Conolly marvelled at how her two-year-old niece (and adopted daughter) Emily associated music with dancing, writing that: 'whenever the girls play upon the harpsichord she sets off and has a notion of turning her little arms over head'.[22] She was discovered 'trotting about' at dances in the house – the purpose of which seems to have been to enable Louisa's numerous teenage nieces and nephews to socialise and practise their steps – delighting everyone by 'holding her petticoats to dance like the company'.[23] Once Emily reached eight years of age, she received professional instruction on the harpsichord and in the rudiments of music as part of her social education; being at the upper echelons of the social ladder, she went on to have lessons with music teachers and dancing masters in London.[24] Music featured too in the lives of her cousins who lived nearby at Carton; they were the Fitzgeralds, children of Ireland's premier peer, the Duke of Leinster.[25] Lady Sophia Fitzgerald, daughter of

21 Ursula M. Rempel, 'The Complete Female: Musical "Accomplishment" in the Late Eighteenth Century', *Man and Nature / L'homme et la nature*, vol. 8 (1989), 39–48, at p. 39.

22 Louisa Conolly to Sarah Napier, 2 February 1785 (Irish Architectural Archive, Conolly Letters, 94/136/2).

23 Louisa Conolly to Sarah Napier, 6 January 1785 (Irish Architectural Archive, Conolly Letters, 94/136/2).

24 Karol Mullaney-Dignam, *Music and Dancing at Castletown, Co. Kildare, 1759–1821* (Dublin, 2011), pp. 51–2.

25 Karol Mullaney-Dignam, '"French Horns Playing at Every Meal": Music at Carton', in Patrick Cosgrove, Terence Dooley and Mullaney-Dignam (eds), *Aspects of Irish Aristocratic Life: Essays on the Fitzgeralds and Carton House* (Dublin, 2014), pp. 92–105.

the 1st Duke, noted in her journal: 'I did get up rather earlier than usual and amused myself playing two or three tunes Harriette had brought me on the harpsichord till breakfast.'[26]

Music was a notable agent of cultural transfer between Irish country houses in the long nineteenth century. Printed sheet music was collected and shared, and many young women spent hours 'writing music' – copying music from printed music sheets – into pre-ruled manuscript music books. Some of these copybooks were started by one family member and used by another, bringing together several copyists' hands or collectors' signatures within a single binding. Tunes were transcribed by or in the company of friends and visitors, music making in a 'private' or domestic setting being a permissible means of display, communication and, in some cases, intimacy.[27] But beyond playing or teaching music in the home there were few, if any, other appropriate outlets for women of the country house to apply their musical skills by the nineteenth century. A professional career was beyond the social constraints of their gender and class. Women who performed as professional actresses, opera singers or ballet dancers were, as Merry E. Wiesner has noted, 'not regarded as honourable women, and many were able to support themselves only by also being the mistress of an artistically inclined male patron'.[28] As a result, upper-class women only ever performed in an amateur and informal capacity and rarely outside the home. Expenditure on musical instruction, goods and services was primarily an investment in their social refinement. They modelled behaviours to other women of lower social status by participating in philanthropic events in the villages or towns on their estates. Thus, in 1875, we find Mary Parsons (1813–85), Countess of Rosse, of Birr Castle, King's County (afterwards Co. Offaly) playing piano duets at an amateur concert in aid of new schools in the locality.[29]

For women on the so-called marriage market, the ability to sing and play music simply, elegantly, and without exhibition, functioned as a measurement of preparation for their future roles as wife, mother and hostess. Important family events in the Irish country house and on the landed estate – marriages, christenings, comings-of-age and harvests – were marked with music and related activities. Music was thus a

26 Journal of Lady Sophia Fitzgerald, 19 February 1783 (National Library of Ireland, Lennox/FitzGerald/Campbell Papers, MS 35,012/1).

27 See Richard Leppert's *Music and Image: Domesticity, Ideology and Socio-Cultural Formation in Eighteenth-Century England* (Cambridge, 1993).

28 Merry E. Wiesner, *Women and Gender in Early Modern Europe* (Cambridge, 2000), p. 188.

29 *Musical Times and Singing Class Circular*, 16 (1875), 788. See also Karol Mullaney-Dignam, 'Irish Country House Music Collections: Birr Castle, Co. Offaly', *Brio: Journal of the International Association of Music Libraries, UK and Ireland*, 49 (2012), 23–36.

significant agent in the formation and expression not only of female identity but also of social and economic status in the eighteenth and nineteenth centuries. A band of musicians was usually hired for a ball or any large or lavish 'public' event for which invitations were widely issued; family members and friends played for more intimate, 'private' gatherings. In rural and urban Ireland, 'visiting' was a fundamental and important aspect of social life, and an important supervised environment for courtship. Evenings were spent chatting, drinking, dining, playing cards, or even dancing with relatives, friends, local landowners or clergymen. In the early twentieth century, the memoirs of elite women such as Elizabeth Plunkett (1866–1944), Countess of Fingall, of Killeen Castle, Co. Meath, still referred to female friends and music making in this context. Recalling a visit to Adare in Co. Limerick, seat of the Earl of Dunraven, around 1903, the countess wrote:

> I shall always remember a night when I listened in the Oak Gallery above the hall to Lady Dunraven and her daughters playing, she at the piano, Rachel and Eileen, the violin and 'cello. And then, Mr Plumstead, the Adare organist, sat down at the organ, and Lady Dudley [wife of the then Lord Lieutenant or viceroy in Ireland], with her lovely voice, sang from the organ loft: 'Oh for the Wings of a Dove!'[30]

Keyboard and string instruments were deemed most suitable for the ladies of the country house, as was singing, but not all landed families could afford to purchase and install an instrument such as an organ; large instruments such as pianos were hired or borrowed when required in the Victorian period.

Interpreting Musical Materials

Some married, and older unmarried, women continued to practise music and acquire musical materials in order to provide mental stimulation, alleviate boredom and pass on their knowledge to younger relatives. The practice of music and acquisition of materials may have permitted them to perform as consumers of music in public, and display their accomplishment in private, but they were dissuaded from engaging with it *too* seriously. To do so was mannish. The music collector, composer and novelist Sydney Owenson, Lady Morgan (*c.*1776–1859), admitted in the nineteenth century that although her father had ensured that she was generally well educated, she had 'studied music rather as a sentiment than a science and drawing as an instrument rather than an art lest I should become a musical pedant, or masculine artist'.[31] Music making

30 Lady Fingall, *Seventy Years Young*, p. 281.

31 Mary Campbell, *Lady Morgan: The Life and Times of Sydney Owenson* (London, 1988), p. 52.

was not a requisite male accomplishment but men with ability were encouraged to study it in a serious or academic way.

Owenson did not hail from a landed family. The daughter of the actor, composer, playwright and theatre manager Robert Owenson (MacOwen), she acquired her title through marriage. She worked for many years as a governess, first at Bracklyn Castle, the home of the Featherstone family in Co. Westmeath, and then at Fort William, the home of the Crawford family in Co. Tipperary. Coming from the middling ranks of society, Owenson probably had different expectations for her life than the country house occupants she tutored, yet she was responsible for preparing them for adulthood. Despite repeated attacks by (male) critics of her novels, she was feted by elite society in Dublin and London, an entrée to which was provided by her popularity and success. She became friends with Lady Abercorn, third wife of the 1st Marquess, and was persuaded to join her as a lady companion at Baron's Court in Co. Tyrone. There, she attracted the attention of the Abercorn's physician, Sir Thomas Morgan, marrying him in 1812 and joining the minor ranks of the gentry.

The names of the majority of women associated with Ireland's country houses are not as well known today as those of Lady Morgan or Lady Louisa Conolly. Generally, women of higher social status, country house inhabitants included, did not participate in politics or business, nor did they typically inherit property; hence, they do not always appear in the public record. Those unmarried or childless were sometimes omitted altogether from authoritative published genealogies. Thus, it is only by investigating extant music collections that some women can be identified and represented. A case in point is provided by the assemblage at Glin Castle, Co. Limerick, home of the Fitzgeralds, Knights of Glin, the majority of which seems to have belonged to a daughter of the 24th Knight, Margaretta Sophia Fitzgerald (*fl.*1838–72). Margaretta's birth date is unknown and, despite the presence of numerous celebrated individual portraits at Glin Castle, none exist of her. This is not unusual, given her life circumstances: not only was she a younger daughter, but she married a policeman and had no children, so did not contribute to extending the family or enhancing its pedigree.[32]

It is only by investigating surviving musical materials that information about Margaretta has been recovered. As of today, the Glin collection consists of eleven bound volumes of music: five compilations of printed music and six manuscript albums. The bound volume is a common feature of a country house music collection and very often the reason the music survives; these volumes, however, are also valuable historical sources, often revealing how women constructed relationships with

32 Karol Mullaney-Dignam, '"Spacious and Splendid": Music, Dancing and Social Life at Glin Castle, 1781–1854', *Irish Architectural and Decorative Studies*, 14 (2012), 16–37.

family members and peers. The printed music volumes at Glin comprise: *A Selection of Irish Melodies with Symphonies and Accompaniments by Sir John Stevenson, Mus. Doc., and Characteristic Words by Thomas Moore, Esqr* (two volumes), *Coomb's Divine Amusement for the use of churches, chapels, schools and private families* (one volume) and selections of piano music (two volumes). The inscriptions on the volumes of *Moore's Melodies* indicate that they originally belonged to Margaretta's mother, Bridgetta, wife of the 24th Knight of Glin, while the volume of devotional music, arranged for the voice, organ or pianoforte by J.M. Coombs, was acquired by Margaretta herself in 1861. One of the two volumes of piano selections bears the inscription 'Margaretta Sophia FitzGerald, Glin Castle, Dec. 24th 1837' and consists of music for both solo piano and piano duets (two performers on one piano). The inscription 'E.U.M. FG, Dec. 1837', found on this volume, suggests that Margaretta's duet partner was her brother Edward Urmston McLeod Fitzgerald (1820–81). Most of the music they played consisted of dances, airs with variations and popular songs arranged for piano. The second volume of piano selections, comprising exercises and scales, bears the inscription 'Margaretta Sophia FitzGerald, Glin Castle, August 30th 1838'. That this printed music was actually played is indicated by a variety of pencil markings and annotations revealing Margaretta to have been a proficient amateur musician. However, it is not known how exactly she acquired the music; some of it was certainly purchased in Limerick, some in Dublin, and the rest further afield, perhaps by her father.

The manuscript music books at Glin, dated 1836, 1839, 1844 (two volumes), 1845 and 1848, contain pieces of music written in black ink by more than one hand. Many of these were transcribed from printed sources for piano; they comprise popular overtures and marches, dance tunes such as quadrilles, polkas, galops and waltzes, and occasional songs with words in English. A military band influence can be detected in pieces like 'My Valentine Galop with vocal chorus – performed by the band of the 81st regiment' and 'Waltz by an officer of the 48th regiment'. Polkas also appear to have been written into the manuscripts by bandmasters of the 74th and 52nd light infantry, who may have been visiting. Military men had a strong presence at Glin Castle, more so than at many other country houses, owing to the unique location of its location beside the River Shannon, which was heavy with traffic and conducive to social activity in the nineteenth century. Most but not all of this manuscript music pertains to Margaretta's life before her marriage in 1847 to William Massy Blennerhassett (*c.*1818–1904), an inspector in the Royal Irish Constabulary. His personal diaries give some indication of his wife's continued relationship with music; she continued to play the piano for many years and had her husband purchase a piano from Pigott's on Grafton Street in Dublin in 1867 at a cost of £50.[33]

Interpreting the cultural practices of those for whom records survive does not, of course, minimise or represent all women's experiences of music in eighteenth- and nineteenth-century Ireland, but it does proffer valuable insights. The documentary evidence pertaining to elite households in Irish country houses – financial records, personal correspondence and diaries – reveals that expenditure on musical experiences, goods and services was not a simple matter of conspicuous consumption; further to that, it formed part of how familial relationships and social expectations were managed. Extant, albeit patchy, musical materials are important too; those ascribed to Margaretta Sophia Fitzgerald, for instance, can be taken as an indication of the music to which she was exposed, either at Glin Castle itself or its social milieu, long before and after her marriage. But her music collection carries more significance than that: it illustrates the social and family ties that domestic music making and its material culture helped to sustain. This also raises questions about the roles of elite men as makers as well as patrons of music, and points to possibilities for further exploring music and gender in elite social networks and local community contexts.

Historical musical things – documents, instruments and iconography – embodied and reflected cultural values, particularly those concerning gender propriety on the part of women. The music tradesmen and the amateur and professional music masters who facilitated music making in the homes of the Irish landed elite also contributed to the gendering of that activity. Music-related references and materials are sometimes the only surviving traces of elite women's lives. Their scholarly study aids the retrieval of those women's lives from obscurity and produces more varied, gender-balanced historical interpretations of the Irish country house. Moreover, where such houses are now open to the public, musical materials can feature not simply as props in the staging of sites as visitor attractions but as cultural heritage objects. Evidencing and understanding how elite women thought about and used their own musical things in the past should have implications for their curation, interpretation and reception today.[34]

33 Diary of William Massy Blennerhassett, 26 August and 7 September 1867 (University of Limerick Special Collections, Glin Papers, P1/22).

34 See Karol Mullaney-Dignam, 'Expanding the Narrative: Public History, Music, and the Irish Country House', in Jeanice Brooks, Matthew Stephens and Wiebke Thormählen (eds), *Sound Heritage: Making Music Matter in Historic Houses* (London, 2021), pp. 247–68.

3

The Development of the Female Musician in Nineteenth-Century Dublin

Jennifer O'Connor-Madsen

> 'Remember this lesson: in every page there are undrawn women, each waiting in her own particular silence.'[1]

In the final decades of the twentieth century there was a growth in feminist musicology and an increased interest in researching female composers and musicians, particularly nineteenth-century figures such as Clara Schumann and Fanny Hensel.[2] This led to a greater awareness of women's contribution to music throughout the ages. However, in Irish musicology the study of female involvement in music remained a neglected field until the early twenty-first century. Initial research into women's role in nineteenth-century Dublin in the early 2000s saw them as names that were referenced but never explored, personalities who had contributed but who were not acknowledged.[3] The common thread was the belief that they were insignificant in comparison to their male counterparts, often dismissed as footnotes in the lives of their male peers. A closer examination led to a palette that painted a different picture – one of contribution, talent, determination and resilience. Their contributions shaped the institutions, performances, festivals and music of nineteenth-century Dublin. Their work was acknowledged and appreciated by their

1 Doireann Ní Ghríofa, *A Ghost in the Throat* (Dublin, 2020).
2 For example: Nancy B. Reich, *Clara Schumann: The Artist and the Woman* (Ithaca, 1985) and Marcia J. Citron, *The Letters of Fanny Hensel to Felix Mendelssohn* (New York, 1987).
3 Several texts and conferences held in Ireland, dating from around twenty years ago, frequently make reference to women but offer little in the way of detail. See, for example, Richard Pine and Charles Acton (eds), *To Talent Alone: The Royal Irish Academy of Music 1848–1998* (Dublin, 1998) and early volumes of the Irish Musical Studies series.

male counterparts, but it was quickly forgotten when the history books were written.

The rise of feminist musicology in the late twentieth century reflected a general development in research dedicated to the involvement of women in the past across disciplines such as history, sociology and anthropology. The position of women in Irish history in a broader sense was similar to that of women in music, they were largely ignored by historians until the late twentieth century, when scholars such as Margaret Ward and Maria Luddy addressed the situation.[4] They set about highlighting the importance of women in history, particularly in the nineteenth century. Ward described the treatment of women as pointing to 'collective amnesia' both in Irish historiography and the Irish mind.[5] During the nineteenth century, women in all areas of Irish society had become more independent and involved in society; Ward, Luddy and others highlighted the importance of women in the development of the country's culture, politics and education since the nineteenth century. The lack of research into women in Irish music until recently has resulted in significant gaps in understanding the development of musical culture in nineteenth-century Dublin. For example, the twentieth century saw several publications on the importance of the Feis Ceoil festival and its role in the development of cultural nationalism in the late nineteenth century, but none refer to its founder Annie Patterson, and initial organisers such as Edith Oldham, in much, if any, detail.[6] Despite the lack of research, the women of nineteenth-century Dublin were significant contributors to the city's musical life and active as performers, composers, organisers and educators. This chapter explores their work and its reception within the musical landscape of that time.

The Musical Landscape of Nineteenth-Century Dublin

With the Act of Union in 1800 many changes occurred in Dublin. The move of parliament back to Westminster resulted in many of Dublin's aristocracy also moving to London. However, this allowed the middle class to emerge as the new ruling class. In terms of music, this led to a continuing development in support and interest throughout the century.

4 Margaret Ward (ed.), *In Their Own Voice: Women and Irish Nationalism* (Cork, 1995); Maria Luddy (ed.), *Women in Ireland, 1800–1918: A Documentary History* (Cork, 1995).

5 Kit and Cyril O'Céirín, *Women of Ireland: A Biographic Dictionary* (Galway, 1996), p. 5.

6 W.H. Grattan Flood, *A History of Irish Music* (Dublin, 1906; reprint: Shannon, 1970); Aloys Fleischmann (ed.), *Music in Ireland: A Symposium* (Cork, 1952). While the Feis Ceoil chapter in the latter book mentions Annie Patterson, it does not credit her with the founding of the competition.

While the eighteenth century was considered the golden age of music in Ireland, particularly with the success of Handel's *Messiah* and audience appreciation for opera and choral music, the nineteenth century is worthy of recognition as a time that shaped the city's musical culture. Throughout the century as music continued to grow, so too did the level of women's involvement and the number of female musicians active in the city. In nineteenth-century Irish society women were subject to many obligations and ideals, as was the case across Europe. The prevailing ideology was that women existed for the benefit of family and that their main role was to attend to the domestic sphere. Women's role in society was generally seen as one of submissive passivity, with prescriptive literature dictating their behaviour, being particularly popular with the clergy. An example of this can be found in a lecture from 1856 given by a well-known Church of Ireland cleric, Reverend John Gregg, entitled 'Women'. He stated: 'there are two things which you ought to desire – which it is your duty to desire – ... and these are excellence and usefulness. Excellence has reference to yourselves and usefulness, to others.'[7] However, the prevalence of such writing suggested unease about the way women were living. In truth, while women were aware of what was expected of them, some resisted these ideals in favour of pursuing careers and philanthropic endeavours. This was certainly true of the many women involved in music. Their gender never seemed to hold them back. In the words of Dr Annie Patterson, 'The daughters and sisters of heroes cannot be bound within the limits of conventionality.'[8]

In 1800 there was little evidence of women working in music; however, they continued to perform, usually as singers in the city's concerts, as they had done in the previous century. As the years progressed music became an acceptable and profitable form of employment for women. They began to appear as 'professors of music', usually teaching the piano. By the mid-century women comprised about 20 per cent of the city's private teachers, and by 1900 this figure had increased to 48 per cent.[9] In many cases they established their own schools of music or musical academies, such as those of Miss Bennett and Mrs Allen. The latter was the daughter of Johann Logier, inventor of the chiroplast and creator of the Logier methods of teaching used by Clara Schumann's father.[10] Mrs Allen's academy at 5 Gardiners Row was set up with her husband but

7 Rev. John Gregg, 'A Clergyman Tells Women What is Expected of Them', cited in Luddy, *Women in Ireland*, p. 13.

8 Annie Patterson, 'Alicia Adelaide Needham', *Weekly Irish Times*, 9 June 1900, p. 4.

9 Jennifer O'Connor, 'The Role of Women in Music in Nineteenth-Century Dublin', (Unpublished PhD dissertation, Maynooth University, 2010), pp. 35–7.

10 *Freeman's Journal*, 13 January 1815.

upon his death in 1833 she became the director, running a school that boasted fourteen pianofortes and several student recitals each year.[11] Mrs Allen managed to run this academy while also raising ten children. Upon her death, the academy passed into her daughters' hands and still existed in 1900.

Women and Music Pedagogy

Mrs Allen and other private teachers began developing the music pedagogy profession for women in nineteenth-century Dublin. With the founding of the Irish Academy of Music and, more importantly, with its reorganisation in 1856, new opportunities emerged for female music teachers in Dublin. It began with the appointment of Fanny Robinson as a professor of piano, second only to her husband, Joseph Robinson. The British-born Fanny Arthur travelled to Dublin to perform in 1849 at a concert in the Antient Concert Rooms.[12] She met Joseph Robinson at the concert and they were married in June of that year. She became well known as a performer in Dublin in the 1850s; she also performed in London and at the Salle Érard in Paris.[13]

In her role in the academy Fanny Robinson oversaw the supervision and organisation of female music students, as well as teaching piano to male and female students. By 1861 she was on the same salary as her husband and Sir Robert Stewart, £100 per annum.[14] This was important, for as the first female member of staff, Fanny Robinson set the precedent for women who followed her. It was also progressive in comparison to female teachers in Britain and Europe because, as Nancy Reich pointed out, 'except for superstars like Clara Schumann, women professors were generally not accorded the respect, rank and salaries of their male counterparts'.[15] An explanation of Robinson's treatment could be that to the academy's board of management she was their superstar. By the time of her appointment to the teaching staff in 1856 she was well known as a composer and pianist, having performed in Dublin, Paris and London. Therefore, it is likely that the board of directors employed Fanny Robinson because she would draw students, much like the appointment of Clara Schumann to the Hoch Conservatory in 1878.

11 O'Connor, 'The Role of Women in Music in Nineteenth-Century Dublin', pp. 41–7.

12 *Freeman's Journal*, 20 February 1849.

13 Jennifer O'Connor, *Robinson, Fanny* <www.sophie-drinker-institut.de> [accessed 9 July 2021].

14 Pine and Acton, *To Talent Alone: The Royal Irish Academy of Music 1848–1998*, p. 85.

15 Nancy B. Reich, *Clara Schumann: The Artist and The Woman*, 2nd edn (London, 2001), p. 284.

The Royal Irish Academy of Music (RIAM) continued this progressive treatment of women. By 1889 it employed twenty-seven teachers, ten of whom were women. All the women taught piano and singing, the two disciplines seen as being suitable for a young lady. They were teaching in the country's only major music academy and earning salaries that equalled and sometimes surpassed those of their male peers.

As well as the successful careers of the those teaching in the RIAM, the influence of the organisation on the education and careers of women and female piano pedagogy worldwide is illustrated in the work of Annie Gregg, who studied with Fanny Robinson at the RIAM. After her time there she moved to Scotland, where she married John Spencer Curwen, the son of John Curwen, the main proponent of the tonic sol-fa method. She went on to author a series of pedagogical manuals for both students and teachers, which were published by her husband's press and known as *Mrs Curwen's Pianoforte Method.*

For Curwen's printing press, Annie Curwen's work was an important addition to the catalogue. Up until the 1880s, the one area that Curwen Press was not targeting was the growing population of female musicians and teachers, but the increase in female involvement in music in the nineteenth century motivated music businesses to respond to the needs of this new demographic in the music pedagogy profession. Many began to produce books and magazines aimed at the female musician.[16] By publishing Annie Curwen, the Curwen Press began to rectify their lack of offerings that would appeal specifically to women. John Curwen's publications on music teaching and the tonic sol-fa method aimed to provide the student and teacher with a 'cheap and accessible' guide to understanding and learning music.[17] Annie Curwen felt that a similar guide that dealt with the pianoforte would be useful. Her preface notes that the guide was 'an experiment' and that she wanted to do for pianoforte teachers what her father-in-law had done for the teacher of singing classes.[18] In the appendix she stated that she was not dealing with technical training and was more concerned with providing a 'better understanding of music, a better kind of teaching of the Elements'.[19] She also referred to her research in preparing to write the book and how she had ascertained through a diligent search of publishers' catalogues and at the British Museum that no one had previously attempted to write anything on this principle for the guidance of the pianoforte teacher.

Annie Curwen's publications provided the ever-growing population of female teachers in Britain, Ireland and, indeed, worldwide with a

16 Nancy B. Reich, 'European Composers and Musicians', in Karin Pendle (ed.), *Women and Music* (Indianapolis, 1991), p. 98.

17 John Curwen, *Musical Theory* (London, 1879), p. ii.

18 Annie Curwen, *Mrs Curwen's Pianoforte Method* (London, 1913), p. iii.

19 Annie Curwen, *Pianoforte Method*, p. 447.

source of professional guidance. Her books exemplify how women not only sought to become involved in the profession but also to improve it. The books provided those interested in teaching with a manual that provided step-by-step guidance in all the necessary areas of teaching. As Curwen herself suggested in the preface to *Curwen's Pianoforte Methods*, the majority of her readers were mothers and female teachers.[20] Her early foundations in the RIAM and experience of music in Dublin helped shape her knowledge of pedagogy, which subsequently supported female musicians and teachers worldwide, who followed her methods diligently. She revolutionised teaching practice around the turn of the twentieth century by endorsing a style of teaching that promoted aural observation alternating with music making. She was one of the first to emphasise psychology and physiology in music pedagogy, with her books including topics such as perception, creativity, and language connotations and denotations.[21] Her methods have been cited as an influence on many twentieth-century educators, including Zoltan Kodály.[22]

The Development of the Female Composer

Although the presence of female composers in nineteenth-century Dublin is rarely discussed, women were successful in this domain throughout the century and into the twentieth century. In his 1903 book *Woman's Work in Music*, Arthur Elson acknowledges the work of several female composers in Ireland. Despite the broad title, the book is primarily concerned with female composers. Elson praises Alicia Needham and Lady Dufferin as 'exceptionally good'; he also lists both Fanny Robinson and Annie Patterson as composers of 'cantata and songs'.[23] While the information on Robinson may be incorrect as there is no record today of her having composed songs, the fact that their work was acknowledged in 1903 illustrates that she and other women were recognised as composers, and not just in Ireland.

When female composers began to appear, their music was appreciated, performed and praised by their male peers in nineteenth-century Dublin. They composed in similar styles and forms as their female European peers

20 Annie Curwen, *Pianoforte Method*, p. v.

21 Debra Brubaker Burns, Anita Jackson and Connie Arrau Sturm, 'Contributions of Selected British and American Women to Piano Pedagogy and Performance', *The International Alliance for Women in Music Journal, IAWM*, 8 (2002), 1–9, at p. 3.

22 M. Lucia Schulte, 'A Study of the Piano Pedagogy of Annie Curwen: Its Correlation and Adaption with the Hungarian Method for the Instruction of Beginning Pianists and Its Implications for Modern Piano Teaching' (Unpublished MA thesis, Catholic University of America, 1971).

23 Arthur Elson and Everett E. Truette, *Woman's Work in Music* (Boston, 1903), p. 152.

and their works were similar in standards and genres to those of Dublin's male composers, such as Joseph Robinson and Sir Robert Stewart. It is difficult to compare the Irish female composers with their British or European counterparts such as Clara Schumann or, later, Ethel Smyth, due to significant differences in their musical experiences and education. Instead, one can examine differences in the reception of their compositions; one can also evaluate the work of Irish composers in its own right, as an important aspect of musical activity in nineteenth-century Dublin. The role of the female composer at that time was to contribute new music for concert life, a role that represents an artistic breakthrough for women. It seems that, in the absence of any significant body of Irish classical music, the works of female composers were embraced because they were Irish – because they provided the city's musical life with something original and unique to Ireland, rather than simply importing productions that had been popular in London. The city was somewhat lacking in both male and female composers, nor was there much training available to those interested in the discipline. Female composers received support and praise from their male peers who, rather than holding them back, were often a factor in their success. However, one characteristic that held true for female and male composers in Dublin, as well as throughout Britain and Europe, was that their careers were nearly always combined with roles as teachers or performers in order to supplement their income.[24] When women did compose, they tended to avoid writing in larger forms such as the concerto or symphony, preferring to concentrate on compositional forms that were more likely to be performed – the same was true for the majority of Dublin's male composers. Nineteenth-century Dublin lacked a full-time professional orchestra, so the possibilities of having large-scale works performed were almost non-existent. The main difficulty for women composing in Ireland during this period was not the lack of support for their work but rather a lack of knowledge and training. Nonetheless, supported by male peers, they had music published and performed. In most cases while their works were popular during their lifetimes, they were quickly forgotten, with no record of performances for much of the twentieth century. Over the past twenty years, revived interest in these women and their music has led to numerous performances in Dublin.[25]

Looking again at the example of Fanny Robinson, we see that she began composing shortly after moving to Dublin. Her knowledge and interest in

24 Deborah Rohr, *The Careers of British Musicians 1750–1850* (Cambridge, 2001), p. 139.

25 This renewed interest began with a concert performed by Elizabeth Pink and Deborah Kelleher on 2 September 2007 in St Ann's Church, Dawsons Street, Dublin. They performed a number of songs at the first Women and Music in Ireland conference at Maynooth University in April 2010.

composition are believed to have originated in her music education with Sir William Sterndale Bennett.[26] Her early piano works, exuding simple stylistic and harmonic qualities, were probably used as teaching pieces for her students. This theory is supported by the fact that the copies of her pieces in the RIAM library bear fingerings and instructions in the composer's handwriting. More complex works such as *Sentiments* and *The Song of the Mill Wheel* gained her greater recognition as a composer. Both were praised by the contemporary press and, coinciding with Robinson's solo performances in Paris, É. Gérard et Cie published the pieces as *Les Pensées* and *Le Chanson du Moulin*.[27] In 1871 Robinson completed her most popular work, the cantata *God is Love*. It was premiered that year by the RIAM choral class and quickly became a favourite in the Dublin cathedrals, receiving many performances in sections as anthems. Its popularity lasted into the early twentieth century.

Another successful female composer of the late nineteenth century was Ellen O'Hea, who studied with Robinson at the RIAM. She showed a talent for composition, which was nurtured by her harmony teacher, Sir Robert Stewart, who critiqued her work. He reportedly said that she 'had her foot firmly on the ladder of fame'.[28] O'Hea composed and performed under the name Elena Norton, probably to distinguish herself from her three sisters who all taught at the RIAM: Margaret O'Hea, another student of Fanny Robinson, who taught piano; Alice O'Shea, a professor of singing and a soprano; and Mary O'Hea, an actress and professor of elocution. Norton's output included several songs and operettas, the most successful of which was a comic opera entitled *The Rose and the Ring*, based on William Thackeray's fairytale of the same name. Premiered on a small scale at the RIAM in November 1876, it was so well received by the audience that a full production with orchestral accompaniment took place in the Antient Concert Rooms in February of the following year.[29] At that point it was conducted by Robert Stewart. The opera was praised by the press, with the *Irish Times* reviewer commenting:

> no female foot has trodden in the ranks of the great composers and that it was not recorded that any lady had produced a successful opera but perhaps Miss Norton may break the spell and inscribe her name on the

26 Peter Horton, 'William Sterndale Bennett, Composer and Pianist', in Therese Ellsworth and Susan Wollenberg (eds), *The Piano in Nineteenth-Century British Culture: Instruments, Performers and Repertoire* (Aldershot, 2007), pp. 119–48.

27 The RIAM library has copies of both versions within their catalogue. The music is the same in both editions.

28 Annie Patterson, 'Miss Margaret O'Hea, Continued', *Weekly Irish Times*, 17 November 1900.

29 *Irish Times*, 11 November 1876, p. 2.

> roll of fame ... where it will be an example and encouragement to the musical sisterhood.[30]

Although Norton appears to have made a significant contribution to Irish composition in her short lifetime, none of her opera scores are extant; without these, it is impossible to judge the extent of her talents. All that survives of her catalogue are copies of two songs, 'Gather ye Rosebuds', with text by Herrick, and 'In a Valley Far Away', which was also known as 'Maurya Vawn Asthore'; both are in the British Library. There is no record of Norton's operas having been published; possibly, they never were. It is regrettable that no evidence remains of works that were so popular at the time. Nonetheless, she achieved something that eluded many composers of that era: she managed to have all her compositions performed, and usually by reputable musicians such as Robert Stewart. Frequently, she also had the opportunity to perform in her works. In most productions of *The Rose and the Ring*, including its 1876 RIAM premiere, she sang the leading soprano role.[31]

In the 1890s, composition in Ireland became caught up in the growing desire for all things nationalist. In the preceding decades, although there had been significant developments in music education, very little music that was distinctly Irish had featured in music lessons at the RIAM or elsewhere, nor had there been real effort to unify composition teaching with Irish themes and subjects. This began to change in the final decade of the century, with the Celtic revival. The idea of Irishness in art became a concern for composers, with Irish literature and folklore used as a source of inspiration by many. One female composer who contributed to this development in Irish art music was Annie Patterson. Patterson's education began at Alexandra College in Dublin, a school that helped herald new directions in education for middle-class girls in the nineteenth century.[32] She subsequently studied at the Royal University of Dublin, graduating with a BA in 1887 and a MusDoc in 1889, making her the first woman to receive a doctorate of music in Ireland and, indeed, the British Isles; she remained the only woman with the title until well into the twentieth century.[33]

Patterson composed many works, ranging from oratorios and operas to piano music, all based on Irish themes and folklore. Unfortunately, only a small number were published, mainly the smaller works, such as her songs and piano arrangements of Irish airs. These included the *Six*

30 *Irish Times*, 11 November 1876, p. 2.

31 *Irish Times*, 11 November 1876, p. 2.

32 Maria Luddy, *Women and Philanthropy in Nineteenth-Century Ireland* (Cambridge, 1995), p. 17. Rhoda Coghill also attended this school.

33 Judith Barger, *Elizabeth Stirling and the Musical Life of Female Organists in Nineteenth-Century England* (Aldershot, 2007), p. 17.

Eithne Ní Pheadair Ollamh Ceóil.

FIGURE 3.1: Dr Annie Patterson, Promotional Pamphlet.
Courtesy of the RIAM Library.

Original Gaelic Songs, *Rallying Song of the Gaelic League* and *King Cormac*. It seems that none of the scores for her larger works have survived. Her list of unpublished compositions includes an oratorio entitled *Meta Tauta*; two Irish operas, *Ardrigh's Daughter* and *Oisin*; a school cantata in Gaelic; an Irish cantata; Irish tone poems; six preludes and fugues for the piano based on Irish folk songs; piano trios that were based on traditional

Irish tunes and original dances; and three sonatas called Tradition, for violin and piano, viola and piano, and cello and piano, respectively.[34] It is a loss that none of these manuscripts survived. However, from the list of titles alone, it is evident that Patterson's output was greatly inspired by Irish themes. She experimented with several of the major genres, combining them with traditional airs and harmonies. The most popular of her published compositions were the *Six Original Gaelic Songs* for solo voice and piano accompaniment (1896), published by Boosey in London. Dedicated to supporters of the Feis Ceoil (the festival Patterson co-founded), they were a means of advertising the festival and were performed several times in the lead-up to the competition. Each song was dedicated to significant patrons of the Feis Ceoil; each bears its title in Irish, with the words printed in Irish and English under the music. In the preface to the songs, Patterson states that the volume can claim to be the first of its kind in three ways. First, it is a collection of new Gaelic lyrics by living authors; second, the melodies are new and original, though 'it is to be hoped that a strong flavour of the composer's nationality will be found in them'; finally, the accompaniments and general structure of the songs are intended to combine the 'characteristic traits of ancient Irish music with the requirements of modern song form'.[35] Through these and all of her compositions Patterson sought to revive the traditional traits of Irish music and popularise the musical traditions that were part of Ireland's heritage. Whether she achieved this is a question beyond the scope of this chapter, but her efforts illustrate her unwavering devotion to Irish music and its revival.

Creating the Feis Ceoil: Female Involvement and Dedication to Culture

Towards the end of the nineteenth century, musicians were aware of the need to continue to increase public interest and involvement in music if they were to advance the city's musical infrastructure. Teachers and musicians also strove to be of comparable standards to their British counterparts. Women in Dublin were accepted in music as they were keen to continue to advance its development, improve standards and increase public interest in the capital's musical life. A thriving scene meant more teaching and concert opportunities for musicians. Women

34 The information on Patterson's publications is from a four-page flyer about her found in a box containing her compositions in the RIAM library. The librarian was unsure of its origins but the information seems to be taken from an edition of *Who's Who*. It is not dated but as it lists work up to 1922 and makes no reference to her 1927 publication, it probably dates from the interim period.

35 Annie W. Patterson, Preface, *Six Gaelic Songs* (Boosey & Co, 1896), p. 3.

set about promoting the expansion and improvement of music through their involvement in several organisations and movements. The late nineteenth century also saw the emergence of a fascination with cultural nationalism, which echoed similar feeling common throughout Europe at that time. Maria Citron has noted that as nations tried to create unity and national pride, they often looked to the past for symbols of heritage, and these were often musical.[36] An example of this can be seen in the work of Patterson and Edith Oldham with the creation of the Feis Ceoil, modelled on the ancient Irish Feiseanna.

Edith Oldham was another female musician who devoted much of her life to the RIAM, with which she was connected for over fifty years through her time as student and then teacher. Oldham began studying there in her early teens, under Margaret O'Hea.[37] In 1883 she was one of three students who received a scholarship to study at the newly opened Royal College of Music (RCM) in London. This scholarship and the subsequent move to London led to one of the most important friendships of Oldham's life, with George Grove. She studied at the RCM from 1883 until 1887. It appears that Grove thought highly of Edith Oldham and, upon her arrival in London as a student of the RCM, they became close friends, a relationship that continued until his death in 1900. This relationship, documented in letters from Grove to Oldham from 1883 until 1899, has generated assumptions about the nature of their involvement. It would be hard to prove the depth of their friendship, particularly as none of Oldham's letters exist, but they provide a valuable window into Oldham's life in London and her subsequent return to Dublin, where she worked with the RIAM and Feis Ceoil.

The Feis Ceoil, Ireland's principal competitive art-music festival, today remains an important annual event, with students from across the country participating in its many competitions. From the beginning, women have been evident in the Feis Ceoil competitions as organisers, adjudicators and performers in the concerts.[38] Patterson is credited by most sources on the subject with playing a role in the founding of the Feis Ceoil competition in 1897, and it is for this that she is best remembered.[39] However, her vital role has often been underestimated, with publications sometimes inaccurately minimising her as simply the honorary secretary.[40] This was a position that it seems she only maintained for the first few months, Oldham being listed as the honorary secretary from

36 Maria Citron, *Gender and the Musical Canon* (Chicago, 2000), p. 37.

37 Percy M. Young, *George Grove 1820–1900: A Biography* (London, 1980), p. 168.

38 Feis Ceoil Programmes, 1897–1917, National Library of Ireland, IR 780941, f2.

39 Pine and Acton, *To Talent Alone: The Royal Irish Academy of Music 1848–1998*, p. 289.

40 Aloys Fleischmann (ed.), *Music in Ireland: A Symposium* (Cork, 1952), p. 212.

1895 in the Feis Ceoil programme of 1897.[41] In many ways, Oldham became the backbone of the competition, particularly in the years that followed the first competition.[42] The labour and dedication of Patterson and Oldham, along with that of many others, helped the competition to grow and gain the position that it maintains today. According to the Feis Ceoil programme of 1897, the idea for the competition arose following a letter by Mr O'Neill Russell to the *Evening Telegraph* in 1894 protesting the neglect of Irish music by the country's leading figures in Ireland. A correspondence followed and, as a result, Patterson approached the Gaelic League in 1894 with the idea of reviving the ancient Irish Feiseanna. This was just one year after the founding of the Gaelic League and two years after the founding of the National Literary Society, so the Feis Ceoil concept tied in with the strong feelings of cultural nationalism stirring at that time. The first general committee meeting took place in 1895, with the committee mainly comprising members of the Gaelic League and the National Literary Society. Patterson shared the role of honorary secretary along with P.J. McCall. In the months that followed, many RIAM staff became involved in promoting the Feis Ceoil. Subscribers included John Spencer Curwen and Sir George Grove. Curwen remained a supporter of the competition into the twentieth century, while his wife, Annie Curwen, was an adjudicator in 1897.[43]

Oldham's legacy rested on her work in the early stages of the Feis Ceoil, undertaken alongside Patterson. They saw the Feis Ceoil as a means of bringing together musicians from across the country to perform and enhance their musical knowledge and interest. They differed on the scope of the competition: Patterson wanted it to serve as a forum solely for Irish traditional music, whereas Oldham pushed for the inclusion of classical genres as well as traditional. In the end, Oldham won out. But although Irish traditional music may not have remained the focus, the festival helped to initiate the inclusion of traditional Irish music into mass schooling and competitive performance. The Feis Ceoil was a lasting achievement for both women and all involved. In the years preceding the first festival they organised meetings, gave lectures, and published articles promoting and illustrating the work of the festival. It was significant as a means of national revival for all music in Ireland. It gave musicians of many disciplines the opportunity to compete and perform irrespective of their class, religion or gender.

41 Feis Ceoil Programme, 1897, National Library of Ireland, IR 780941, f2.

42 An examination of the *Irish Times* from 1897 to 1905 shows she appeared at every meeting that was held regarding the Feis.

43 '1st Feis Ceoil, Dublin 1897', Feis Ceoil Programmes, National Library of Ireland, IR 780941, f2.

Conclusion

The nineteenth century saw Dublin begin to develop as a musical city in significant part due to the work of women. As music was a field in which they were allowed to seek employment and where their defiance of social ideals of the time was tolerated, it was an appealing profession for women and a means of making a good salary. On the question of why they managed to gain such a level of equality in Dublin, there were several reasons. At the beginning of the nineteenth century, Dublin was lacking a culture of music education. With the opening of the RIAM, the board of governors were eager to create a centre of music similar to institutions in England and Europe and were accepting of anyone who could aid in the success of that venture. It was an area where the cultural, socia, and economic needs seem to have outweighed social expectations of women. It is also worth noting that many of the successful European composers and performers came from musical families where they grew up with music and guidance in the discipline. This was not the case for the women working in music in Dublin, with the exception of Mrs Allen. In comparison to women in other areas of Irish society, female pedagogues and composers experienced treatment that was progressive, particularly in terms of their salaries and status. By 1861 there was no other profession open to a woman in Ireland where she could receive the same salary as a male co-worker. In reference to the Feis Ceoil, the success of that competition, which was primarily organised by women, became an example to women in other areas beyond music.

Virginia Woolf, a favourite author of Patterson, claimed that 'a woman must have money and a room of her own'. The female musicians of nineteenth-century Dublin had earned both: a room for teaching or composing, a good salary and, perhaps most importantly, good social standing that allowed them to develop and progress in their careers. Much of the work that has been done on exploring the contribution of these women and their female successors in the twentieth century has been completed by women in the twenty-first century. One wonders if their disappearance from the history books tells us more about the gender bias of those working in the twentieth century than of the male peers in the nineteenth century who appear to have welcomed the contributions of women. Throughout the past two centuries, the work of women in music seems to have frequently been championed by peers only to be omitted by those who write the histories and research the outcomes. The increased wealth of research in the past twenty years has been largely women championing women. Perhaps the next twenty years will see a greater balance appear where the work of musicians, composers and educators is championed by all, regardless of gender.

4

Family, Filial Bonds and Forging Careers as Female Musicians in the Nineteenth Century: The Story of the Glover Sisters

Mary Louise O'Donnell

A Strong Paternal Influence

Erminia (Mary), Lina (Madeline) and Emilie (Emily) Glover were steeped in music from early childhood. Their father John William (1815–99) was organist at St Mary's Pro-Cathedral;[1] professor of music at the Central Model Schools of the Board of National Education; founder of the Royal Choral Institute;[2] lecturer on the history of Irish music; composer of cantatas, songs and instrumental pieces; and arranger of one hundred airs for Patrick Weston Joyce's seminal collection *Ancient Irish Music* (1873). Glover, along with the German cellist Wilhelm Elsner,[3] the violinist/conductor Richard M. Levey,[4] and the conductor/composer/

1 Glover was a prolific composer of sacred and secular music, including six masses, organ voluntaries, and an opera based on Oliver Goldsmith's *The Deserted Village*. For more information, see Paul Collins, 'John William Glover', in Harry White and Barra Boydell (eds), *The Encyclopaedia of Music in Ireland* (Dublin, 2013), vol. 1, p. 435.

2 The Royal Choral Institute (RCI) was founded in1851 by John William Glover 'to bring before the public in general the great choral compositions of the ancient and modern masters together with the training of a numerous body of choristers for that purpose'. For further information see Adèle Commins, 'Royal Choral Institute', in White and Boydell (eds) *Enyclcopaedia*, vol. 2, p. 897.

3 Wilhelm Elsner (*c.*1822–84) was appointed cello teacher at the Irish Academy of Music (IAM) in 1851. The IAM became known as the Royal Irish Academy of Music (RIAM) from 1872.

4 Richard Michael Levey [O' Shaughnessy] (1811–99) was a violin teacher at the IAM from 1848 and compiler of the two-part collection *The Dance Music of Ireland* (1858/1878). See Ita Beausang, 'Levey Family', in White and Boydell (eds), *Enyclcopaedia*, vol. 2, pp. 587–8.

lecturer Sir Robert Prescott Stewart,[5] formed part of an elite group of musicians and intellectuals who dominated musical life in Dublin from the 1840s onwards. Several of John William's children pursued successful careers as musicians, including his sons Ferdinand (1836–59) and William (*d.*1917). This chapter focuses on the lives and careers of his three daughters, namely Erminia (*c.*1838–83), Lina (*c.*1847–1929) and Emilie (*c.*1848–1917). It explores how they contributed to the vibrant music scene in Dublin and further afield in the latter half of the nineteenth century; it also traces how, through collaborations with their father, they enabled him to realise his personal, musical and patriotic vision.

John William was a devoted teacher to his children and, in addition to piano and voice lessons, he provided them with a strong foundation in the rudiments of compositional technique. Ferdinand, in particular, exhibited exceptional talent and musical ability from an early age. In his late teens, he decided to pursue a career in music and left Dublin to study composition, vocal technique, repertoire and performance in Naples. Following his critically acclaimed debut at the Teatro Nuovo in Naples in 1856, he was appointed principal baritone at that theatre until July 1857.[6] He returned to London in August 1857 to join the Pyne and Harrison English Opera Company for performances at the Lyceum and Covent Garden theatres. He subsequently took principal roles in William Vincent Wallace's *Maritana*,[7] and Michael William Balfe's *The Rose of Castille*.[8] In October 1857, his first cantata, *The Fire Worshippers*, which was based on Thomas Moore's orientalist romance *Lallah Rookh*, was premiered at the Royal Irish Institution in Dublin. Widely regarded among his peers as a 'versatile musical genius',[9] it seemed that Ferdinand was destined for a brilliant career. Unfortunately, he contracted smallpox and died at the age of twenty-three on 22 April 1859.[10] Despite his short career, Ferdinand's reputation endured, particularly in England, long after his death.

For the Glover family 1859 was a year of mixed emotions. Two weeks before the death of Ferdinand, his father's edition of Thomas Moore's *Irish Melodies* had been published in Dublin by James Duffy. The publication was the culmination of many years of meticulous editing and

5 For a detailed account of the personal and professional life of Prescott Stewart, see, Lisa Parker, 'Robert Prescott Stewart (1825–94): A Victorian Musician in Dublin' (Unpublished PhD thesis, Maynooth University, 2009).

6 'Ferdinand Glover', *Leinster Express*, 25 October 1856, p. 3.

7 William Vincent Wallace (1812–65) was a composer and violinist born in Waterford. He wrote several operas, including *Maritana*, *Matilda of Hungary* and *Lurline*.

8 Michael William Balfe (1808–70) was a Dublin-born composer and singer. He composed twenty-eight operas, including his most popular work, *The Bohemian Girl*.

9 'Ferdinand Glover', *Freeman's Journal*, 4 August 1857, p. 3.

10 'Theatrical Chit Chat', *Reynold's Newspaper*, 1 May 1859, p. 9.

revision of the proof sheets of Moore and Sir John Stevenson. Glover was an ardent admirer of Moore's oeuvre; he and his family spent much of their careers promoting the popularity of Moore's musical compositions in Ireland, Britain and North America.

A few months after Ferdinand's death, his sister Erminia married James Mackey, a commercial traveller who was a town commissioner in Kingstown,[11] and occasionally sang *basso profundo* at liturgies in the Church of Our Lady of Mount Carmel (Whitefriar Street Church), Dublin.[12] Erminia and James had three children, James (Jimmy), Michael and Mary, but their marriage was not a happy one. James was a supporter of the Irish Republican Brotherhood (the Fenians) and was one of several Fenian sympathisers who assisted with the Richmond Prison breakout of their leader James Stephens in 1865.[13] On that occasion, Mackey was accompanied by his four-year-old son Jimmy, who was frequently used as a ruse to hide his father's clandestine activities. Following a raid on the family home in November 1865, James was incarcerated in Mountjoy Prison for several weeks. A few months later he was declared bankrupt, the Mackey family lost their home and James fled, leaving Erminia with no option but to move back with their children to her parents' home at 14 Talbot Street.

Before her marriage, Erminia had established a reputation as one of the leading Catholic church musicians in Dublin. She was resident organist at the Church of St Paul of the Cross, Mount Argus, Dublin, and organist at St Michael's Church in Kingstown. In addition to her role as organist at St Michael's, she acted as musical director for performances of Mendelssohn's *Elijah* and other sacred works at the church; these performances featured renowned visiting singers such as Giovanni Vizzani, Zélia Trebelli and Thérèse Tietjens. Equally accomplished on piano and harp, Erminia performed regularly at concerts in Dublin and provincial towns throughout Ireland from the 1860s onwards. She was also a respected teacher who taught piano and pedal harp privately for many years before her appointment as the first harp teacher at the Irish Academy of Music in 1871.[14] Amongst her most famous students

11 Kingstown is now known as Dún Laoghaire.

12 James M. Glover, *Jimmy Glover, His Book* (London, 1911), p. 2.

13 For further information on James Stephens and Fenianism, see Marta Ramón, *A Provisional Dictator: James Stephens and the Fenian Movement* (Dublin, 2007) and Eva Ó Cathaoir, *Soldiers of Liberty: A Study of Fenianism 1858–1908* (Dublin, 2018).

14 Richard Pine and Charles Acton (eds), *To Talent Alone: The Royal Irish Academy of Music, 1848–1998* (Dublin, 1998), pp. 143–4. In 1871, harp classes were introduced at the IAM, a year before Queen Victoria accepted the invitation to be patron and the Academy was titled 'Royal'.

was George Buckley Byng, later a composer and musical director at the Alhambra Theatre in London.[15]

Emilie commenced harp lessons with her sister Erminia but later studied with the Welsh harpist John Thomas.[16] By her late teens, Emilie was a formidable force in musical life in Dublin as a soloist, accompanist and composer. The first reference to a performance by her dates to November 1865 when she, Lina and Erminia provided musical illustrations for one of their father's lectures on Moore's *Irish Melodies* at the Sussex Hall in Dublin.[17]

Glover was a consistent champion of his daughters' talents, giving them every encouragement and opportunity to further their fledgling careers and develop their performance skills. Erminia, Lina and Emilie assisted their father at talks and recitals throughout Ireland and further afield. In March 1866, Lina accompanied her father to England where she provided musical illustrations for his lectures on Irish music at the Marylebone Literary and Scientific Institution, London. In December 1867 John William was joined by his three daughters at a lecture on Irish music at the Town Hall in Waterford.[18]

Emilie and Lina's Fledgling Careers

By the mid-nineteenth century, Glover had established his reputation as a multi-instrumentalist par excellence and composer of works that incorporated Irish airs or Irish idioms into classical forms. Emilie emulated her father; two of her earliest compositions for harp and piano duet, *Erin* and *La Traviata*, were published by Duncan, Davison & Co in London in October 1867 (Figure 4.1). *Erin* is a fantasia for harp and piano that combines three Irish airs, namely, 'Let Erin Remember', 'Fly Not Yet' and 'Love's Young Dream'. Her reputation as a composer, however, was overshadowed by her prolific career as a pianist and harpist. On 4 October, her debut performance with the Italian Opera Company at the Exhibition Palace, Dublin was well received, with her accompaniments described as 'exquisitely performed' and 'worthy of the honourable

15 Although George Wilford Buckley Byng (1861–1932) was born in England, he moved to Dublin at the age of seven to study at the IAM. Byng was a piano student of Erminia Mackey and her father John William Glover.

16 John Thomas (1826–1913) was a Welsh harpist, composer and music historian. He was named 'Chief of the Welsh minstrels' in 1861 and was a professor of harp at the Royal College of Music and Guildhall School of Music in London. He was appointed harpist to Queen Victoria in 1872. See Roslyn Rensch, *Harps and Harpists*, rev. edn (Bloomington, 2007), p. 171. See n. 24 on his younger brother, Thomas (Aptommas).

17 'Professor Glover's Concert', *Irish Times*, 14 November 1865, p. 4.

18 'Waterford Mechanics' Institute', *Munster Express*, 14 December 1867, p. 2.

FIGURE 4.1: Excerpt from *Erin* by Emilie Glover.
Author's collection.

position assigned to her'.[19] On that occasion Emilie accompanied the German soprano Thérèse Tietjens. It was the first of many collaborations in Ireland and Britain between Emilie, the renowned soprano and the Italian Opera Company.

Tietjens was well-known to the Glover family. Lina regularly attended vocal classes with her in London and Dublin; she also dedicated *Lina*

19 'Harp Music by Emilie Glover', *The Musical World*, 45, 12 October 1867, p. 704.

Glover's Singing Tutor to her mentor in 1867 in appreciation of her support and encouragement over many years. Lina's vocal tutor was an introductory singing manual that included solfège exercises used by her brother Ferdinand, as well as information on breathing techniques, pronunciation, diction and ornamentation; a glossary of expression markings in Italian and examples of Irish airs were included as appendices. It was reviewed as 'very pithy, very direct, and so strikingly simple from first to last, as to be certainly intelligible to the least experienced or least ready student of the art of singing'.[20] The tutor was published in London by d'Almaine & Co., and in Dublin by her father under the title of Glover & Co, 14 Talbot Street.

The family home at 14 Talbot Street was an important performance space for the Glover children. It offered a relaxed and familiar setting to showcase their performance skills and broaden their repertoire beyond Irish airs and compositions by Thomas Moore to include pieces and songs by Handel, Rossini and von Flotow.[21] In 1868, Emilie and Lina, along with their father on violin, performed there on 14 and 21 March.[22] Following the success of these concerts, Emilie was engaged as soloist at the second Grand National Concert of Irish Music on the 23 June at the Exhibition Palace, Dublin.[23] On that occasion she performed her composition *Erin* and *Sounds of the Emerald Isle* by the Welsh harpist/composer Aptommas,[24] who was a frequent visitor to Dublin from the 1860s onwards.

From 1868 to 1869 Emilie and Lina gained invaluable experience and confidence by organising and promoting regular performances at their family home and various other venues throughout Dublin. Their success prompted the sisters to plan an ambitious series of harp and vocal concerts at the Exhibition Palace, Dublin on the evenings of 20 and 21 December and the afternoon of 23 December 1869. Although the specific objective of these concerts was to celebrate and popularise the harp as a 'national instrument',[25] it should be noted that Emilie played pedal harp

20 'Music', *The Nation*, 17 July 1869, p. 12.

21 Friedrich von Flotow (1812–83) was a German composer of ballets, incidental music and operas. His most famous opera, *Martha*, was first performed in 1847.

22 'Harp Recital', *Freeman's Journal*, 17 March 1868, p. 3.

23 'Exhibition Palace', *Freeman's Journal*, 23 June 1868, p. 1.

24 Thomas Thomas (Aptommas) (1829–1913) was a Welsh harpist and composer who performed extensively throughout Europe and the United States; he also authored books on the history and pedagogy of the harp. Aptommas was a younger brother of John Thomas (see n. 16). For more information on Aptommas and his performances in Ireland, see Mary Louise O'Donnell, 'In the Shadow of Bochsa: A Study of Three Foreign Virtuoso Pedal Harpists in Dublin (*c.*1850–1900)', in Helen Lawlor and Sandra Joyce (eds), *Harp Studies II: World Harp Traditions* (Dublin, forthcoming).

25 'Harp and Vocal Concerts', *Freeman's Journal*, 3 December 1869, p. 1. For

rather than any kind of Irish harp. In fact, the recital repertoire included few examples of music that could be classified as part of the 'Irish' or 'national' repertoire. Lina sang Thomas Moore's 'The Harp that Once' at each concert, but the only pieces that incorporated Irish airs, albeit in a classical compositional structure, were *Irish Fantasia* by Aptommas and Emilie's composition *Erin*. The choice of programme for these concerts undoubtedly reflected contemporary musical tastes, but it is noteworthy that when Irish or 'national music' was performed in these settings it was invariably presented in a form that was more palatable to contemporary Dublin audiences.

Although the programme was changed for each concert, the overall format remained the same. The first part, which always consisted of sacred repertoire, was followed by a performance of *Erin* between the parts; a selection of miscellaneous music concluded each concert. The first concert included the following: a performance by Wilhelm Elsner and John William Glover of a transcription for cello and *orgue expressif* of excerpts from Rossini's *Stabat Mater*, Charles Gounod's *Nazareth* sung by Lina, and a fantasia based on themes from Jacques Offenbach's *Orphée aux enfers* for harp and *orgue expressif*. The concert on 23 December featured extracts from Handel's *Messiah*, a duet for harp and cello by von Flotow entitled *Hymne aus Stradella*, a fantasia on airs from Gounod's *Faust* composed by John William Glover, and selections from *The Tempest* by Henry Purcell. The concerts concluded with a harp medley of Scottish airs such as *The March of the Cameron Men* and *Tullochgorum*.

Erminia: A Mother and Musician

While Emilie and Lina were attempting to forge successful careers in music in the late 1860s, Erminia was struggling with the breakdown of her marriage to James Mackey. She, along with her parents, cared for her three young children at the family home in Talbot Street. Glover took charge of the musical education of his three grandchildren, particularly that of his grandson Jimmy. Recognising his considerable talent, Glover took Jimmy on a lecture tour of provincial towns in Ireland. At eight years of age, Jimmy, or 'the Celebrated young boy Vocalist Master Williams the Boy Mario', provided musical illustrations for his grandfather's talks, as his mother and aunts had done for many years. As well as singing some of Moore's *Irish Melodies* and other Irish airs he assisted his grandfather in carrying and unpacking luggage, setting up the *orgue expressif* and collecting money from ticket sales.[26] Jimmy's father, resenting the increasing influence of the extended Glover family on his eldest son,

further information on these recitals, see, Mary Louise O'Donnell, *Ireland's Harp: The Shaping of Irish Identity c.1770–1880* (Dublin, 2014), pp. 129–30.

26 Glover, *Jimmy Glover*, pp. 4–5.

insisted that the boy take a job as a druggist's apprentice at the age of thirteen. He worked for ten hours a week but also acted as deputy organist at St Mary's Pro-Cathedral and at Whitefriar Street Church – positions secured for him by his grandfather. James Mackey had minimal contact with his three children, leaving Erminia to manage their upbringing. When John William suggested taking Jimmy on an extended trip to France to learn languages, gain musical experience and 'to end the insecurity and unprofitableness of [his] earlier existence', Erminia enthusiastically agreed.[27] Jimmy, who later changed his surname to Glover as a mark of respect to and appreciation of his grandfather, wrote about the influence John William had on him and his career:

> There was one person, however, who played a very important part in my early life, and to him I owe my present position. It was he who taught me everything I know. It was he who, against my will, physically thrashed my musical education into my brain, who rescued me from the menial service of the druggist counter, and at his own expense, albeit contrary to my father's wishes, placed me in a position to earn my living. Whether it be writing for the Press, the ability to speak several languages, my knowledge of the piano, the violin, or the organ; I owe it all to him.[28]

Musical Collaborations

The Glover family collaborations continued in 1870 with the first in a series of performances of John William's oratorio *St Patrick at Tara*. Howard E. Smither described the work as 'an isolated' example of an Irish national oratorio influenced by contemporary national German oratorios inspired by the lives of famous historic figures.[29] The large-scale work for choir and orchestra, based on excerpts from the *Life of St Patrick* by James Henthorn Todd,[30] was first performed on 30 May 1870 for the benefit of Mercer's Hospital at the Antient Concert Rooms, Dublin, with the composer conducting an orchestra and chorus of over two hundred performers. Lina took the role of Fethelema, one of the daughters of the King of Tara; Richard M. Levey led the orchestra and Emilie was principal harpist. The work focuses on the arrival of St Patrick to the court of the high king of Tara and his conversion of the princes, nobles, knights and

27 Glover, *Jimmy Glover*, p. 32.

28 Glover, *Jimmy Glover*, p. 4.

29 Howard E. Smither, *A History of the Oratorio, vol. 4: The Oratorio in the Nineteenth and Twentieth Centuries* (Chapel Hill, 2000), p. 256. It should be noted that some editions of the score and newspaper reviews describe the work as a cantata.

30 See G.O. Simms, 'James Henthorn Todd', *Hermathena*, 109 (1969), 5–23.

warriors assembled there for a great feast. *St Patrick at Tara* is divided into two parts with eighteen movements in the first part and thirteen in the second part. The harp as an accompanying instrument plays an integral role in the work, in particular in the sublime alto solo 'I Often Wish', the tenor aria 'Give Me That Strain' and the rousing 'Strike the Lightly Trembling Lyre' for duet and chorus. Fethelema's solo, titled 'Irish melody',[31] is strikingly plaintive and formed part of Lina's repertoire throughout her career.

The premiere of *St Patrick at Tara,* eagerly anticipated by Dublin audiences and much hyped in contemporary newspapers, was enthusiastically received. The work was an important vehicle for Glover to promote Emilie and Lina to audiences in Ireland and Britain. In early 1871, Lina moved to London where her first official engagement was to perform Italian and English songs at a concert organised by the Schubert Society at the Beethoven Rooms in Harley Street on 15 February.[32] In March of that year, Emilie and her father travelled to London for the English premiere of *St Patrick at Tara* at St George's Hall, in aid of the French Refugees' Benevolent Fund. Lina sang 'The Song of Inisfail' with 'a sweet well-modulated voice', while Emilie was described as 'brimful of talent ... quite as brilliant and accomplished a pianist as harpist ... [who] played with extraordinary execution and delicacy of touch'.[33] In general, Glover's composition was less enthusiastically welcomed by London audiences than it had been in Dublin the previous year. Several critics were unimpressed by the work, with many commenting on the poor overall structure and lengthy movements. One reviewer even noted that 'there was too much eccentricity mixed up with a modicum of ability to treat the numbers of [Glover's] composition ... seriously'.[34]

Despite the mixed reception in London, *St Patrick at Tara* was reprised in Dublin on 29 May 1871 at the Exhibition Palace on a larger scale than the previous year: the forces comprised organ, full orchestral accompaniment and over five hundred voices. Lina and Emilie were joined for the performance by their brother William on the organ. The concert was part of an impressive spectacle that also included ornamental fountains, statues, grottos and military bands.[35] The following day, the Glover family marked the anniversary of Thomas Moore's birth with an event in the Antient Concert Rooms. Erminia performed her father's work *Fantasia on Irish Melodies* on piano, Emilie and her father played *Erin,* Lina sang 'Farewell to thee, Araby's Daughter' from *Lallah Rookh* and 'The Romaika'

31 This song was also known as 'The Song of Innisfail'.
32 'Fine Arts and Music', *The Tablet,* 18 February 1871, p. 212.
33 'Professor Glover's New Cantata', *Morning Advertiser,* 16 March 1871, p. 3.
34 'Musical Gossip', *The Athenaeum,* 25 March 1871, p. 377.
35 'Public Amusements', *Freeman's Journal,* 16 May 1871, p. 1.

from *Evenings in Greece* by Thomas Moore. Selections from *The Fire Worshippers* by their late brother Ferdinand were also performed.

By early 1872 Lina had settled permanently in London. Amongst her engagements that year was a performance at a musical festival in aid of the friends of the Royal Dramatic College on 14 February,[36] and a concert of Irish ballads at St James's Hall on 16 March.[37] The highlight of Lina's professional career was undoubtedly her engagement to sing at a series of concerts at the Royal Albert Hall in May and July 1872. She joined artists such as Edith Wynne and the London Glee and Madrigal Union to perform for audiences that included the Duke of Edinburgh and his brother Prince Arthur.[38] During this time, Emilie also attempted to establish her reputation in London musical circles. Although based in Dublin, where she spent most of the year teaching and performing, she gave a number of critically acclaimed performances in London. In July, Emilie arranged a concert entitled 'The National Music of Ireland' at St George's Hall, at which Lina sang and her father spoke about each of the pieces performed. In 1873, Emilie and Lina travelled back and forth to Dublin from London for engagements. Emilie played with the Philharmonic Society for their second grand concert of the season,[39] and for Sophia Flora Heilbronn's concert at the Antient Concert Rooms in July.[40] There was another performance of their father's work *St Patrick at Tara* at the Antient Concert Rooms on 15 March, in aid of the Mansion House Central Coal Fund. Lina reprised her role as Fethelema, Emilie and Erminia played harps, and a choir and orchestra of two hundred people performed.

On 9 March 1874, Lina was joined by Emilie and William for a performance at the Pimlico Rooms in London;[41] a few days later she married William Arthur Gedge of Claverton Street, St George Hanover Square, London. Lina's first performance as Madame Gedge was at the Exhibition Palace, Dublin on 15 March; advertisements for the concert described her as 'a lady highly distinguished in London musical circles'.[42] Following her return to London, she was engaged by Charles Sleigh to sing at the Concert Hall of the British Musical and Dramatic Institute on 25 April.[43] She visited Dublin the following month to sing at a concert in the Antient Concert Rooms. The intense concert schedule and frequent commutes between Britain and Ireland eventually took its toll on Lina. With the

36 'A Grand Musical Festival', *The Morning Post*, 8 February 1872, p. 4.
37 'Tonight – Irish Ballad Programme', *The Standard*, 16 March 1872, p. 1.
38 'Fashion and Varieties', *Freeman's Journal*, 23 July 1872, p. 2.
39 'Philharmonic Society', *Irish Times*, 1 February 1873, p. 3.
40 'Public Amusements', *Irish Times*, 21 July 1873, p. 1.
41 'New Music', *The Era*, 15 March 1874, p. 12.
42 'The Oratorio of St Patrick at Tara', *Freeman's Journal*, 11 March 1874, p. 3.
43 'The British Musical and Dramatic Institute', *The Era*, 19 April 1874, p. 9.

exceptions of a concert marking the centenary of Moore's birth in Dublin in 1879, at which her father's grand choral fantasia *One Hundred Years Ago* was premiered, and two concerts at the Antient Concert Rooms in June 1880, Lina retired from concert performance in Ireland and Britain. She moved to Southampton with her husband and remained there until her death in 1929.

Following Emilie's marriage to Samuel Grey of Colchester Street, Eaton Square, London on 30 May 1875, her career went from strength to strength. Her composition *Ukrania*,[44] a fantasia based on Russian airs, was dedicated to the Duchess of Edinburgh and published by Duncan Davison & Co. An appointment as principal harpist with the Imperial Italian Opera Company followed and, as part of that, a series of concerts in London in October 1876,[45] and at the Ulster Hall, Belfast in March 1877.[46]

From the time that Emilie moved to London in the early 1870s, Erminia was in constant demand throughout Ireland as an accompanist both on piano and harp. She often featured on the programme for her father's concerts and, at a performance of *St Patrick at Tara* at the Exhibition Palace on 15 March 1875, she was the only one of John William's children who performed on that occasion. She played at the premiere of her father's cantata *Patria* in Louth in 1876,[47] and that of Paul McSwiney's opera *Amergin* in Cork on 23 February 1881.[48] During her stay in Cork, she gave lessons on harp and piano.[49] She performed regularly with touring opera companies but was also a respected soloist; her performance of Charles Oberthür's *Fantasie sur des thèmes de l'opéra 'Martha'* was always popular at recitals. Erminia, Owen Lloyd and Swedish harpist Adolf Sjödén led a choir of pedal harpists performing national airs from Ireland, Scotland, Wales, England, Norway and Sweden at the Irish Harp Revival Festival that took place at the Rotunda, Dublin on 6, 8 and 10 May 1879.[50]

As the decade progressed, musical collaborations between members of the Glover family became infrequent. The centenary of Thomas Moore's birth in 1879, however, was an opportunity for the family to celebrate with a fitting musical tribute to their father's friend and idol. A concert of

44 'New Music', *Irish Times*, 9 April 1874, p. 2.

45 'Public Amusements', *Liverpool Mercury*, 28 September 1876, p. 1.

46 'Morning Concert in the Ulster Hall', *Belfast News-Letter*, 9 March 1877, p. 3.

47 'Gossip: Music and the Drama', *Irish Times*, 17 January 1876, p. 6.

48 Paul McSwiney (1856–90) was born in Cork but emigrated to New York in the early 1880s. For more on McSwiney's opera and its reception, see Axel Klein, 'Stage-Irish, or the National in Irish Opera, 1780–1925', *The Opera Quarterly*, 21 (2005), 27–67, at p. 44 and p. 46.

49 'Mrs Mackey, Harpist', *Cork Examiner*, 17 February 1881, p. 1.

50 An Irish piper and Mr Smith, one of the last surviving celebrated blind Irish harpers also performed at these concerts. For more information on the Irish Harp Revival Festival, see O'Donnell, *Ireland's Harp*, p. 130.

popular Moore's *Irish Melodies* took place on 28 May with a chorus of two hundred voices, soloists and a band of harps. *One Hundred Years Ago*, the piece that their father composed to mark the centenary, was premiered; the band of harpists played 'The Harp that Once', Emilie and Erminia performed a selection of pieces for harp and piano including Carolan's Concerto, 'The Young May Moon' and 'The Last Rose of Summer', and Lina sang 'The Song of Innisfail'. The concert was preceded by a grand literary and musical celebration in the large Concert Hall of the Exhibition Palace and followed by a performance of selections of Irish music by combined bands totalling one hundred instrumentalists.[51] The success prompted a repeat event with reduced audience numbers on 31 May.

On 7 and 8 June 1880, Lina was joined by Erminia and her father for her final concerts in Dublin at the Antient Concert Rooms. It was undoubtedly a deeply poignant occasion for John William and his daughters as it marked the end of over two decades of Glover family collaborations. The tradition of family performances, however, was continued by Erminia and her children. On 25 April 1881, she performed in public for the first time with her son Michael at Mrs Lalor-Ireland's debut concert at the Antient Concert Rooms; on that occasion they played a harp and piano duet entitled *Sonnambula* by John Thomas.[52]

The Glover Sisters: The Final Years

Erminia's last public performance occurred at the Royal University Buildings on 18 May 1883 at a concert in aid of Steevens' Hospital. She died suddenly a few weeks later and was buried on 11 June; her daughter, sons, father and brother William were the chief mourners at her funeral. She was described in the *Irish Times* as 'one of the greatest harpists of modern Ireland' and her death left a void in the pedal harp tradition.[53] Although foreign virtuosi such as Aptommas and his student Madame Priscilla Frost were active in Ireland in the 1880s,[54] it was left to Owen Lloyd, a virtuosic pedal harpist from Co. Clare, to assume the role of interpreter and promoter of Irish melodies on the pedal harp.[55] Erminia had taught her daughter Mary to play the harp; she, like her mother, pursued a music career. She performed Irish airs and selections from

51 'Notes on News', *Irish Times*, 21 May 1879, p. 4. See *The Standard*, 29 May 1879 for a detailed account of events organised to mark the centenary of Thomas Moore's birth.

52 'Public Amusements', *Irish Times*, 23 April 1881, p. 2.

53 'Death of Mrs Mackey', *Irish Times*, 8 June 1883, p. 5.

54 Madame Frost was a harpist with Charles Hallé's Band and harp teacher at the RIAM.

55 For more information on the life and work of Owen Lloyd, see Mary Louise O'Donnell, 'Owen Lloyd and the de-Anglicization of the Irish Harp', *Éire-Ireland*, 48 (2013), 155–75.

Moore's *Irish Melodies* arranged by her grandfather, and compositions by her aunt Emilie, including *La Traviata* and *Erin*. She composed some pieces for harp, for example, *The Artisanerie Polka*, and gave music lessons at Messrs Pohlmann's premises at Dawson Street, Dublin.[56] Her brothers Michael and Jimmy similarly pursued music careers;[57] Jimmy became a respected performer, composer and conductor, serving as director of music at the Theatre Royal, Drury Lane in London from 1893 to 1923.[58]

Following Erminia's untimely death and Lina's retirement from the music profession, Emilie and her brother William were left to carry on their father's legacy. From the 1880s onwards, there are only sporadic references to performances by Emilie in Ireland and Britain. She played at the opening of the new Leinster Hall on 2 November 1886 when she was listed as being part of 'Her Majesty's Opera'.[59] Although she returned to Dublin to perform and teach for a few months each year, extant concert programmes suggest that the Irish airs and Moore's *Melodies* that she favoured in her early career were gradually replaced by repertoire and a style of playing espoused by nineteenth-century romantic virtuoso harpist/composers from England and France, such as John Thomas and Alphonse Hasselmans.

Emilie was part of the royal entourage that accompanied Queen Victoria on her visit to Dublin in June 1897, after which she remained in Dublin for a few months to give lessons.[60] At some stage in the late 1890s she emigrated to the United States under the patronage of Maurice Grau, opera impresario and manager of the Metropolitan Opera in New York from 1896 to 1903. She played in the Metropolitan Opera orchestra for several seasons and was also principal harpist with the St Louis Symphony Orchestra. She died in October 1917, a few weeks after her brother William.[61]

The Glover sisters were destined from a young age to have careers as musicians and, with the support and encouragement of their father, they succeeded. Erminia, Lina and Emilie were born at a time when, because of an increase in the number of public concerts and demand among the middle classes for music education, male and female musicians could make a viable living from performing and teaching in large urban areas. Musicological research on female composers and performers in Ireland

56 'School, Lesson, &c.', *Freeman's Journal*, 14 January 1886, p. 1.

57 Michael produced a performance of his grandfather's work, *St Patrick at Tara*, in Dublin in December 1902. See 'St Patrick at Tara', *Irish Times*, 24 November 1902, p. 8.

58 For further information on the life and career of James Mackey, better known as Jimmy Glover, see *Jimmy Glover and His Friends* (London, 1913) and *Hims Ancient and Modern* (London, 1926).

59 'The Opening of the New Leinster Hall', *Irish Times*, 1 November 1886, p. 5.

60 'Madame Emilie Grey', *Irish Times*, 29 November 1897, p. 6.

61 'Late Professor Glover', *Freeman's Journal*, 6 November 1917, p. 2.

in the nineteenth century has shown that many women were active in musical life at this time, particularly in Dublin.[62] The story of the Glover sisters, therefore, is not exceptional but it is important to document the contribution of Erminia and Emilie to the development of a distinctly Irish tradition of pedal harp performance. Together with Lina, their father and brother, they responded to the need to sustain excellent standards in musical life in Dublin and further afield in the latter half of the nineteenth century.

62 See Jennifer O'Connor, 'The Role of Women in Music in Nineteenth-Century Dublin' (Unpublished PhD thesis, Maynooth University, 2010).

Part II

Women and Practice in Irish Traditional Music

5

The Daghdha, the Minstrel Boy and Convent Schools: Reflections on Gender and the Harp in Ireland

Helen Lawlor

Introduction

The Irish harp has occupied a place in the Irish psyche for centuries, both musically and ideologically.[1] An identifiably Irish instrument, its repertoire and style have provenance in Ireland since at least the ninth century AD, thus bolstering its import in terms of cultural and ideological associations. Its high status in early Gaelic Ireland dissipated in the seventeenth and eighteenth centuries, although harpers found employment by travelling to the houses of the gentry performing and composing music.[2] Several attempts to revive the harp tradition in the late eighteenth and early nineteenth centuries failed to instigate a popular revival and the harp's impact in Irish musical spheres was minimal until later in the twentieth century.[3] The twentieth-century revival has led to widespread growth in harping in Ireland and abroad, particularly over the past twenty years. Today there are more harpers than at any time in the past two hundred years active as performers, teachers and students.[4] Irish harping throughout the twentieth and into the twenty-first century (particularly in the form of the ('neo')-Irish harp) has been a predominantly

1 This chapter is based on papers presented at the Women and Music in Ireland conference (17 April 2010) and at the UCD Seminar in Musicology (2 November 2017).

2 Edward Bunting, *The Ancient Music of Ireland* (Dublin, 1840); Gráinne Yeats, *The Harp of Ireland: The Belfast Harpers' Festival, 1792, and the Saving of Ireland's Music by Edward Bunting* (Dublin, 1980); Joan Rimmer, *The Irish Harp*, 3rd edn (Dublin, 1984); Mary Louise O'Donnell, *Ireland's Harp: The Shaping of Ireland's Identity, c.1770–1880* (Dublin, 2014).

3 Helen Lawlor, *Irish Harping, 1900–2010* (Dublin, 2012).

4 Toner Quinn, *Report on the Harping Tradition in Ireland* (Dublin, 2015).

female pursuit.[5] The most publicly visible harpers in the twentieth and twenty-first centuries have been women, save for a small proportion of well-known male harpers. This manifestation of the tradition is vastly different to that of the earlier centuries when the harp, while not exclusively a male tradition, was heavily dominated by men. The present gender imbalance is much at odds with the earlier history of the harp and shows a disparity with other instruments in the Irish musical tradition. This chapter traces the changing gender trajectory of the harp, beginning with the role of the instrument in Irish mythology. The chapter appraises myth, poetry, visual art and contemporary musical artistic practice, and considers the implications of the modern-day gender imbalance for the development of the tradition into the future.

Myth and Folklore

The origin of the harp is told in mythology by Marbhan and recounted in Eugene O'Curry's *On the Manners and Customs of the Ancient Irish* (1873). The harp has an almost ethereal origin in this folk tale and is credited with sleep-inducing abilities:

> There once lived a couple [a man and his wife] [...] the wife conceived a hatred to him, and she was [always] flying from him through woods and wildernesses and he continued to follow her constantly. And one day that the woman came to the sea shore of Camas, and was walking over the strand, she met a skeleton of a whale on the strand, and she heard the sounds of the wind passing through the sinews of the whale on the strand; and she fell asleep from the sounds. And her husband came after her [and found her asleep]; and he perceived that it was from the sounds the sleep fell upon her. And he then went forward into the wood, and made the form of the Cruit; and he put strings from the sinews of the whale into it and that was the first Cruit that was ever made.[6]

The harp is literally and metaphorically man-made in this folk tale. The beautiful sonority of the instrument is analogous to the confluence of the fruits of the ocean, the wind and land that induces sleep in the flighty if willful wife. The harp is imbued with a magic quality that gives power to its creator. While it is unlikely that tellers of folk tale in the past millennium may have been concerned with the underlying

5 Terms in common usage to describe the 34-string lever harp include 'Irish', 'neo', 'celtic' and 'non-pedal'. For a further discussion see Anne-Marie O'Farrell, 'The Chromatic Development of the Lever Harp: Mechanism, Resulting Technique and Repertoire', in Sandra Joyce and Helen Lawlor (eds), *Harp Studies: Perspectives on the Irish Harp* (Dublin, 2016), pp. 209–38, at p. 210.

6 Eugene O'Curry, *On the Manners and Customs of the Ancient Irish* (London, 1873), p. 236.

gender subjugation of the woman in this tale, what is important in this context is actually the creation myth itself: this is an instrument borne of nature, similar in metaphoric proportions to the whale and capable of special feats.

In Irish mythology the harp as musical instrument is associated with key mythic figures including the Daghdha and Lúgh, both of whom were symbols of male virility, courage and magic. The Daghdha was a 'leading mythic character in Irish literature'.[7] He was one of the Tuatha Dé Dannan who, according to Padraic Colum: 'lived in the northern isles of the world, learning lore and magic and druidism and wizardry and cunning, until they surpassed the sages of the arts of heathendom'.[8]

The Daghdha was considered the 'principal deity in ancient times'. He was the father-god and indeed was father of many, thus fulfilling an important role in establishing the familial lineage of many of the Tuatha Dé Dannan. He lived at Brugh na Bóinne (the tumulus at Newgrange) and was also identified with the sun-deity among the western Celts.[9]

The Battle of Moytirra (Cath Maige Tuired) is a central story in Irish mythology, recounting the battle between two supernatural groups, the Túatha Dé Dannan and the Fomhóire. Written texts date to the eighth century with multiple versions existing due to translation and oral transmission practices.[10] The Fomhóire of the underworld were in possession of Ireland, forcing the Tuatha Dé Dannan to use much sorcery and magic (including the Daghdha's magic harping) to regain the land. The following extended extract outlines the mythic qualities of the harp and shows its use by the Daghdha as a powerful weapon in his armoury:

> And Lugh and Dagda and Ogma followed after the Fomor, for they had brought away the Dagda's harp with them [...] And they came to a feasting-house [...] and there was the harp hanging on the wall. And it was in the harp the Dagda had bound the music, so that it would not sound till he would call to it. And sometimes it was called Dur-da-Bla, the Oak of Two Blossoms, and sometimes Coir-cethar-chuin, the Four-Angled Music.
>
> And when he saw it hanging on the wall it is what he said: 'Come summer, come winter, from the mouth of harps and bags and pipes.' Then the harp sprang from the wall, and came to the Dagda, and it killed nine men on its way.
>
> And then he played for them the three things harpers understand, the sleepy tune, the laughing tune, and the crying tune. And when he

7 Dáithí Ó hÓgáin, *The Lore of Ireland: An Encyclopaedia of Myth, Legend and Romance* (Cork, 2006), p. 151.

8 Padraic Colum, *A Treasury of Irish Folklore* (New York, 1967).

9 Ó hÓgáin, *The Lore of Ireland*, p. 151.

10 Gerard Murphy, *Saga and Myth in Ancient Ireland* (Cork, 1971), p. 23.

> played the crying tune, their tearful women cried, and then he played the laughing tune, till their women and children laughed; and then he played the sleepy tune, and all the hosts fell asleep. And through that sleep the three went away through the Formor that would have been glad to harm them.[11]

Descriptions of the Daghdha in this epic tale convey 'hugeness, generosity and a voracious appetite'.[12] Other descriptions in the literature describe the Daghdha as exhibiting 'cunning, sternness and strength'.[13]

The Daghdha was not alone in his harping. Lúgh was another mythical hero in Irish folklore, with a reputation as the Samhildánach, meaning 'the one who possesses all the arts'. He was a Celtic deity and sanctuaries dedicated to Lúgh have been found in Western and Northern Europe with several place names deriving from his name, including Lugudunon (fortress of Lugus) and Lyon.[14] Dáithí Ó hÓgáin describes Lughnasadh as 'an assembly held by him [i.e. Lúgh] at the beginning of harvest each year'.[15] The fullest account of Lúgh's harping occurs in the eleventh-century Irish text *Cath Maige Tuiread*.[16] The following excerpt describing Lúgh's arrival at Tara is taken from Murphy's *Saga and Myth in Ancient Ireland* (1961):

> The doorkeeper saw an unknown troop approaching him. A fair and shapely warrior, with a king's trapping was in the forefront of that band … The doorkeeper asked the Samhildánach: [possessing many crafts, at the same time/master of all crafts] …
>
> Question me, doorkeeper: I am a smith, warrior, a poet and a historian, a sorcerer, cupbearer and metal-worker … I am a harper … Ask the king whether he has one single man who possesses all these arts, and if he has I shall not enter Tara.[17]

This text, and others like it, include the harp as a virtuous trait of the mythic Celtic gods.[18] Notably, these are male gods who exhibit superhuman strength, generosity and skills. This set a mythical and ancient precedent for the high status of the harpers in early Gaelic Ireland, who were second only to the *file* (poet) in social status.

11 Lady Gregory, *Complete Irish Mythology* (London, 1994), pp. 52–3.
12 Ó hÓgáin, *The Lore of Ireland*, p. 153.
13 Ó hÓgáin, *The Lore of Ireland*, p. 153.
14 Ó hÓgáin, *The Lore of Ireland*, p. 311.
15 Ó hÓgáin, *The Lore of Ireland*, p. 311.
16 Ó hÓgáin, *The Lore of Ireland*, p. 312.
17 Witley Stokes, 'The Second Battle of Moytura', *Revue Celtique*, 12 (1891), cited in Murphy, *Saga and Myth*, pp. 29–30.
18 See also Deirdre Nic Chárthaigh, '*Cia an Saoi lé Seinntear an Chruit*: A Bardic Poem to a Harper', in Helen Lawlor and Sandra Joyce (eds), *Harp Studies II: World Harp Traditions* (Dublin, forthcoming).

The Harp in Gaelic Ireland

The ancient Gaelic harp tradition has been the subject of much scholarly inquiry, including the works of Ann Buckley, Ann Heymann and Paul Dooley.[19] The most famous and extant example of the early Gaelic harp is the Trinity College harp (often inaccurately called 'The BrianBorú' harp). This harp in particular typifies the early Gaelic model, which was strung with brass strings on a quadrangular sound box hollowed out of a single piece of willow. These instruments rested against the left shoulder and were about 70cm in height with a string span of *c.*thirty strings, diatonically tuned over four octaves. While we have some knowledge of the construction of early harps through extant instruments, iconography also offers an avenue for the study and interpretation of early harp images, such as depictions of harpers on high crosses.[20] Ann Buckley's work on instruments in Ireland from the ninth century remains seminal in this area, although she urges caution when extrapolating meanings from such iconographical sources:

> musical instruments are usually depicted as one element of a scene in religious carvings: not for the purpose of conveying information of a musicological nature but to preach the Christian message, portraying scenes of adoration and ritual of which music was a component.[21]

We may, however, in attempting to decode the gender trajectory of the musical instrument, utilise and interpret some of the extant imagery to contribute to the analysis. Paul Dooley proposes in *Harp Studies* that 'the earliest reliable reference to an Irish harp [...] comes from Giraldus Cambrensis', drawing from his well-cited text *Topgraphia Hibernica* (*c.*1188):

> It is only in the case of musical instruments that I find commendable diligence among these people; on them they are incomparably more skilled than any people we have seen [...] the most important element in their art appears to be in veiling it, as if 'it were the better for being hidden; art revealed brings shame'.[22]

19 Ann Buckley, 'Musical Instruments in Ireland from the Ninth to the Fourteenth Centuries', in Gerard Gillen and Harry White (eds), *Irish Musical Studies, vol. 1: Musicology in Ireland,* (Dublin, 1990), pp. 13–57; Ann Heymann, 'Harp', in Fintan Vallely (ed), *The Companion to Irish Traditional Music* (Cork, 1999), pp. 175–81; Ann Heymann, 'Three Iconic Gaelic Harp Pieces', in Joyce and Lawlor (eds), *Harp Studies*, pp. 184–208; Paul Dooley, 'The Harp in the Time of Giraldus', in Joyce and Lawlor (eds), *Harp Studies*, pp. 21–58.

20 Simon Chadwick, 'The Early Irish Harp', *Early Music*, 36: 4 (2008), 521–31.

21 Buckley, 'Musical Instruments in Ireland from the Ninth to the Fourteenth Centuries', p. 14.

22 Extracts from the translation of *capitulum* xi given by Ann Buckley, in 'Music in Ireland to *c.*1500', in Dáibhí Ó Cróinín (ed.), *A New History of Ireland I:*

The accompanying images in Dooley's article of illustrations from two extant manuscripts that were possibly supervised if not drawn by Cambrensis give a historically accurate rendering of the bards, if not the harps themselves (even taking Buckley's caution into account).[23] In these illustrations we observe well-dressed male musicians tuning their harps in an ecclesiastical setting. Dooley, citing Michelle Brown, concludes that:

> Michelle Brown remarks that both 'preserve an image of the characteristic Irish bard, a resplendent chap with elaborate garb […] and flowing beard […]'. According to Scott these illustrations are definitely the work of someone who knew the dress and appearance of the Irish. Thus it would appear that the artists paid some attention to detail in depicting the players.[24]

Clearly the existence of these images does not preclude female performers but rather identifies the harp at that time as a male occupation and esteemed pursuit, as was the case for harpers detailed in the Brehon Laws, outlined by O'Curry:

> the Cruitire, or harper, is recognized as one of the distinguished artists, in a special clause in the following words: 'A Cruit; that is, this is a Cruit in place of a Timpan, or a Cruit in its own proper state. This is the only species of music; that is, it is the only profession of music, which is entitled to be ennobled; that is, which is entitled to Enechland; [that is, to a fine in right of insult to the honour, as well as for personal injury to the performer], even though it does not attend on the illustrious, that is, although it is not retained by a nobleman, but it noble in its own.'[25]

This special status lasted throughout Gaelic Ireland but dissipated with socio-political changes that led to the decline of the bardic order. These changes were accelerated and intensified after the Treaty of Limerick in 1691 and the introduction of the Penal Laws to Ireland. Not long before this seismic shift in Irish life, the harp had enjoyed popularity amongst wealthy households in both Ireland and England. Public presentation of harp music in the seventeenth century remained a male-dominated sphere. John Cunningham, for example, provides names of six harpers, all male, who held 'official posts in the Royal Music at the English court during the first half of the seventeenth century, at least four of whom are known to have played the Irish type of instrument'.[26] In his article,

Prehistoric and Early Ireland (Oxford, 2005), pp. 760–2, cited in Dooley, 'The Harp in the Time of Giraldus', p. 32.

23 Dooley, 'The Harp in the Time of Giraldus', pp. 50–1, fns 97 and 98.

24 Dooley, 'The Harp in the Time of Giraldus', pp. 50–1.

25 O'Curry, *On the Manners and Customs*, pp. 265–6.

26 John Cunningham, '"Irish Harpers are Excellent, and their Solemn Music is Much Liked of Strangers": The Irish Harp in Non-Irish Contexts in the

Cunningham makes a convincing case for the short-lived expansion of the harp into a chromatic instrument through various methods (such as extra rows of strings, as is the case with the Dalway harp) and in the context of English consort music.[27] The rise and fall of popularity of the harp in a new context may have accelerated its subsequent demise in Ireland too:

> The cultural assimilation of the Irish harp allowed the instrument to participate simultaneously and successfully, for albeit a brief period, in the realms of both Irish and English music. However, the cultural crossover of the Irish harp could not be sustained once the cultural network of the Stuart court had been dismantled in the late 1640s and 1650s. It is perhaps no coincidence that once the Irish harp ceased to be an untenable participant in the English consort the tradition's need for modulation notes dissipated, and the Irish harp largely returned to its diatonic (and Irish) origins by the end of the century.[28]

Musically and socially, the Irish harp started to trail behind as a relic of a past age. The chieftains of Gaelic Ireland had lost any remaining vestiges of power and their court system belonged to a different time. However, the harpers still found favour amongst the landed gentry, both Catholic and Protestant, in the seventeenth and eighteenth centuries. Harpers were still received as esteemed guests and travelled around the country staying for between a week and a month in the homes of the gentry. There they performed music for occasions and composed for their patrons. Turlough Carolan (1670–1738) is probably the most well-known exponent of this tradition. A blind harper, he was patronised by the McDermott Roe family of Longford and gained repute as a composer of harp music in both the traditional and 'modern' styles.[29]

In addition to socio-political factors, musical factors also contributed heavily to the decline in popularity of the instrument. In comparison with continental compositional and organological developments that underpinned the changing musical styles of late Baroque into early Classical, the Irish harp was largely a solo diatonic instrument incapable of fully embracing the totality of new musical trends. What followed after Carolan's death was a decline in uptake of the instrument, compositional output and viable patronage, so that by the 1790s the harp had almost become wholly symbolic in its cultural import. Despite the failed

Seventeenth Century', in Barra Boydell and Kerry Houston (eds), *Irish Musical Studies, vol. 10: Music, Ireland and the Seventeenth Century* (Dublin, 2009), pp. 62–81, at p. 62. These harpers are listed with their harp types as: Cormack MacDermott, Daniel Cahill, Philip Squire, Lewis Evans (Irish harp); Malcombe Goate (Scottish harp?); Jean le Flelle (triple harp?).

27 Simon Chadwick, 'The Cloyne Harp', *Early Gaelic Harp Info* <http://www.earlygaelicharp.info/harps/cloyne.htm> [accessed 11 July 2022].

28 Cunningham, '"Irish Harpers are Excellent"', p. 80.

29 Edward Bunting, *The Ancient Music of Ireland* (London, 1840) p. 71.

attempts to revive the tradition, such as the Granard Balls, Belfast Harp Festival, and the harp schools at Dublin, Drogheda and Belfast – often borne out of misguided musical if ideologically sound motivations – a vital sustaining thread in the continuation of harping has been the published works of Edward Bunting.[30] Bunting was initially hired to transcribe the music played by harpers present at the 1792 Belfast Harp Festival but continued his work long after the event, publishing three phenomenally important collections of tunes with essays, descriptions and analyses of the harping tradition.[31]

Bunting's inclusion of Denis Hempson's biography is a tremendously important resource for scholars today. Bunting writes of Hempson's harp tuition: 'He lost his sight at the age of three years by the small-pox; at twelve years old he began to learn the harp under Bridget O'Cahan; "for," as he said, "in these old times, *women* as well as men were taught the Irish harp in the best families, and every old Irish family had harps in plenty."'[32] Bunting makes brief mention of these two female performers in the preface to his 1840 volume:

> Although formerly it was very usual for females to apply themselves to the harp, yet at this epoch [late eighteenth century] there were but two female performers of any repute in Ulster. These were Catherine Martin, a Meath woman, who delighted greatly in the tunes composed by Parson Stirling, of Lurgan; and Rose Mooney, a pupil of Elliot's, who attended the Granard and Belfast Meetings. The latter died at Killala, just after the landing of the French there, under very lamentable circumstances.

While Bunting lamented the decline of the harpers from the corpus of active practitioners of Irish music by the mid-nineteenth century, he did so without considering the contemporaneous shift in appreciation of the harp in the popular consciousness. Perhaps that sorrowful decline in the ancient Gaelic tradition freed the harp from its direct musical associations and allowed it to become reimagined in nineteenth-century symbolism and poetry.

Literature and Poetry

Recent scholarship has begun to redress the dearth of research on harping in the nineteenth century, particularly the work of Mary Louise O'Donnell, whose book *Ireland's Harp* assesses the musical, cultural and

30 Colette Moloney, *The Irish Music Manuscripts of Edward Bunting* (Dublin, 2000).

31 Edward Bunting, *A General Collection of the Ancient Irish Music* (London, 1796); Edward Bunting, *A General Collection of the Ancient Music of Ireland* (London, 1809); Bunting, *The Ancient Music of Ireland*.

32 Bunting, *The Ancient Music of Ireland*, p. 74.

symbolic history of the harp in that century.[33] Despite the attempts of antiquarians and musicians in the nineteenth century to reignite interest in the Gaelic harp tradition, festivals and harp schools did not succeed in creating a sufficient platform for new musical creation and a proliferation of harp activity on a sustainable national level. In poetry and literature, the harp found a place as a malleable trope for romanticism and nationalism.[34] O'Donnell describes how Sydney Owensen, for example, treats the harp as a central device in her novel *The Wild Irish Girl*:

> For Owenson, the instrument and its music are elements of a complex three-part trope involving the harper, harp, and harp music [...] She recognised that the harp without the harper was powerless – with the harper, the instrument could be a dynamic utopian icon serving 'to rally Ireland as a nation ready to look forward to the future'. Owenson (in the guise of Glorvina) enthusiastically assumed the role of harper both literally and figuratively.[35]

Indeed, Owenson played an Egan harp, which itself was visually impactful as a symbol of Irishness.[36] The harp in literature became increasingly distant from contemporary performance practice over the course of the early to mid-nineteenth century, a separation that allowed for poetic imaginings of the harp to represent ideologies rather than music; this ultimately distanced the instrument from the very tradition that had musically sustained it for eight hundred years. Thomas Moore's *Irish Melodies* accelerated this transition as he returned to the harp frequently as a symbol of freedom in the post-union era.

Drawing on Harry White's analysis of the development of Moore's bardic persona in the *Irish Melodies*,[37] I examine three excerpts of Moore's poetry to show how the harp is objectified as a symbol of femininity and how the power to make it sound rests in the hands of the male bard.

33 O'Donnell, *Ireland's Harp*; Mary Louise O'Donnell, 'The Bengal Subscription: Patriotism, Patronage and the Perpetuation of the Irish Harp Tradition in the Early Nineteenth Century', in Joyce and Lawlor (eds), *Harp Studies*, pp. 75–89; Nancy Hurrell, 'The Royal Portable Harp by John Egan', *Journal of the Historical Harp Society* (2003).

34 Emily Cullen, 'Tempering the Stereotypes of Irishness Abroad: The Irish Harp as Golden Lever of Temperance and Respectability', in Joyce and Lawlor (eds), *Harp Studies*, pp. 105–20.

35 O'Donnell, *Ireland's Harp*, p. 51.

36 For a fuller investigation of the work of Egan and his successors see: Nancy Hurrell, *The Egan Irish Harps: Tradition, Patrons and Players* (Dublin, 2019). Of note in gendered traditions is that Egan's daughter created a successful harp-making business following her father's death, surpassing the work of her brother.

37 Harry White, 'The Lyre of Apollo: Thomas Moore and the Irish Harp', in Joyce and Lawlor (eds), *Harp Studies*, pp. 90–104.

In 'The Minstrel Boy', from volume five of the *Irish melodies*, published in 1813, the brave minstrel marches to war with 'his wild harp slung behind him'. After his capture he preserves the virtue of the harp and its symbolic home:

> The Minstrel fell! – But the foeman's chain
> Could not bring that proud soul under
> The harp he lov'd ne'er spoke again
> For he tore its chords asunder
> And said 'No chains shall sully thee
> Thou soul of love and brav'ry!
> Thy songs were made for the pure and free,
> They shall never sound in slavery!'[38]

The male protagonist is at the centre here, his fearless final act exhibiting strength, courage and integrity. This fast-paced and dynamic poem sees the harp in action even if it meets a deathly end. By contrast, in 'Dear Harp of My Country', the harp meets a sorrowful if more peaceful end: 'The cold chain of silence had hung o'er thee long' and:

> […]
> Go, sleep with the sunshine of Fame on thy slumbers,
> Till touch'd by some hand less unworthy than mine.
> If the pulse of the patriot, soldier, or lover,
> Have throbb'd at our lay, 'tis thy glory alone;
> I was but as the wind, passing heedlessly over,
> And all the wild sweetness I waked was thy own.[39]

White articulates:

> He is addressing the harp as an icon of Irish culture, as a symbol of repressed political autonomy, as a vital agent of his own poetic discourse. But he is scarcely concerned in any literal sense with the instrument itself. As in the famous painting of Moore at his study in Sloperton Cottage, the harp lies to one side (or on its side).[40]

Following the 1798 rebellion, Moore visited Kilmainham Gaol to see Edward Hudson who was imprisoned there. Linda Kelly describes how 'Moore showed courage in going to visit him [Edward Hudson], in Kilmainham Gaol […] A good painter as well as a musician, Hudson had whiled away his time making a large charcoal drawing of the mythical origins of the Irish harp on the wall of his cell. Moore used the subject –

38 <http://www.musicanet.org/robokopp/moore.html> [accessed 11 July 2022].
39 <http://www.musicanet.org/robokopp/moore.html> [accessed 11 July 2022].
40 White, 'The Lyre of Apollo', p. 99.

sea-nymph who falls vainly in love with a mortal, and is transformed into a harp – for one of his Irish melodies, "The Origin of the Harp".'[41]

'Tis believed that this Harp, which I wake now for thee
Was a Siren of old, who sung under the sea;
And who often, at eve, through the bright waters roved,
To meet, on the green shore, a youth whom she loved.
But she loved him in vain, for he left her to weep,
And in tears, all the night, her gold tresses to steep,
Till heaven look'd with pity on true-love so warm,
And changed to this soft Harp the sea-maiden's form.
Still her bosom rose fair – still her cheeks smiled the same
While her sea-beauties gracefully form'd the light
And her hair, as, let loose, o'er her white arm it fell,
Was changed to bright chords uttering melody's spell.
Hence it came, that this soft Harp so long hath been known
To mingle love's language with sorrow's sad tone;
Till thou didst divide them, and teach the fond lay
To speak love when I'm near thee, and grief when away.[42]

Moore, inspired by Hudson, reinvents the origin of the harp, still emerging from the sea (previously a whale carcass) but now as beautiful sea maiden, no longer man-made but divinely created. She is an elusive and tragic figure who is immortalised as the harp. The poetry created by Moore here was realised visually by painter Daniel Maclise, who illustrated this poem in 1842 in his 'The Origin of the Harp'. Mary Helen Theunte posits that:

> Although some supernatural women in *aislings* had musical voices and streaming hair, Moore's tale of the origin of the harp transcends Irish tradition by evoking popular visual images of sirens and mermaids with streaming hair and the birth of Venus rising from the foam of the ocean. Moore's celebration of the image of ancient bard and plain harp, often referred to as the Brian Ború harp, no doubt accelerated that image's popularity.[43]

Moore effectively reinvents the creation myth of the harp to fit with his aesthetic, portraying the romantic and idealised *female* harp.

Into the later nineteenth century the Irish harp's status was so low that its presence in literature and poetry becomes further distant from

41 Linda Kelly, *Ireland's Minstrel: A Life of Tom Moore: Poet, Patriot, and Byron's Friend* (London, 2006), p. 29.

42 <http://www.musicanet.org/robokopp/moore.html> [accessed 11 July 2022].

43 Mary Helen Thuente, 'The Origin and Significance of the Angel Harp', in Patricia A. Lynch, Joachim Fischer and Brian Coates (eds), *Back to the Present, Forward to the Past: Irish Writing and History Since 1798* (Amsterdam and New York, 2006), pp. 181–208, at p. 203.

any musical awakenings; instead, it played a deeply symbolic role. The harp becomes the languishing Ireland, the fateful Caitlín Ní Úallacháin, glorified in the poetry, song and literature of the nation and indeed the diaspora.[44] The organological developments, most notably the harps produced by John Egan of Dublin, coupled with its representation in poetry, literature and art, created a radically different musical reality for the instrument.[45]

O'Donnell further acknowledges the musical displacement and ideological freedom of harp representations in the later nineteenth century:

> images of aged bards and mute harps, and strains of melancholy harp music dominated the perception of the Irish harp for the remainder of the century. As the contemporary tradition was further dislocated from the glorious golden age of Irish harp patronage and performance described by Moore, the symbolic value of the Irish harp and harper was exploited by the next generation of Irish nationalists who looked to this Irish Arcadia and its utopian icon, the harp, as a source of inspiration in imagining a new unified Irish nation.[46]

The new popularity of the Irish harp as a drawing-room instrument, echoing the context of the European pedal harp, lent an element of bourgeois respectability to the instrument and furthered its association as an instrument for music making in the home. It came to be considered a ladylike instrument, a transformation that began in pedal harping when Queen Marie Antoinette took up the harp in France and spread its popularity in European drawing rooms.[47] This trend was embedded in societal ideologies of gender roles and marriage, as articulated by Ellen Koskoff:

> Certainly, from the eighteenth century to the present, again in the areas of the world that supported a court system, the home, a semiprivate, protected environment, became the most important context for women performers as noted in the literature. Unmarried women, often viewed as property to be transferred from father to husband, perfected skills there that would make them desirable to potential mates; males, in positions of economic and social power (relative to women of their class), on the other hand, generally had access to musical training and to public, even professional environments for musical performance.[48]

44 Cullen, 'Tempering the Stereotypes of Irishness Abroad'.

45 Hurrell, *The Egan Irish Harps*.

46 O'Donnell, *Ireland's Harp*, pp. 62–3.

47 Lawlor, *Irish Harping*, pp. 142–57.

48 Ellen Koskoff, *A Feminist Ethnomusicology: Writings on Music and Gender* (Urbana, Chicago and Springfield, 2014), p. 125.

In the Irish case, the harp was popularised as an instrument appropriate for young ladies to play in convent schools, with Loreto Abbey, Rathfarnham and Dominican College, Sion Hill (Dublin) emerging later in the twentieth century as centres for harping. This context intensified the female uptake of the harp so that by the second and third decades of the twentieth century there was minimal evidence of male performers. In the mid-century the revival of the tradition was pioneered by visionary harpists such as sisters Róisín and Máirín Ní Shéaghdha, Sheila Larchet Cuthbert and Gráinne Yeats. (For a discussion of Larchet Cuthbert and Yeats see Teresa O'Donnell, Chapter 7, this volume.)

Arts Practice Today

In the 2014 *Report on the Harping Tradition in Ireland*, commissioned by the Arts Council, author Toner Quinn provides a snapshot of the gender divide in contemporary practice. Of the respondents 347 were female and 46 male, representing an 88.3 to 11.7 per cent breakdown.[49] These figures do not distinguish between performers of the wire-strung/pedal/ or neo-Irish harp, which is important because, colloquially, evidence suggests that the wire-strung harp community has a far more balanced gender divide. Perhaps this is due to the legacy of the 'great' male harpers as Gaelic bards. The response to that survey is not surprising: the harping tradition throughout the twentieth century has been pioneered, reimagined, revived and organised primarily by women. Furthermore, they as women musicians, often in a professional or semi-professional capacity, subverted the gender norms and expectations of their generations by forging musical careers, not just as teachers but as performing artists, arrangers and broadcasters. For example, Mother Attracta Coffey published her arrangements, *Irish Melodies for Harp*, in 1904, followed by her successor at Loretto Abbey Rathfarnham, Mother Alphonsus O'Connor, who also published arrangements. O'Connor taught Sheila Larchet Cuthbert, one of the founding members of Cairde na Cruite. Larchet Cuthbert's efforts, particularly from the 1960s onwards, provided a driving force to the harp revival. The Ní Sheaghdha sisters (one of whom taught Mary O'Hara) were also centrally involved in the repopularisation of the harp through their own performance, teaching and broadcasting careers. O'Hara had an international profile from the 1950s to the 1990s (even sharing a manager with Bob Dylan), rising to global stardom as a singer and harpist. In the late 1970s Máire Ní Chathasaigh and Janet Harbison both began playing traditional music on the Irish harp to popular acclaim.[50] Teachers, performers and advocates for the harp including Laoise Kelly, Denise Kelly-McDonald, Gráinne Hambly,

49 Quinn, *Report*.
50 Lawlor, *Irish Harping*.

Aibhlín McCrann, Michelle Mulcahy, Áine Ní Dhubhghail, Eithne Benson, Deirdre Ní Bhuachalla, Ann-Marie O'Farrell, amongst many others, have significantly enhanced performance and participation. In comparison, only a few male professional harpers have gained prominence over the same period, in particular, Derek Bell, Michael Rooney, Cormac De Barra and Paul Dooley. The harp for much of the twentieth century was a marginalised instrument both in art and traditional music communities of practice. The intensive feminisation of the instrument is a possible barrier to uptake where a perceived identification with a single gender exists. While noteworthy that there exists a growing number of young male harpers in Ireland, to date their impact on gender diversity remains limited. Diversity in gender is a welcome factor in any musical tradition.

In *Feminine Endings*, Susan McClary argues that:

> The codes marking gender difference in music are informed by the prevalent attitudes of their time. But they also themselves participate in social formation, insomuch as individuals learn how to be gendered beings through their interactions with cultural discourses such as music. Moreover, music does not just passively reflect society; it also serves as a public forum within which various models of gender organization (along with many other aspects of social life) are asserted, adopted, contested and negotiated.[51]

Her argument is still relevant. The Irish harp is at a high point in terms of uptake with young students, opportunities for professional performers, and its representation at formal learning institutions and through vehicles such as Music Generation. As public gender performativity is partially disseminated through musical codes, it is perhaps time to further target focused positive interventions to benefit the diversification of the harping tradition in Ireland. The gender associations over the past 120–150 years have arisen from the harp's unique interpretive symbolism and its place in Irish cultural history. If, through music, as McClary argues, 'individuals learn how to be gendered beings', then to prevent the ultimate 'othering' of the harp as a vehicle for women's music making only, opportunities and supports for young male harpers need to be continually supported to redress the obvious gender imbalance as it presently exists. Activity and (re)negotiation are stressed by McClary here – there is nothing fixed or permanent in terms of gendering of music; rather, public discourses help to shape and define gender norms at any given historical moment. In this interpretation, appreciation of how gender codes are formed offers a route to expanding the gender diversification of the harp tradition.

The recent history of the harp offers a very different perspective on gender and Irish traditional music. Tes Slominski emphasises the

51 Susan McClary, *Feminine Endings*, 2nd edn (Minneapolis, 2002), pp. 7–8.

importance of rendering women musicians visible in the written and oral histories of Irish music.[52] Reconsidering the history of the Irish harp through the lens of gender provides an opportunity to reintegrate women into the cannon of artistic activists, teachers and culture bearers in traditional music scholarship. It also demonstrates how the gender associations of this instrument have changed radically over time. Through its long and complex history, the harp has been a vehicle for the expression of cultural values and identities, offering a unique lens through which to study music and gender both in terms of its sonic and ideological manifestations.

52 Tes Slominksi, *Trad Nation* (Middletown, 2020), p. 43.

6

'No Longer Second Fiddle': Due Recognition for Josephine Keegan

Daithí Kearney

Introduction

Until recently, the history and study of Irish traditional music has been dominated by men, creating an impression that female musicians are not as important in the tradition. Josephine Keegan (*b.*1935), a fiddle and piano player as well as a composer, now living in Mullaghbawn (or Mullaghbane) in south Armagh, exemplifies the different roles played and challenges faced by female Irish traditional musicians in the twentieth century. Keegan's musical life and output highlight the role and influence of women in the tradition, knowledge of which contributes to a fuller understanding of the tradition. As Keegan has been overshadowed by the attention paid to her contemporaries and collaborators, including Seán McGuire (1927–2005) and Joe Burke (1939–2021), this chapter considers her multiple achievements: as piano accompanist to male soloists, fiddle soloist of note in her own right, collector and composer of Irish traditional music, and pedagogue. She was an innovator in the context of her solo recordings and corresponded widely with her contemporaries. The male dominance of the tradition, particularly in the past, may be explained by social and cultural norms including attitudes to appropriate behaviour and the presence of women in pubs, attitudes that Keegan challenged and overcame as a pioneering female performer in a male-dominated society. Informed by debates in musicological discourse and music journalism, this chapter recognises changing attitudes in recent years towards a greater appreciation of female performers and composers in Irish traditional music.

The invisibility of women in narratives of Irish traditional music misrepresents their presence and influence. The masculinity of space and gender norms in Irish society had a significant impact on the visibility of women musicians.[1] P.J. Curtis writes: 'There were in fact a great number of superb women musicians and singers up and down the country, but their talents were restricted to the privacy of their own homes.'[2] Christina Dolphin highlights the absence of women in the literature from many of the seminal texts on Irish traditional music in the twentieth century,[3] such as those by Breandán Breathnach,[4] Ciarán Carson,[5] Tomás Ó Canainn,[6] Francis O'Neill[7] and Seán Ó Riada.[8] When revising his *Pocket History of Irish Traditional Music* for republication in 2017,[9] Gearóid Ó hAlmhuráin included a new section on women in music, recognising the omission from the first edition and the fact that, despite their absence from the narratives, women contributed significantly to the development, transmission and performance of Irish traditional music.[10] Perhaps most notable in exploring issues of gender in Irish traditional music is Tes Slominski, who has highlighted the roles of some of Keegan's contemporaries in the development of Irish traditional music.[11] (See Slominski, Chapter 15, this volume.)

Attitudes to women entering pubs, the principal space for the performance of Irish traditional music, affected the visibility of women musicians in Irish traditional music.[12] Lucy Farr suggests that the pub was a place where women 'sort of felt that you shouldn't be',[13] with Helen O'Shea noting the necessity of 'having a powerful male mentor' or 'demonstrating a talent that is considered virtuosic' in order to be accepted.[14] Many women engaged in Irish traditional music did so in their roles

1 Helen O'Shea, *The Making of Irish Traditional Music* (Cork, 2008); Helen O'Shea, '"Good man, Mary!" Women Musicians and the Fraternity of Irish Traditional Music', *Journal of Gender Studies*, 17: 1 (2008), 55–70; Gearóid Ó hAlmhuráin, *A Short History of Irish Traditional Music* (Dublin, 2017).

2 P.J. Curtis, *Notes from the Heart: A Celebration of Traditional Irish Music* (Dublin, 1994), p. 125.

3 Christina Dolphin, 'Reels, Heels and Glass Ceilings: Women Musicians in the Professional Sphere of Irish Traditional Music' (Unpublished MA dissertation, University of Limerick, 2013).

4 Breandán Breathnach, *Folk Music and Dances of Ireland* (Dublin, 1971).

5 Ciarán Carson, *Pocket Guide to Irish Traditional Music* (Belfast, 1986).

6 Tomás Ó Canainn, *Traditional Music in Ireland* (Cork, 1993).

7 Francis O'Neill *Irish Minstrels and Musicians* (Cork, 1987).

8 Seán Ó Riada, *Our Musical Heritage* (Portlaoise, 1982).

9 Gearóid Ó hAlmhuráin, *Pocket History of Irish Traditional Music* (Dublin, 1997).

10 Ó hAlmhuráin, *Short History*, pp. 186–91.

11 Tes Slominski, *Trad Nation: Gender, Sexuality, and Race in Irish Traditional Music* (Connecticut, 2020).

12 Seán Williams, *Focus: Irish Traditional Music* (London, 2010), p. 201; Slominkski, *Trad Nation*.

13 Fintan Vallely and Charlie Piggott, *Blooming Meadows: The World of Irish Traditional Musicians* (Dublin, 1998), p. 74.

14 O'Shea, *The Making of Irish Traditional Music*, p. 110.

as mothers and teachers, transmitting the music in local areas without gaining significant public profile or acclaim. At different times during her life, Keegan fulfilled various roles and sometimes challenged what was expected of a woman in Irish traditional music contexts.

Rina Schiller brought the issue of gender and Irish traditional music to the table at *Crosbhealach an Cheoil* in 1996, observing that 'the role model of the 1960s Irish traditional group was exclusively male'.[15] Drawing comparisons with Irish society in the 1960s, Liz Doherty studied women musicians in Cape Breton traditions, documenting how mothers and sisters acted as piano accompanists for male relatives on the fiddle.[16] Slominski has focused on some notable historical female figures in Irish traditional music, including fiddle players Treasa Ní hAlpín and Julia Clifford.[17] Slominski comments that 'many women musicians were visible at one time but have since been forgotten outside their families and immediate communities'.[18] Echoing the concept of second-degree visibility presented by Slominski,[19] and commented on by Doherty,[20] Naila Ceribašić considers relationships between men and women musicians in Croatian folk music, emphasising how a kinship relationship with a man 'often made it possible in the past, and still makes is possible for women to enter into the field of instrumental music in a more permanent, serious, and professional way'.[21] Keegan benefited from her father's participation in Irish traditional music and is often considered in relation to prominent male performers, chiefly Burke and McGuire, but deserves recognition for her individual contributions.[22]

15 Rena Schiller, 'Gender and Traditional Irish Music', in F. Vallely et al. (eds), *Crosbhealach an Cheoil: The Crossroads Conference* (Dublin, 1996), pp. 200–5, at p. 204.

16 Liz Doherty, 'The Paradox of the Periphery: Evolution of the Cape Breton Fiddle Tradition *c.*1928–1995', (Unpublished PhD dissertation, University of Limerick, 1996), pp. 77–83.

17 Tes Slominski, 'Music, Gender, and the Public Sphere in Twentieth-Century Ireland', (Unpublished PhD dissertation, New York University, 2010); Slominski, *Trad Nation*.

18 Slominski, 'Music, Gender', p. 72.

19 Slominski, 'Music, Gender'; Slominski, *Trad Nation*.

20 Doherty, 'The Paradox of the Periphery'.

21 Naila Ceribašić, 'Social Canons Inherited from the Past: Women Players of Folk Music Instruments in Croatia', *Studia Musicologica Academiae Scientiarum Hungaricae* T. 44, Fasc. 1/2 (2003), pp. 147–57, at p. 149.

22 It is worth noting that Burke and McGuire were accompanied by Keegan on the recording *Two Champions* (Outlet SOLP1014, 1971); the title refers to the two male musicians but this should be read in the context whereby accompanists were often unnamed. The LP cover is notable as it features the names of the two male musicians but Keegan, unnamed, is in the foreground seated at the piano.

Influenced by general questions posed by Bruno Nettl regarding the ethnomusicological study of women and music,[23] the following chapter provides a brief biography of Josephine Keegan. I reflect on Keegan's success as a fiddle performer and recording artist. Separately, I consider her piano playing and the second-degree visibility she experienced. Alongside her performing career, I outline Keegan's contribution to Irish musical traditions as a collector and composer, activities she pursued for much of her life. Finally, I trace the belated recognition for Keegan's achievements in the twenty-first century, symbolic of the generally increasing recognition for women in Irish traditional music.

Josephine Keegan

Born in Dundee, Scotland, Keegan moved with her family to Co. Armagh, Northern Ireland in 1939 and later to Mullaghbawn in 1950.[24] Keegan's father Joe (*d*.1973) was a notable flute player. From Derryvilla near Portarlington, he learnt music from his mother Anne Delaney before joining the Bishopswood Flute Band, with whom he learned to read and write music.[25] He broadcast as a solo artist on Radio Éireann in the 1950s.[26] Keegan's mother Alice Kelly (*d*.1963) came from Rassan, Co. Louth, an area near the border between Monaghan in the Republic of Ireland and Armagh in Northern Ireland. Alice had a basic knowledge of piano technique and music theory; Keegan credits her mother with teaching her the rudiments and introducing her to the piano.

Josephine's two older sisters, Maymie and Eilish, had already begun to play piano.[27] Her father taught her tin whistle, introduced her to the flute and started her on the fiddle. Keegan attended the Convent of Mercy, Bessbrook and Our Lady's Grammar School in Newry. At Bessbrook she took piano lessons with Sister M. Paul (Hicks) and violin lessons with Sister M. Therese (Martin). She progressed to competition success at the Newry Feis and Castleblayney Feis.[28] She won the Oireachtas fiddle competition in 1955 and competed in Fleadh Cheoil na hÉireann in Boyle in 1960.[29]

23 Bruno Nettl, *The Study of Ethnomusicology: Thirty-One Issues and Concepts* (Illinois, 2005), p. 405.

24 Tommy Fegan, 'Josephine Keegan', in Fintan Vallely (ed.), *Companion to Irish Traditional Music* (Cork, 2011), p. 377.

25 Josephine Keegan, *The Keegan Tunes Cuid a Dó* (Mullaghbawn, 2006).

26 Ceol Camlocha, *Aoibhneas na Bealtaine: The Sweets of May: the Céilí Band Era, Music & Dance of South Armagh* (Armagh, 2008), p. 9.

27 Maymie married Andy Cross in 1960 and lived in Rathangan, Co. Kildare until her death in 2011. Eilish (Dayap) emigrated to the United States where she married.

28 Keegan, *The Keegan Tunes Cuid a Dó*, p. 25.

29 Fegan, *Companion*, p. 377.

Keegan's early musical milieu involved house sessions and céilís, as is captured as part of the book and CD project *The Sweets of May*.[30] Concertina and melodeon player Paddy Murphy (1901–73) hosted evenings of music with his wife Mary in Creggandufff, while the Keegan family home also hosted evenings of music. While still at school in the 1940s, Keegan travelled to the Newry Feis where she first met piano player Seán O'Driscoll and experienced a céilí band performance by Ceol an Iubhair. With local fiddlers John (1929–96), Peter (1940–93) and Pat Murphy, she became involved in the John Murphy Céilí Band. She also played occasionally with the Dunreavy, Vincent Lowe and Johnny Pickering Céilí Bands. Early performances included playing céilís locally from 9pm until 3am for which the musicians received a modest fee, signifying their involvement in a semi-professional scene. These bands developed their repertoire to include waltzes and more modern music, but not everyone agreed with the inclusion of this repertoire.[31]

Keegan moved to Belfast to study education at St Mary's Training College before returning to teach in Mullaghbawn. During the late 1950s she developed a wide musical network by attending events such as Fleadhanna Cheoil and corresponding with other musicians. In the early 1960s she sought to bring together some of these musicians for a concert in Mullaghbawn Parish Hall. At this time, Keegan was married and teaching locally; with the support of the local parish priest and community, a night of music was held and a recording made of the night.[32]

England

Keegan moved to London in 1963 and toured throughout England with musicians including Seán McGuire and Joe Burke. This decision and career path were highly unusual at that time for a woman from a rural Irish background. In contrast with the session scene documented by Reg Hall,[33] Keegan was primarily engaged in formal performances in venues where audiences would sit and listen. Writing about this period, Antóin MacGabhann records the musical collaboration between McGuire and Burke: 'Together with Josephine Keegan on piano they toured around Ireland and the Folk Clubs and Festivals of England, Scotland and Shetland. Seán had already formed a musical partnership with Josephine

30 Ceol Camlocha, *Sweets of May*.

31 *Cherish the Ladies*, first broadcast on RTÉ Radio 1, July 2006.

32 The quality of this recording is impaired by the enthusiasm of a dancer located near the microphone.

33 Reg Hall, 'Irish Music and Dance in London, 1890–1970: A Socio-Cultural History, Parts I and II' (Unpublished PhD dissertation, University of Sussex, 1994).

Keegan, herself a great fiddle player, who provided expert and sensitive piano accompaniment for most of his playing career.'[34]

McGuire is an important figure in Keegan's career,[35] but is also implicated in her second-degree visibility.[36] Born in 1927 in Belfast, McGuire studied in Belfast with George Vincent and later his bowing style was influenced by May Nesbitt.[37] An extravagant player, he won the Oireachtas in 1949, achieving 100 per cent from all judges.[38] As well as gaining prominence as a soloist, he played in the Malachy Sweeney Céilí Band with his father and Johnny Pickering.[39] The development of Keegan's musical relationship with McGuire is important in understanding her significance in Irish traditional music and emergence as a professional artist during the 1960s. Like many aspects of her early life, her awareness of McGuire was influenced by her father. He had heard the young fiddler on the radio around 1946–47 and when Josephine left for college in Belfast, he insisted: 'you're going to have to make it your business to meet this man'.[40] Josephine called twice to McGuire's house where she met his mother, who told her he was not around. Shortly afterwards, McGuire's father John (Jack) called to the college and invited her to visit Seán again. Keegan and McGuire went on to play and record together regularly throughout the 1960s and 1970s.

While in London, Keegan occasionally played in a number of bands, including the Galtymore and Fulham. She gigged regularly on a Monday night in The Plough on Harrow Road with McGuire and Roger Sherlock.[41] The significance of the Plough sessions may be understood from acknowledging those in attendance; the audience included members of the Birmingham Symphony Orchestra and many jazz musicians. Frank Lee and Leo Redmond, renowned céilí band musicians, also played there. Richie and Finbarr Dwyer, Paddy Taylor and Jimmy Power were also part of a community of musical practice in London at that time. Other female musicians on that London scene included Julia Clifford and Lucy Farr,

34 Antóin MacGabhann, 'Seán McGuire', in *Honouring Seán McGuire and Kilcogy Musicians* (Dublin, 2012), pp. 13–16, at p. 14.

35 Christened Maguire, Seán later changed his name; both names appear on recordings and ephemera.

36 'Traditional Fiddler who Opposed the Purists', *Irish Times*, 2 April 2005, p. 12.

37 Geoff Harden, 'The Passing of the Fiddler', *Fortnight*, 436 (2005), 10–11.

38 Martin McGinley, 'A Presence Wherever Folk Music is Played on the Fiddle', *Treoir*, 2005.

39 Seán MacConnell, 'Death of Fiddler Sean McGuire', *Irish Times*, 25 March 2005, p. 8.

40 Josephine Keegan, 'There Will Never Be Another One!', in *Honouring Sean McGuire and Kilcogy Musicians* (Dublin, 2012), p. 7.

41 Roger Sherlock, 'My Memories of Sean McGuire', in *Honouring Sean McGuire and Kilcogy Musicians* (Dublin, 2012), p. 18.

who feature on Reg Hall's recording *Paddy in the Smoke*, recorded at the Sunday morning sessions at The Favourite in Holloway in 1967.

Back to Ireland

On return to Ireland around 1969, Keegan continued to perform in pubs with McGuire, with whom she had established a personal relationship. It was not a common occurrence for women to be present at, never mind perform in, what was then the male-dominated space of the pub. Initially, Keegan and McGuire were invited to play in a hotel in Glencolmcille, Co. Donegal for a night. They were invited back for a weekend, then a week, and then for ten nights from Christmas until New Year. There were bar extensions every night and people travelled significant distances to hear them.

In 1971, after being spotted at a session in the Readypenny Inn near Ardee, Co. Louth, Keegan and McGuire were invited to the Céilí House bar in Oldcastle, Co. Meath.[42] By this time, the pair were widely known from their recordings and radio broadcasts. They played with publican Michael Lynch on double bass every Monday night for the rest of the decade and Lynch remembers people travelling from all over the world to listen to them. Photographs in Lynch's personal collection emphasise the importance of this space in the east of the country to Irish traditional music during the 1970s, contrary to a focus on the west of Ireland in narratives about the tradition.[43] The Lynch family's own musical network, developed through regular performances in Dublin, was influential in attracting musicians to Oldcastle, but the Keegan and McGuire duo are remembered as a 'star attraction'.[44]

Escaping the violence of the Northern Ireland 'Troubles', Keegan and McGuire moved to Ballinagh and later Mountnugent, then Mullagh, all in Co. Cavan.[45] McGuire's father was from Cavan and a monument in his memory stands in the village of Kilcogy. During the mid-1970s the potential for Irish traditional music to attract tourists was recognised and groups of American tourists would listen to Keegan and McGuire in Oldcastle and other nearby venues.[46]

At this time, McGuire was undoubtedly the more recognisable personality who received most of the attention, but Keegan's role should not be underestimated. In addition to accompanying McGuire, Keegan helped create a musical identity for the pair. John Daly asserts that 'Josephine

42 Michael Lynch, interview, 21 September 2017.

43 Daithí Kearney, 'Towards a Regional Understanding of Irish Traditional Music' (Unpublished PhD dissertation, University College Cork, 2009).

44 Lynch, interview, 21 September 2017.

45 MacGabhann, 'Seán Maguire', p. 13; Lynch, interview, 21 September 2017.

46 Lynch, interview, 21 September 2017.

was an integral and defining part of the "McGuire package". She sought to create something from his technical talents and her musicality.'[47] Indeed, Lynch remembers McGuire asking Keegan to play through tunes for him to learn. McGuire could sight read and learn by ear, but Keegan's distinctive sense of phrasing was something he sought to develop in his own playing.[48] Despite the fact that Keegan taught many students throughout the years, Kevin Loughlin remembers her insisting that 'you could never teach anyone music, you could simply help them'.[49]

Recording

Keegan is a prolific recording artist in the context of Irish traditional music from the 1960s until the 1980s. Her impact in the recording world was initially as accompanist to musicians including Seán McGuire (1968, 1969, 1978), Joe Burke (1971), Roger Sherlock (1963, 1971), Séamus Tansey (1971), Kevin Loughlin (1971) and Jim McKillop (1980). In addition to these albums, further unreleased recordings were made during her time in London.[50] Prior to 1976 she tended to play piano predominantly in these recordings, but between 1977 and 1982 she recorded five solo albums on the fiddle (and providing her own piano accompaniment).[51] Some of these recordings feature newly composed pieces by Kevin Loughlin, Finbarr Dwyer, Brendan McGlinchy, Brian O'Kane, Paddy Taylor, Jimmy McHugh, Jim McKillop and several by Cavan-born composer Ed Reavy, some of which were first released on these recordings. Keegan also recorded sixteen of her own compositions.

While celebrated widely as an accompanist, Keegan's five solo albums between 1977 and 1982 are valuable in establishing her identity as a fiddle player and solo artist. According to the cover notes for *Reels, Jigs and Hornpipes*: 'On this recording she is no longer "second fiddle". She is "first fiddle" and plays her own accompaniment.'[52] Many of the composers showcased by Keegan were friends and musical collaborators. Like Keegan, who had been awarded the Gold Medal at the Oireachtas in 1955, many of those she accompanied had also won competitions. While McGuire's accomplishments have been mentioned, he was never

47 John Daly, interview, 14 September 2017.
48 Lynch, interview, 21 September 2017.
49 Kevin Loughlin, interview, 1 October 2017.
50 Paddy McGinty, interview, 1 October 2017.
51 Josephine Keegan, *Irish Traditional Music*, LP, Outlet SOLP1033 (1977); *Irish Traditional Music: Reels, Jigs, Hornpipes, Airs*, LP, Outlet, OAS 3030 (1980); *Traditional Irish Music: Reels, Jigs, Hornpipes, Airs*, LP, Outlet SOLP1040 (1980); *Irish Traditional Music: Reels, Jigs, and Hornpipes*, LP, Outlet OAS 3037 (1982); *Josephine Keegan*, LP, Outlet SOLP1044 (1983).
52 Josephine Keegan, *Reels, Jigs, Hornpipes, Airs* (Belfast: Outlet SOLP 1040 – 1980).

a champion at Fleadh Cheoil na hÉireann, the competitions organised by Comhaltas Ceoltóirí Éireann. In these competitions, Séamus Connolly won senior fiddle titles in 1961 and 1963, while Brendan McGlinchy triumphed in 1962 and Jim McKillop in 1975. Kevin Loughlin won the senior competition for the three-row button accordion in 1964, as well as miscellaneous competitions in 1967 and 1968. Joe Burke secured senior button accordion titles in 1959 and 1960; Séamus Tansey received top prize in the senior flute competition in 1965. Flute player Roger Sherlock was a member of the 1966 All-Ireland winning Glenside Céilí Band (1966) and later the Thatch Céilí Band, who were successful in 1986 and 1987; like Burke, he toured the United States with Comhaltas in the 1970s.[53] Thus, the musicians Keegan accompanied on these recordings were of the highest calibre and duly recognised during this period.

On some of the releases by Outlet Records in Belfast, McGuire served as producer; it was he who decided that Keegan should perform as the accompanist.[54] The influence of Keegan's recordings with McGuire on the Irish traditional music soundscape continued when Keegan returned to the studio to accompany Jimmy Power on his 1985 LP *Fifty-Odd Years*. Reg Hall writes in the liner notes:

> Jimmy has long admired the recordings of McGuire, so when Tom Power conceived this celebration of his father's half century in music he arranged for McGuire's accompanist, Josephine Keegan, to come over from Belfast for the recording. Josephine's unique and superb style of piano accompaniment is probably due to the complete understanding she holds for the fiddle, for she is indeed an excellent fiddle-player in her own right and pursues a busy career as a full-time music teacher in her native Northern Ireland.[55]

Keegan returned to recording her own compositions in the twenty-first century, with albums such as *Lifeswork* (2001) and *The Keegan Tunes* (2002), which feature over thirty musicians mostly drawn from the area around south Armagh.[56]

53 Reg Hall, *A Few Good Tunes: A History of Irish Music and Dance in London, 1800–1980 & Beyond* (Topic Records, 2016), p. 610.

54 Loughlin, interview, 1 October 2017.

55 Hall also notes Power's regard for the playing of Seán McGuire in *A Few Good Tunes*, p. 898.

56 Other later recordings include: Josephine Keegan, *The Nightingale and Other Lesser Spotted Tunes* (2006); *The Fairy Bridges* (2006); *A Few Tunes Now and Then* (2011); Josephine Keegan, *Around and About* (2012).

Piano

In her dissertation *The Ivory Bridge*, Aileen Dillane states: 'An instrument can imply a gender status, becoming tied up with a specific sex. Historically, the piano was associated with the female. The taking of piano lessons was traditionally seen as an effeminate pursuit for boys.'[57] Dillane continues: 'When musicians in Ireland began to absorb the piano into their sound world – no doubt in part due to the influence of the 78rpm recordings – very few male pianists were available. As a result, women filled the gap and female pianists in Ireland enjoyed prominent positions in many groups and céilí bands.'[58] Keegan is part of this musical society and, in some ways, stereotyped as a pianist despite her excellence as a fiddle player. Dolphin's recognition that a modern trend is to 'Put the woman in the front' is in stark contrast to that of Keegan's era where she was so often in the background or to the side, as the piano accompanist to much more famous male counterparts.[59]

Keegan's career was shaped by a growing commercial music recording industry in the 1970s. Dillane notes: 'When the making of commercial recordings of Irish music began in Ireland, many musicians opted to include piano accompaniment.'[60] This extends to recordings made by Irish traditional musicians in England in the latter half of the twentieth century. Keegan regularly accompanied men, something that she recognises was a common practice; for example, her London-based friends Martin and Theresa MacMahon both played accordion, but in most instances Theresa would accompany her husband on piano.[61] Johnny Pickering's wife was also a pianist; the couple played with McGuire in the Malachy Sweeney Céilí Band.

Keegan had received rudimentary instruction from her mother and schoolteachers, but the first major influence on her traditional piano style was Seán O'Driscoll. While accompanying a school friend at a dancing feis in Newry, she heard O'Driscoll play and asked to look over his shoulder. Back at boarding school she persuaded fellow students to play simple melodies while she worked out chords in the bass, attempting to imitate O'Driscoll. Later she became influenced by Shetland piano

57 Aileen Dillane, 'The Ivory Bridge: Piano Accompaniment on 78rpm Recorded Sources of Irish Traditional Dance Music in America *c.*1910–1945' (Unpublished MA dissertation, University of Limerick, 2000), p. 57.

58 Dillane, 'The Ivory Bridge', p. 169.

59 Dolphin, 'Reels, Heels', p. 12.

60 Dillane, 'The Ivory Bridge', p. 179.

61 Teresa MacMahon also recorded with Finbarr Dwyer: Finbarr Dwyer with Teresa McMahon, *Pure Traditional Irish Accordion* Music (also issued as *Irish Traditional Accordionist*), Outlet Label PTICD 1004.

players, particularly Ronnie Cooper (1934–82)[62] and Violet Tulloch,[63] the latter known as the Queen of Shetland. It was with McGuire that Keegan first encountered Shetland fiddle music and they travelled to Shetland in 1972. McCann states: 'The talented trio of McGuire, Keegan, and Burke made annual trips to Shetland for a decade. They played in Lerwick to capacity, enthusiastic and knowledgeable audiences.'[64] On these trips Keegan returned to playing fiddle, having primarily played piano in the years prior to that.[65]

Keegan's approach to piano playing was valued by many of her contemporaries. Discussing her style and approach to accompaniment on the radio series *Cherish the Ladies*, Keegan states:

> I think it's a different sort of thing to play accompaniment to different people. You know each one is different … the instrument's different, the person's different, their interpretation of the music is different. And, ah, as an accompanist that's what you have to follow, rather than look for things you have to listen to what's there and adapt the accompaniment really to that.[66]

On the album cover for *At Their Best* is written: 'As ever the accompaniment of Josephine Keegan superbly unifies the ensemble playing and heightens the solos.'[67] Reflecting in 2012, Joe Burke wrote: 'Josephine Keegan's musicianship and her very creative piano accompaniment had a very positive effect on our music.'[68] While Keegan is usually considered a 'sympathetic' and 'understated' accompanist, Siobhán Long describes her style in accompanying Séamus Tansey as vigorous.[69] (For another discussion of women as accompanists, see Watson, Chapter 11, this volume.)

62 Nicol McLaren, 'Ronnie Cooper' <https://boxandfiddlearchive.weebly.com/ronnie-cooper-1982.html> [accessed 1 March 2021].

63 Gussie Angus, 'Violet Tulloch "The Star"' <https://boxandfiddlearchive.weebly.com/violet-tulloch.html> [accessed 1 March 2021].

64 Kevin McCann, 'Scottish Fiddle Playing and Its Irish Connections', *Box and Fiddle*, 19: 03 (1995) <https://boxandfiddlearchive.weebly.com/scottish-fiddle-playing-and-its-irish-connections.html> [accessed 11 July 2022].

65 Keegan's decision to return to the fiddle was partly due to McGuire's misfortune; he broke his wrist in the lead-up to a tour on Shetland with Keegan and Burke.

66 *Cherish the Ladies*, RTÉ Radio 1, 18 July 2006.

67 *At Their Best: Sean McGuire and Roger Sherlock*, Outlet SOLP 1008 (1971).

68 Joe Burke, 'He Made Great Music … He Made History!' *Honouring Sean McGuire and Kilcogy Musicians* (Dublin, 2012), pp. 8–9.

69 Siobhán Long, 'The Best of Seamus Tansey: Traditional Irish Flute', *Irish Times*, 5 February 2010.

Collecting

Keegan began collecting Irish traditional music while in boarding school. Her methods of collecting involved communicating with other musicians throughout the country, such as Frank O'Higgins, Leo Rowsome and Paddy Canny. Nicholas McAulliffe and Anne Sheehy sent tapes, as did their fellow Kerry musician Paddy Cronin, who had emigrated to Boston. There was an abundance of tune collections in the Keegan household but Josephine recognised that her father knew many more tunes not in the collections. Keegan also compiled four collections entitled *Irish Tunes by the 100*, which were published under the names of Keegan and McGuire by Dave Bulmer in 1975. Daly interprets these publications as an effort to create a dual identity, as too often Keegan remained in McGuire's shadow.[70] The books outline four aims in presenting the tunes for publication:

1 To preserve a number of tunes that might otherwise have been lost, by committing them to paper.
2 To circulate these and the other tunes accurately because we feel that the written note is the surest way of communicating music.
3 Hopefully to expand and enrich the repertoire of the reader.
4 To satisfy the appetites of those who would like to share these tunes with us, and in doing so give pleasure to our musical friends, young and old, old and new.[71]

Sources for the music include Jack McGuire and Joe Keegan, Seán and Josephine's fathers; further recognition is given to composers, many of whom hail from Ulster or Scotland, such as James McMahon, Paul Murphy and Keegan herself.

Composition

Since 2002, Keegan has published four collections of her own compositions. She was awarded the TG4 Composer of the Year award in 2005. Despite composing since childhood, she asserts that she did not consider herself a composer until TG4 (a television channel that broadcasts predominantly in the Irish language) approached her in relation to the award. Recognition for Keegan the composer has increased through the inclusion of her work on numerous recordings more recently. These compositions are often considered difficult by instrumentalists in the tradition. Murphy posits that this is because many were initially written

70 Daly, interview, 14 September 2017.

71 Seán McGuire and Josephine Keegan, *Irish Tunes by the 100* (Lincolnshire, 1975).

at the piano and then reimagined for the fiddle.[72] An examination of the tunes reveals technical challenges relating to fingering, and leaps that require skipping over strings.

Although Keegan had included her own compositions on various recordings and published some in *Irish Tunes by the 100*, it was not until 2002 – encouraged by Tommy Fegan and Ciarán Burns, two local musicians with whom she had worked on *The Sweets of May* project – that she published her first collection of compositions. Subsequent volumes followed in 2006, 2010 and 2012. Notes on the tunes provide insight into Keegan's life, particularly on people and places meaningful to her. In conversation with me, Keegan was unable to elaborate on the motivation or inspiration for tune titles but suggests that tunes are like an autobiography or a gathering of friends. In my experience, many musicians perform Keegan's compositions without knowing their origin or knowing much about Keegan herself.

A distinctive aspect of Keegan's compositions is the influence of a 'Scottish style', often in tunes composed for Scottish friends. Born in Dundee, Keegan never returned to the city of her birth but travelled extensively elsewhere in Scotland, particularly Shetland where she was influenced by the music and approach to transmission and performance. In her second collection of compositions, Keegan states: 'I hasten to add that before deciding to include these Scottish style tunes I had them approved by a few knowledgeable musicians.'[73] Keegan remained a popular figure in Shetland, returning to perform at the Shetland Accordion and Fiddle Festival in 2005, 2007 and 2014.

Home in South Armagh

Keegan asserts her identity as an Armagh woman in the notes she provided to accompany her compositions.[74] Yet she retains a great love of Scottish music. Her record collection features LPs by several Scottish fiddle players, including Willie Hunter and Aly Bain. Influenced by the Shetland fiddlers, especially Tom Anderson, she gathered a group of fiddle players in Mullaghbawn in the early 2000s, accompanied by piano and guitar. Attempting to create a unified sound rather than the heterophony typical of an Irish session, Keegan chose less well-known tunes and wrote them out for the musicians to sight read, thereby imitating the Shetland tradition.

Martina Murphy, a member of the Keegan fiddle group, remembers it as a social and relaxed gathering each week. Keegan recounted her

72 Niall Murphy, interview, 7 June 2017.

73 Keegan, *The Keegan Tunes Cuid a Dó*, p. 13.

74 For example, in relation to 'Burren Hill', Keegan asserts: 'I'm from Armagh' (*The Keegan Tunes*, 2002), p. 18.

experiences in Shetland. The venue was a building behind O'Hanlon's Bar in Mullaghbawn, a popular session venue. Amongst the members were Martina and her son Niall; Betty and Goretti Molloy from Moy, Co. Tyrone; Paula Rafferty; Niamh Gallagher; Joanne Millar; Shauna Hughes; Marie Savages; Ursula Byrne; the Carragher sisters from Crossmaglen; the Savage sisters from Outlacken; and Donal O'Hanlon from Newry on guitar.[75] The membership highlights the presence of families and a willingness to travel to participate.

The group's repertoire included compositions by Keegan, Paddy O'Brien, Ed Reavy and Charlie Lennon, among others. The decision to include old local tunes such as 'The Three Tunes', 'The Sweets of May' and 'Betty Black' demonstrated a sense of local cultural awareness that was replicated in the book and CD *The Sweets of May*. The group learnt the repertoire using sheet music.[76] Gradually, younger members left the area for university, prompting the group to disband, but some former members continue to teach and perform.

Recognition

Keegan had performed in Canada in the late 1960s, playing with Jean Carrignon and Phillipe Bruno;[77] later, in 1972, she completed a coast-to-coast tour of the United States with Dermot O'Brien and the Clubmen, Larry Cunningham and Nita Norrie. Nevertheless, she had left the public eye by the 1980s, when she focused on teaching and, to some extent, became forgotten. Despite her long musical life, it is primarily in more recent years that Keegan has received recognition for her achievements. Writing in *Irish Music Magazine*, Seán Laffey explains:

> Due fame has somehow eluded her outside of the knowing fraternity of discerning players [...] Maybe it's because for many years she was seen as an accompanist, maybe living in Armagh, Northern Ireland she is somehow cut off from the main media movers in Dublin and Belfast, maybe because her most sustained and prolific recording output is just now emerging, but more should be written about her and her music.[78]

In 2003, Keegan received an award from Boston College in appreciation of her lifelong dedication to Irish traditional music and invaluable

75 Martina Murphy, correspondence, 23 September 2017.

76 Murphy, interview, 7 June 2017.

77 Miles Krassen identifies the influence of McGuire on the musical style of Carrignon. See Miles Krassen, 'An Analysis of a Jean Carignan Record', *Canadian Journal for Traditional Music* (1974); also noted by McGuire in Harden (2005), pp. 10–11.

78 Seán Laffey, 'Review: Josephine Keegan *The Fairy Bridges*', *Irish Music Magazine*, 13: 5 (2007), 65.

contribution to Irish cultural preservation. In addition to the TG4 Composer of the Year award, her work was further celebrated in 2005 by the Newry and Mourne District Council. In Co. Louth, Dundalk Institute of Technology's Traditional Music Ensemble granted Keegan honorary membership in 2013. She garnered local recognition once more in 2018 as recipient of the Musical Icon Award at the Iúr Cinn Fleadh. In 2006, Keegan featured in the radio series *Cherish the Ladies*, presented and produced by Aoife Nic Cormaic.[79] The other women featured were Liz Carroll, Rosie Stewart, Liz and Yvonne Kane, Josephine Marsh and Kitty Hayes – all of whom reinforce the argument for a greater understanding of the role of women in Irish traditional music.

Conclusion

Josephine Keegan was not the first Irish female musician to achieve prominence, but the multifaceted nature of her contribution to Irish traditional music sets her apart. She learnt to live in a man's world, in part through her relationship with Seán McGuire and her father's influence. Despite her skills as a fiddle player, she often took up a secondary position as piano accompanist. Keegan challenged social norms by playing professionally in pubs at a time when Irish traditional music and women were new to these spaces. She was an exceptional musician who gradually became invisible. Late in life, however, Keegan's career and reputation have grown. She has become a role model for the next generation, cited in Liz Carroll's acceptance speech for her 2006 TG4 Composer of the Year award. In examining Keegan's contribution to Irish traditional music, it becomes clear that a better understanding of the tradition requires a more thorough awareness and knowledge of the roles and lives of the women involved.

79 *Cherish the Ladies*, RTÉ Radio 1, 18 July 2006.

7

Ireland's Female Harping Triumvirate: The Legacy of Sheila Larchet Cuthbert, Mercedes Garvey and Gráinne Yeats

Teresa O'Donnell

From the middle of the twentieth century, three female harp players – Sheila Larchet Cuthbert (*b.*1923), Mercedes Garvey (1925–2013) and Gráinne Yeats (1925–2013) – were pivotal to the evolution of the harp in Ireland. As friends, teaching colleagues and lifelong members of Cairde na Cruite (Friends of the Harp), they transformed harp performance and pedagogy in Ireland for the remainder of the twentieth century. The harping landscape in Ireland at this time was dominated by female players. Larchet Cuthbert, Garvey and Yeats enjoyed distinguished harping careers at home and abroad; they did not relinquish their successful careers after marriage and/or having children, unlike many women of their generation. They shared a desire to improve standards in harp performance and teaching, and to expand the repertoire of the Irish (or lever) harp. Their commissioning and premiering of contemporary works for the Irish harp, in particular, were vital steps in the development of the instrument. Many of these works pushed the boundaries of the harp, enhancing its potential and capabilities. In this chapter, I evaluate the contribution of Larchet Cuthbert, Garvey and Yeats to the harp in Ireland and assess their influence and legacy through an examination of five main areas of activity: pedagogy, performance, commissioning, recording and publishing in the latter half of the twentieth century.

Harping Context

The main centres for harp learning in Ireland in the 1950s were Catholic convent schools, a tradition that can be traced back to the end of the nineteenth century. Recent research by Mary Louise O'Donnell into the attempts of the Gaelic League (Conradh na Gaeilge) to revive the harp in the late nineteenth century has afforded an important context to our understanding of Irish harp revivals from the 1950s onwards, in particular, the emergence of a predominantly female tradition and the crucial role played by various religious orders in the dissemination of Irish language and culture in this period.[1] This symbolic alliance of the Catholic church with the Irish harp was a critical influence on the subsequent Irish harp revival in the mid-twentieth century, which was promoted in Catholic convent schools, most notably, Dominican College, Sion Hill, Dublin. The harping infrastructure provided by these convent schools had a seminal influence on the careers of Larchet Cuthbert (who studied at Loreto Abbey, Rathfarnham) and Yeats, who was taught by Larchet Cuthbert and Garvey.

Yeats expounded a melancholic panorama of Irish harping in the 1950s, noting that 'the harp had fallen into such disuse that it seemed a somewhat exotic instrument to most people'.[2] Apart from the difficulty of sourcing the instrument, she explained that there was a paucity of published music for it as well as the challenge of finding 'an audience willing to listen' to harp music.[3] Ancillary to these obstacles was the fact that the harp was often dismissed as a cabaret instrument, used by singers for a 'genteel' accompaniment. Some commentators, including Yeats, argue that this perception of the harp and its players negatively affected the image of the harp for many years and arrested its development. It should be noted, however, that many singers who accompanied themselves on harp enjoyed considerable national and international success at this time – for example Máirín and Róisín Ní Shéaghdha, and, not least, Mary O'Hara.

Singer/harpists of this period played a pivotal role in creating awareness of the Irish harp worldwide and sowed the seeds for the imagining of a new identity for the harp. Unquestionably, some singer/harpists accompanied themselves with what was commonly referred to as the 'three-chord trick', i.e. the use of tonic, subdominant and dominant chords, which required only a basic knowledge of harp technique. Others, however, such as Mary O'Hara, who studied pedal harp with Garvey, experimented with more complex arrangements, pushed the boundaries of the instrument and explored new performance spaces for the instrument. With her critically acclaimed concerts in Carnegie Hall, London's Royal Festival and Royal Albert Halls during the 1970s and 1980s, O'Hara was one of the first Irish musicians to achieve worldwide success on the Irish

1 For further information on harping initiatives of the Gaelic League see Mary Louise O'Donnell, 'Owen Lloyd and the De-Anglicization of the Irish Harp', *Éire-Ireland*, 48: 3 and 4 (2013), 155–75.

2 Gráinne Yeats, 'The Rediscovery of Carolan', in Bernard Harris and Grattan Freyer (eds), *Integrating Tradition: The Achievement of Seán Ó Riada* (Ballina, 1981), p. 80.

3 Yeats, 'The Rediscovery of Carolan', p. 98.

harp. There were other well-trained harpists performing in Ireland at this time, many of whom are too often occluded from the debate on harping of the period and too often dismissed and demeaned as cabaret harpists. The author's teacher, the late Sr Eugene McCabe (1931–99) studied pedal harp with Mother Alphonsus O'Connor at Loreto Abbey, Rathfarnham to diploma standard, held diplomas in piano and organ, graduated with a BA from University College Dublin, and later taught herself the Irish harp. Sr Eugene taught pedal and Irish harp, piano and musicianship at Mount Sackville Secondary School, Dublin. She arranged liturgical and traditional Irish music and transcribed classical music for solo harp and harp ensemble. Like her colleagues, Larchet Cuthbert, Garvey and Yeats, Sr Eugene spent her life promoting the Irish harp as an instrument with no limitations, as a legitimate solo instrument in the literacy-based art music tradition for which there existed a rich and varied repertoire of traditional Irish, classical and contemporary music.

Performance and Pedagogy

Larchet Cuthbert, Garvey and Yeats were classically trained multi-instrumentalists and hailed from culturally active families. Sheila Larchet Cuthbert was born in Dublin in 1923. Her father John F. Larchet (1884–1967) was a distinguished composer and conductor, director of the Abbey Theatre (1908–35), professor of harmony and counterpoint at the Royal Irish Academy of Music (RIAM) (1920–55) and professor of music at University College Dublin (1921–58); her mother, Madeleine (née Moore), was a violinist and taught at the RIAM for forty years. Sheila's sister, Máire, was principal viola player with the Radio Éireann Symphony Orchestra, while her brother Gerard played the French horn. Larchet Cuthbert studied cello and piano at the RIAM. She was educated at Loreto Abbey, Rathfarnham and, at the suggestion of Mother Alphonsus O'Connor, commenced harp lessons there, continuing with O'Connor for one year after finishing school. Following this, Larchet Cuthbert studied with French harpist Tina Bonifacio in Manchester and received a BMus from University College Dublin in 1944. She was principal harpist at the Liverpool Philharmonic for two years, became the first permanent harpist with the Radio Éireann Symphony Orchestra from 1948, and spent two years with the Hallé Orchestra, at the request of conductor Sir John Barbirolli.

In the review of RTÉ Symphony Orchestra's performance of Debussy's *Prélude à l'après-midi d'un faune*, under the baton of Jean Martinon, Larchet Cuthbert's 'fine playing' was praised for the 'succession of lovely tone colours and poetical impression'.[4] As a member of the Prieur Instrumental

4 'Concert', *Irish Press*, 4 August 1947, p. 10.

Ensemble, Larchet Cuthbert played alongside her violist sister, Máire, in a performance of Debussy's Sonata for Flute, Viola and Harp at the Archbishop Byrne Hall, Dublin in 1953. Critic Joseph O'Neill praised the ensemble's 'pleasurable performance', which captured the 'excellent balance and unanimity' of the work.[5] In 1958, Larchet Cuthbert toured the United States and Canada with the Irish Festival Singers, where she met her future husband, James Cuthbert, a member of the vocal group. She collaborated with Donal O'Sullivan, author of *Carolan: The Life, Times and Music of an Irish Harper* (1958), on a series of programmes for Radio Éireann, arranging music by the harper composer Turlough Carolan (1670–1738) and other harpers.

Larchet Cuthbert's standing as one of the leading pedal harpists in Ireland at this time was acknowledged when she and Mercedes Garvey were invited to join the committee of the inaugural Israeli Harp Festival in 1959. In an interview with the *Irish Press*, Larchet Cuthbert reported that she and Garvey had been invited to join the British Honorary Committee. Larchet Cuthbert politely pointed out that she and Garvey deemed this inappropriate 'as Ireland was an independent republic', but 'would be very honoured to represent Ireland'.[6] The festival committee conveyed their apologies for the error, adding that '[t]hey had, of course intended us to represent Ireland'.[7]

Larchet Cuthbert established classes in Irish and pedal harp at the Municipal School of Music (subsequently part of the Dublin Institute of Technology, now known as TU Dublin) as well as teaching at the RIAM. Apart from an eminent performing and teaching career, Larchet Cuthbert's greatest legacy is *The Irish Harp Book: A Tutor and Companion* (1975), discussed below. In recognition of her contribution to music in Ireland, she was awarded an honorary doctorate from the Dublin Institute of Technology in November 2013. In the 1960s, Larchet Cuthbert was replaced by Nancy Calthorpe as Irish harp teacher at the College of Music (now TU Dublin). Calthorpe is probably best known for her arrangements of music and songs for Irish harp solo and Irish harp and voice, including four volumes of *The Calthorpe Collection: Music for the Irish Harp*, *Begin the Harp* (1988) and *A Celtic Bouquet for the Harp*, arranged for voice or violin and harp (1977).[8]

5 'Ensemble's Fine Recital', *Irish Independent*, 24 January 1953, p. 7. Members of the Prieur Instrumental Ensemble included Andre Prieur (flute), Zola Cerulli (violin), Máire Larchet (viola), Maurice Meulien (cello) and Sheila Larchet (harp).

6 'Harpers' Festival in Israel', *Irish Press*, 17 February 1959, p. 10.

7 'Harper's Festival in Israel'.

8 Calthorpe (1914–98) had previously taught voice and piano at Ursuline Convent, Sligo; Loreto Abbey, Rathfarnham; and Dominican College, Sion Hill, where she took harp lessons with Máirín Ní Shéaghdha.

Mercedes Garvey (née Bolger) was born in Gorey, Co. Wexford in 1925. Her mother, Mercedes Bolger McGrath, was an accomplished violinist, having studied with Madeleine Larchet at the RIAM and Dettmar Dressel in London and Dresden. In later life, her mother became interested in the Irish harp and its history, and arranged traditional Irish music for the harp. Garvey herself studied cello from the age of four years and commenced harp lessons at the RIAM aged fourteen. After receiving a double first in cello and pedal harp (under Gwendolen Mason) from the Royal College of Music, London, she played one season as cellist and second harpist with the Scottish National Orchestra. Following this, Garvey returned to Dublin to assume the position of principal harpist and soloist with the Radio Éireann Light Orchestra (RÉLO) and, later, the Radio Telefís Éireann Symphony Orchestra. As a member of the RÉLO, she played the first harp part in Balfe's opera *The Rose of Castille* at the first Wexford Opera Festival (Festival of Music and the Arts), 'and as a staunch Wexford woman that made her very happy'.[9] On 11 February 1953, Garvey and flautist André Prieur performed Mozart's Flute and Harp Concerto in C major, K. 299 with members of the RTÉ Symphony Orchestra at Cork City Hall. The performance was described as 'delightful' and a critic applauded the decision to feature on the programme a work for flute and harp.[10]

Garvey commissioned and premiered many contemporary Irish compositions for the Irish harp, including T.C. Kelly's *Fantasia for Harp and Orchestra on Two Irish Airs* (1958) and Brian Boydell's *Four Sketches for Two Irish Harps* (1961–62), which she performed with Gráinne Yeats. Garvey performed Kelly's *Fantasia* with senior students from the RIAM under the baton of Max Thöner at the Dagg Hall, RIAM in June 1960. The reviewer praised Garvey's performance, describing the work as 'the best item of the whole evening'.[11] One year later, on 12 June 1961, Garvey performed the work again at the RIAM, this time for Prince Rainier and Princess Grace of Monaco, as part of the Dublin Musical Festival. She was described as a 'dexterous and musicianly soloist'.[12] *Four Sketches for Two Irish Harps* was premiered by Garvey and Yeats at a concert on 11 March 1962 at the Eblana Theatre, Dublin. This concert marked a significant juncture in the evolution of the Irish harp in the twentieth century; it further underscored both Garvey's and Yeats's commitment to pushing the boundaries of the instrument and introducing it to a new audience. At this concert the duo also performed *Lough Swilly Suite for Two Irish Harps*

9 Taken from Aibhlín McCrann's eulogy for Mercedes Garvey delivered at St Patrick's Church, Glencullen, Co. Dublin on 23 November 2013 (private papers of Aibhlín McCrann).

10 'Enjoyable Concert', *Irish Examiner*, 14 February 1953, p. 8.

11 'Students' Enjoyable Recital', *Irish Independent*, 28 June 1960, p. 7.

12 'Intimate Occasion', *Irish Press*, 13 June 1961, p. 7.

by Ruth Mervyn and *Two Arabesques* for solo harp by T.C. Kelly. As Mary Louise O'Donnell has pointed out:

> [t]o say this evening was a defining moment in the history of the Irish harp in the twentieth century is not an exaggeration. The premiering of works by contemporary Irish composers changed the perception of the Irish harp and introduced the instrument to audiences and composers who hitherto had shown no interest in it.[13]

Cairde na Cruite also commissioned works on behalf of Garvey and Yeats, including *Introduction and Air for Two Irish harps* by Joan Trimble and *Spanish Arch* by James Wilson. The duo regularly performed countrywide as part of the Music Association of Ireland's regional and schools' concerts. Garvey toured extensively in Europe, made numerous recordings of Irish music and was professor of harp at the RIAM for many years.

In 1960 she married Michael Garvey, a director of programmes at RTÉ. After the birth of their only child, also named Mercedes, Garvey approached Yeats to replace her as harp teacher at the RIAM. Yeats was reluctant to accept the position but was eventually persuaded.[14] Due to Yeats's increasing touring commitments in the United States, she subsequently asked Elizabeth Hannon to replace her. Hannon, like Yeats, was concerned about her limited harping skills; nevertheless, she remained at the RIAM for five years. This scenario is perhaps indicative of the limited number of qualified harp teachers in Ireland at the time. Garvey and Yeats organised harping weekends and workshops, and established harp schools as far apart as Derry and Wexford. They organised a group of teachers (working on a rota basis) to travel to various parts of Ireland and devised a method of teaching employing pedal harp technique to be used in all centres. Addressing the lack of printed music available for the Irish harp, Garvey and Yeats made new arrangements of Irish traditional music and other repertoire for their students. Together, they edited four volumes of *Sounding Harps* for beginners, junior to intermediate, intermediate and senior levels. In partnership with her former student Elizabeth Hannon, Garvey co-edited a collection of her mother's arrangements entitled *My Gentle Harp* (1992) for moderate to upper-intermediate harp players, which included pieces such as *As I Roved Out*, *Tree of Liberty*, *Blind Mary*, *Cill Chais*, plus the harp duets *The Flaxen Shirt* and *Déirín Dé*.

Garvey died on 20 November 2013. Aibhlín McCrann, chair of the recently established Cruit Éireann Harp Ireland (national umbrella organisation for the harp in Ireland), described Garvey as 'a woman of many

13 Mary Louise O'Donnell, 'Heavenly Harps, Heavenly Cloths', in Barra Boydell and Barbara Dignam (eds), *Brian Boydell Centenary Essays* (Dublin, 2021), p. 124.

14 Interview with Yeats on 4 August 2011. Mairéid Sullivan, *Celtic Women in Music: A Celebration of Beauty and Sovereignty* (Ontario, 1999), pp. 65–86.

FIGURE 7.1: Mercedes Garvey. Courtesy of Mercedes Garvey.

colours: deeply spiritual, kindness personified; an accomplished cellist and harpist, then a mother, home-maker, harp teacher, editor; an iconic person in the Irish harp world in the quietest, most unobtrusive way.'[15]

The third avant-garde harp player, Gráinne Yeats, née Grace Ní hÉigeartaigh, was born in Dublin on 14 April 1925. She was the youngest child of Cork-born historian, editor and civil servant P.S. O'Hegarty and Derry native Wilhelmina (Mina) Rebecca Smyth. Her parents were politically active: her mother was a member of Cumann na mBan (Irishwomen's Council) and her father was a member of the Supreme Council of the Irish Republican Brotherhood and Sinn Féin. She was educated at Alexandra College, Milltown, Dublin, and later Trinity College Dublin, graduating with a history degree. She met her future husband, Michael Yeats, son of W.B. Yeats, at an event organised by TCD's Cumann na nGael (Gaelic Society); they married in 1949 and had four children: Caitríona, Siobhán, Pádraig and the late Síle.

Yeats studied voice and piano at the RIAM and was a multiple prize-winner in both at the Feis Ceoil. She was also a member of the Dowland Consort (1959–69), a semi-professional vocal ensemble founded by Brian Boydell, which specialised in Renaissance music. Concert programmes from the late 1950s reveal that she appeared as a solo soprano with the Clontarf Choral Society, singing oratorios by Purcell and Handel. Yeats complemented her classical music education with an impressive repertoire of Irish language songs that she learned during family holidays to the Kerry Gaeltacht. Her first introduction to the harp was at gatherings and functions organised by the Gaelic League, where the harp was predominantly used to accompany the voice. Unlike Larchet Cuthbert and Garvey, Yeats's foray into the world of harping did not occur until her late twenties, following a harp performance by Abbey Theatre actress Joan O'Hara, sister of Mary. Due to the scarcity of Irish harps at the time, sourcing a harp was challenging. After much searching, she eventually located a second-hand harp made by Henry Briggs of Glasgow. Subsequently, she commenced lessons with Larchet Cuthbert and Garvey.

Yeats toured extensively in Europe, the United States, India and Japan. Her 'beautiful soprano voice' and 'fine musicianship' were noted in her debut at the Wigmore Hall, London, on 16 March 1966.[16] In the same year, she was presented with the Harriet Cohen International Award for solo instruments. In 1969, her international reputation was affirmed when she secured an appearance on the CBS *Ed Sullivan Show* (12 March 1969). Yeats had an impressive repertoire of classical, traditional Irish and contemporary vocal and instrumental music, which she enriched with her knowledge of Irish history and the harp. Her repertoire included

15 Aibhlín McCrann, 'Mercedes Garvey – A Tribute', *An Cruitire*, 12 (2013), 4–5.
16 'Wigmore Hall Recital by Gráinne Yeats', *Irish Times*, 18 March 1966, p. 8.

songs and arias by Bartlet, Galilei, Dunstable, Mudarra, Fuenllana and Respighi, transcriptions of English and French lute music, Irish songs, arrangements of music by Carolan and other harpers, music from Wales and Brittany, and contemporary music by Irish composers. Through her membership of the Dowland Consort, Yeats had access to composers such as Boydell and Joseph Groocock, both of whom composed and arranged for her. Groocock wrote *Three Pieces for Voice and Harp* (1962) and *Six Pieces for Irish Harp* (1962) for her, while Boydell set a number of works to texts by Yeats's father-in-law: for example, *Three Yeats Songs* (1965), the RTÉ commission *Musician's Song* (1965), and *Love is an Immoderate Thing* (1965). Yeats performed many of these works at the annual Yeats Summer School, Sligo. Writing in 1968, the reviewer Charlotte Brooks observed that Yeats rarely repeated her programme, and celebrated Yeats's inclusion of Irish songs and instrumentals in the second half of her concerts.[17] In 1987, Yeats became the first harpist from Ireland to perform at the World Harp Congress in Vienna and was invited to perform at the 1993 Congress in Copenhagen.

Yeats's pioneering endeavour to revive the wire-strung harp remains her outstanding legacy. She researched the techniques, playing styles and repertoire of the old harpers and arranged pieces from Edward Bunting's collection *The Ancient Music of Ireland* (1796, 1809 and 1840) and other manuscripts. Procuring a wire-strung harp proved even more difficult than an Irish harp. As she noted, 'good modern harps were difficult enough to find, but a traditional harp was unheard of'.[18] During a concert tour to the United States, Yeats met Jay Witcher, an American harp-maker, and commissioned a replica of the Sirr harp from him.[19] In attempting to reproduce the technique of the old harpers, who played with their fingernails, she experimented with growing her nails long, applying false nails and testing various plectrums. She extensively researched the history of the harp in Ireland, especially the life and music of Turlough Carolan and Derry harper Denis Hempson (1695–1807); she published her findings in 'Some Thoughts on Irish Music' (1973) and *The Harp of Ireland: The Belfast Harpers' Festival, 1792 and the Saving of Ireland's Harp Music by Edward Bunting* (1980 and 1992), the companion book to her groundbreaking album *Féile na gCruitirí Béal Feirste: The Belfast Harpers' Festival, 1792*.[20] Interestingly, despite her mastery of the instrument, Yeats described the

17 'Grainne Yeats in Sligo', *Irish Times*, 24 August 1968, p. 12.

18 Yeats, 'The Rediscovery of Carolan', p. 84.

19 The Sirr harp dates from the late seventeenth or early eighteenth century and is preserved in the National Museum of Ireland.

20 Gráinne Yeats, 'Some Thoughts on Irish Music', *Ceol*, 4: 2 (1973), 37–50. For further information on Yeats's research, see Teresa O'Donnell, 'Gráinne Yeats: A Modern-Day Bard Remembered', *The American Harp Journal* (2014), 15–21.

wire-strung harp as 'too troublesome, too inflexible, and too difficult to make its way into the modern world'.[21]

Yeats recorded three albums. The first, *Irish Folk Songs*, released by the New York label Spoken Arts in 1962, included Irish and English songs such as 'Down by the Sally Gardens' and 'An Raibh Tú ar an gCarraig?' Her second album, *A Rogha Féin*, was released in 1983 by Gael Linn, Dublin and featured the music of Carolan, music from the Bunting Collection, and Irish and Welsh songs. Unquestionably, Yeats's most significant recording was *Féile na gCruitirí Béal Feirste: The Belfast Harpers' Festival, 1792* (1980 and reissued in 1992.) She performed on four different harps strung with wire or gut strings for the 1980 recording; a gut-strung harp made by Daniel Quinn (1967), an Aoyama (1972), a Maldwyn Thomas reproduction of the Trinity College harp, and Witcher's wire-strung Sirr harp (1975).[22] The 1992 edition featured forty-two tracks on two CDs.

Cultural Activism

As mentioned above, Larchet Cuthbert, Garvey and Yeats were lifelong members of Cairde na Cruite. The organisation's history has been told in numerous sources, notably Helen Lawlor's monograph.[23] To revisit this briefly: the genesis to establish an organisation to promote the Irish harp initially came from three non-harp players: Cearbhaill Ó Dálaigh (former President of Ireland), Irish scholar Fionnán MacColuim and singer Colm Ó Lochlainn. These cultural activists espoused the revival of the harp through the medium of the Irish language. Cairde na Cruite sought to restore the Irish harp to its former place of honour through the following four aims: to hold public performances and concerts of harp music and to organise a harp festival; to foster the learning of the Irish harp; to publish available harp music; and to provide and publish a harp tutor and to encourage the composition of music and arrangements of tunes for the harp. This last aim was suggested by committee member and Irish language activist Eibhlín Ní Chathailriabhaigh, due to the paucity of published material for the Irish harp. She worked tirelessly to fundraise for the publication. Larchet Cuthbert was appointed to compile and edit the book, which was eventually published by Mercier Press in 1975. *The Irish Harp Book: A Tutor and Companion* heralded 'a new and exciting era' for the harp. It realised:

21 Yeats, 'The Rediscovery of Carolan', p. 80.
22 The 1980 release featured twenty-eight tracks, while the 1992 reissue featured forty-two tracks in total on two CDs.
23 Helen Lawlor, *Irish Harping: 1900–2010* (Dublin, 2012).

> a long held desire to provide not only a comprehensive course of study for a student of the Irish harp but also an introduction to much lovely music, mainly unknown, and spanning some four hundred years to the present time. A deeper appreciation of our own culture and tradition must inevitably follow.[24]

The text is divided into twelve lessons, each containing detailed instruction on fingering, technique, scales, studies, pieces based on skills explored in the lessons, and a song or songs with harp accompaniment. It also addressed harp maintenance, tuning, replacement of strings and blades, correct posture and position at the harp, provided diagrams of the harp and other relevant information. *The Irish Harp Book* features 27 *Studies* and *Tutor for the Irish Harp* by Mother Attracta Coffey (Mother Alphonsus O'Connor's harp teacher), solo and ensemble pieces, songs, arrangements of Irish airs, songs and music from the Bunting and Petrie collections, and an unprecedented number of contemporary compositions. Larchet Cuthbert contacted several composers inviting them to create 'a new literature for our national instrument' by composing in one of the following five styles: original piece for solo Irish harp; arrangement of an Irish melody for solo Irish harp; original song with harp accompaniment; arrangement of an Irish song (in English or Irish) with harp accompaniment; or an original composition for two or more harps, and/or other instrument(s).[25] Composers were furnished with a chart of possible key changes suitable for an Irish harp tuned in E flat major and samples of fingering exercises. Remarkably, this was the only communication Larchet Cuthbert had with the composers until their works were completed.[26] Table 7.1 lists contemporary works in *The Irish Harp Book*, several of which were commissioned and premiered by Yeats and Garvey.

TABLE 7.1. Contemporary works in *The Irish Harp Book*.

Composer	Work	Genre
T.C. Kelly	*Interlude*	harp solo
John Kinsella	*Allegro Giocoso*	harp solo
Gerard Victory	*Three Pieces for Irish Harp*	harp solo
A.J. Potter	*Étude Bitonal*	harp solo
Aloys Fleischmann	*An Cóitín Dearg*	harp solo

24 Sheila Larchet Cuthbert, *The Irish Harp Book: A Tutor and Companion* (Cork and Dublin, 1975), p. 5.

25 Copy of letter sent by Eibhlín Ní Chathailriabhaigh on behalf of Sheila Larchet Cuthbert to composers, 6 July 1966, Cairde na Cruite Archive.

26 Interview with Sheila Larchet Cuthbert by the author on 22 May 1999.

TABLE 7.1. *continued.*

Composer	Work	Genre
Daniel McNulty	*Fantasia* *Berceuse* *Rondo*	harp solo
James Wilson	*Spanish Arch*	harp duet
Brian Boydell	*Two Sketches:* (i) *Dance for an Ancient Ritual* and (ii) No. 2 of *Four Pieces for Two Irish Harps*[27]	harp duet
Seóirse Bodley	*Scintillae*	harp duet
Joan Trimble	*Duet*[28]	harp duet
Anne Crowley	*Suite of Four Pieces for Harp Trio*	harp trio
Edgar Deale	*For the Children:* (i) *Songs without words* (ii) *Set Dance*	harp and voice/ instrument

Arrangements of Irish music by renowned harpers, harpists, composers and organists also featured in the tutor; these included Charlotte Milligan Fox, Herbert Hamilton Harty, Charles Villiers Stanford, Treasa Ní Chormaic, Máirín Ní Shéaghdha, Mercedes Bolger McGrath, Mercedes Garvey, Gráinne Yeats, Éamon Ó Gallchobhair, Cian Ó hÉigeartaigh, J. Redmond Friel, Havelock Nelson, John F. Larchet and Gerard Meyer.

Larchet Cuthbert invited composer Seán Ó Riada to arrange the Irish air 'Sliabh na mBan' for *The Irish Harp Book*, however she was unable to secure a score from him. Notwithstanding the fact that Ó Riada did not compose for the Irish harp, Yeats noted that 'he stimulated an interest in it among a large number of people who had never heard it before' and brought the music of the harpers to a wider audience.[29] Larchet Cuthbert was not the first harp player to request a harp composition from Ó Riada. Yeats had previously approached him to compose for the instrument in the 1960s, prior to her interest in the wire-strung harp. He agreed to write a piece, but only for the wire-strung harp as he disapproved of the gut-strung harp favoured by harp players at the time.[30]

27 These later became movements iii and ii, respectively, of *Four Sketches for Two Irish Harps*.

28 Also known as *Introduction and Air for Two Harps*.

29 Yeats, 'The Rediscovery of Carolan', p. 91.

30 Ó Riada used the harpsichord to re-create the sound of the wire-strung harp in his folk orchestra Ceoltóirí Chualann (1961–69).

The Irish Harp Book was well received in musical and cultural circles when first published. The critic Charles Acton opined that it would 'provide a real incentive for young players to find out more' about playing the harp rather 'than just a ladylike accompaniment for arrangements of traditional tunes'.[31] He praised the quality of the typesetting and complimented Larchet Cuthbert for her 'self-effacing' inclusion of music by harping colleagues, contemporary composers and use of research by American harpist and historian Roslyn Rensch.[32] Nevertheless, Acton suggested amendments for the next edition of the book, which he believed would sell out quickly. He queried Larchet Cuthbert's use of the term 'tutor' to describe a book that was not a 'teach yourself' book, asserting that the proposed method for tuning the harp was only achievable by experienced musicians and not beginners to whom the book was directed. He further questioned the lack of biographical information regarding the composer Viner, whose studies grace the book, and noted inconsistencies in the recommended hand position, namely, the use of the tips of the fingers rather than the side of the fingers as illustrated in the example Zabel's *Method*. Despite this criticism he applauded the clarity of Larchet Cuthbert's 'expositions and the firmness of her technical advice and instruction'.[33]

Harping Legacy

The commissioning, premiering and publishing of contemporary works for the Irish harp by Larchet Cuthbert, Garvey and Yeats transformed the instrument and its repertory and provided the Irish harp with a contemporary identity. As renowned exponents of their instrument(s), boasting national and international musical careers as soloists and orchestral musicians, they were well placed to stimulate harping activity and composition in Ireland. Most importantly, this triumvirate shared a desire to acknowledge and celebrate the rich tradition of the harp in Ireland while also updating the repertoire and image of the harp, and consolidating the Irish harp as a modern and multifarious instrument. They fostered an awareness of the harp by bringing it to a wider audience, improved standards of teaching, created a demand for harps, and encouraged composers to write for the harp. Each of these elements was essential in forging a new identity for the harp and developing a new infrastructure for the instrument. Further, their cultural activism – involvement in Cairde na Cruite and its annual summer school, An Cúirt Chruitireachta (established in 1985), harp competitions at Dublin's Feis Ceoil and other harping competitions and festivals around Ireland – continued the

31 'The Irish Harp for Players', *Irish Times*, 3 December 1975, p. 8.
32 'The Irish Harp for Players'.
33 'The Irish Harp for Players'.

legacy of a larger movement dating back to the late eighteenth century, whose proponents attempted to stimulate interest in the harp as a living tradition. The fruits of these women's cultural and musical endeavours are evident in the harp's current variegated existence. The harping tradition has undergone numerous iterations of itself over the years – constantly redefining itself; responding to historic, social and musical imperatives; engaging with classical, Irish traditional, world and early musics. Larchet Cuthbert, Garvey and Yeats contributed to this transformation and their legacy is evidenced in the thriving harping tradition of the twenty-first century. In Yeats's own words:

> Nowadays, things have changed. There are numerous good professional and amateur players, whose performances are popular at home and abroad. There is a goodly number of promising young students, a reasonable supply of printed music for them to play, and there are plenty of good harps to be obtained, both in Ireland and in foreign countries. As a result of all this the standard is getting better all the time.[34]

34 Interview with Gráinne Yeats by the author on 4 August 2011.

Part III

Gaps and Gender Politics in the History of Twentieth-Century Women Composers and Performers

8

'A Daughter of Music': Alicia Adélaïde Needham's Anglo-Irish Life and Music[1]

Axel Klein

The subject of this chapter is an Irish female composer who died in 1945 without leaving any major impact on Irish musical history or its corresponding historiography. Given these circumstances, the question as to why she would be of interest to readers in the twenty-first century is not unjustified. The facts are that Alicia Adélaïde Needham used to be a household name in musical circles on both sides of the Irish Sea from about the 1890s to 1920. In terms of how frequently her works were performed, she may have equalled or perhaps surpassed male colleagues such as Charles Villiers Stanford or Hamilton Harty – who remained incomparably more famous than her, not least because they wrote more large-scale music, whereas Needham preferred the small forms of songs and piano music. In contrast to her reputation one hundred years ago, knowledge today about this composer and her work is very limited. This alone justifies her rescue from oblivion.[2]

Needham was born on 31 October 1863 in Oldcastle, County Meath;[3] her maiden name was Montgomery.[4] She attended Victoria High School,

1 The article is based on a presentation of the same title held at the joint annual conference of the Society for Musicology in Ireland and the Royal Musical Association at University College Dublin, 9 July 2009.

2 My narrative focuses on Needham's typescript autobiography cited and explained below. The main contemporary sources about Needham are three articles by Annie Patterson: 'Alicia Adelaide Needham', *The Weekly Irish Times*, 9 June 1900, p. 4; (as 'A.W.P.') 'Coronation Music: A Triumph for Ireland', *The Irish Times*, 21 June 1907, p. 7; and (as 'Eithne Ní Peadair') 'Alicia Adelaide Needham', *The Leader*, xxiii (1916), 14, pp. 227–8.

3 Gregory Blue confirms Needham's date of birth was 1863 (not 1872 as erroneously stated elsewhere). See Gregory Blue, 'Needham, (Noël) Joseph Terence Montgomery (1900–1995)', in *Oxford Dictionary of National Biography* <https://www.oxforddnb.com/> [accessed 4 March 2021].

4 She called herself 'Ada Montgomery' in her early diaries; see Cambridge

a boarding school in Derry, for four years, the exact period of which is unknown. Following this, she spent a year in Castletown on the Isle of Man. She studied at the Royal Academy of Music (RAM) in London, at first for one year only, most likely the academic year 1880–81: her teachers included Frank Davenport (harmony and counterpoint) and the Irish pianist and composer Arthur O'Leary (piano); occasionally, she received lessons from George Macfarren and Ebenezer Prout. It is not known what she did in the intervening three years before she resumed her studies at the RAM in 1884; in any case, she graduated in 1887 and became a Licentiate of the Royal Academy of Music (LRAM) in 1889. In 1893 she further passed the examinations to the Associateship of the Royal College of Music (ARCM). In the meantime, she married the London-based physician Joseph Needham in 1892 and gave birth to their only child, also called Joseph, in 1900.[5]

Actively supported by her husband who organised concerts for her and secured her earliest publications, Needham began her professional musical career in 1894 with a number of publications and recitals of piano music and songs. She allegedly wrote some seven hundred compositions, most of which were songs, but there are also vocal duos, trios and quartets with piano accompaniment, piano music (including the *Four Pianoforte Sketches*, Op. 30), orchestrations of songs, choral hymns, marches for brass bands, and one church service.[6] More than two hundred published works can be found in the British Library, some of which are song cycles and similar collections, each featuring up to twelve pieces. She seems to have stopped composing before 1920, however, and little was heard of her henceforth. She died, largely unnoticed by the public, on 24 December 1945.

Thanks to her son's later fame as a highly distinguished biochemist and sinologist, his private papers, which extended to his mother's papers, were archived, initially at the University of Bath, and now at Cambridge University.[7] Thus, it is in connection with her identity as the mother of a famous scientist that researchers may access detailed information on this composer today. The portion of the 'Joseph Needham Papers'

University Library, Joseph Needham Papers, item A.99.

5 Details sourced in the Needham autobiography manuscript discussed below.

6 The number of compositions is given in *Irish Times*, 26 June 1933, p. 6. Michele Esposito used two of her songs in the production of his 'romantic comedy' *Peggy Machree* at the Broadway Theatre, New York, between 21 December 1908 and 23 January 1909. The performance included *Maureen* in Act 1 and *The Exile's Return* in Act 2; see Internet Broadway Database <https://www.ibdb.com/broadway-show/peggy-machree-7014> [accessed 11 July 2022].

7 http://www.lib.cam.ac.uk/collections/departments/manuscripts-university-archives/significant-archival-collections/needham; accessed 11 July 2022. Section A ('Biographical') is the largest section in this collection and within this section the material relating to Alicia Needham is by far the largest.

relating to Alicia Needham encompasses published music; private and professional correspondence for the period 1877 to 1921; extensive diaries spanning the years 1879 to 1924; photographs, notebooks and similar items. These sources are vital to retracing and reconstructing the composer's biography. This chapter, although guided to an extent by information published in newspapers during the composer's lifetime, is mainly based on her typescript autobiography, entitled 'A Daughter of Music', archived in Cambridge among the Joseph Needham Papers as 'Ms Needham: A.97'.

This autobiography is a strange document. Obviously intended for publication, it was completed at a time when the composer's star had fallen very low. It ends by describing events of 1926, and although Needham mentions her intention to write a second volume, this does not seem to have been realised. The typescript itself, however, appears to date from 1935 or later, as can be deducted from a sentence on page 68 where she says that after her husband's death (in 1920) she moved into a flat where she stayed for fifteen years. As I shall try to explain here, it seems rather unlikely that either in 1926 or by 1935 she would have found a large readership for her autobiography. Although the typescript is constructed as a roughly chronological account, there are few actual dates in it, which leaves the reader to guess how old the author may have been at any specific point in her narrative. She does not even specify when or where she was born, when she studied, and so on – she omits all the factual details that would form the basis of any appreciation today, be it academic or biographical. One is tempted to suspect that she did not intend her autobiography to be a subject of future academic research at all. Instead, she must have been convinced that her readers would indeed be more interested in the personal anecdotes, travel accounts and tales of encounters with blue-blood celebrities that comprise much of this volume.

Formally, the autobiography is a typescript of 122 pages, divided into fifteen chapters that are very uneven in length and style (see Table 8.1). Apart from a relatively substantial chapter six, the page length averages about five or six; the text is mainly devoted to her childhood and upbringing, education, artistic successes and her family life. But towards the end it turns into a travelogue about her repeated journeys to Germany, Austria and Italy, and the chapters grow considerably longer. These are private travels, not concert-giving tours, so for a reader interested in her work as a musician, at least half of the typescript is not directly relevant to this theme.

Table 8.1: Formal overview of the chapters in Needham's autobiography manuscript, 'A Daughter of Music'.

Ch.	Page nos	Length (pages)	Contents
1	1–5	5	Birth, early childhood, family history
2	6–13	8	Family move to Co. Down, school, discovery of her musical talent, toys and games, processions at St Patrick's Day and the 12 July marches
3	14–20	7	School, visits to Belfast, boarding school in Derry, recreations, to Gloucester via Liverpool, ambitions as pianist, year on Isle of Man, well-known families among acquaintances
4	21–5	5	First year at RAM, teachers, holidays, musical acquaintances, marriage, honeymoon in Scotland
5	26–32	7	London home and neighbourhood, her music room, prolific composing, return to RAM, Feis Ceoil successes, language studies at Oxford, women's achievements, suffragette movement
6	33–43	11	Son's birth (1900) and godfathers/ godmothers, recital at Cork Exhibition (1902), Coronation Prize Song for Edward VII with concert, songs, Army and Navy Song Cycle, approaching war
7	44–8	5	Son's childhood; Pan-Celtic Meetings in Edinburgh, Wales and Belfast; president at Eisteddfod, banquet for famous women of Ireland, serious illness
8	49–53	5	Holiday in Italy (1910): Venice; meeting Lord Kitchener; Rome and Vatican (audience with Pope Pius X); Genoa, Pisa, Paris
9	54–6	3	Stinie Morrison murder case
10	57–60	4	Her pets
11	61–6	6	Son to boarding school; outbreak of First World War: husband in medical service, herself in Red Cross (1915); playing piano to wounded soldiers

Ch.	Page nos	Length (pages)	Contents
12	67–9	3	Son to Cambridge University (1918), husband dies (1920), break-up of home and looking for flat, holiday in Scotland including Iona
13	70–83	14	Europe (1922): Oberammergau Passion Play, Munich, Freiburg, Nuremberg, Vienna, Salzburg, Freiburg, Bonn, Cologne
14	84–103	20	Europe (1925): Brussels, Cologne, Hanover, Berlin, Potsdam, Dresden, Leipzig, Prague, Munich, Oberammergau, Graz, Vienna, Munich, Heidelberg
15	104–22	19	Italy (1925–6): through Switzerland to Milan (December 1925), Rome (January 1926), Bordighera (funeral of Queen Alexandra), Rome and Vatican (Pope Benedict), Naples, Perugia, Siena, Assisi, Bordighera, Ventimiglia; rise of Fascism; French Riviera; Monte Carlo

There is also a curious break in her chronological narrative between chapters six and eleven, in between which she jumps back ten years before she returns to her description of events during the First World War (during which Needham volunteered with the Red Cross; see Figure 8.1). This unevenness, in combination with a dwindling potential readership of people who would remember her by the mid-1930s, may have contributed to her manuscript not finding a publisher, if indeed she had tried so at all.

Her autobiography also excludes any personal sentiments that would not be expected from a woman of her (former) social standing. For instance, the overview of the 'Joseph Needham Papers' at Cambridge mentions that her extensive diaries reveal a very unhappy marriage, but there is no word about it in the autobiography, probably because personal details of this kind would not have been socially acceptable. Obviously, at the beginning of the relationship she appreciated her husband's support of her musical career, but later he does not seem to have played any major role in her life, except, it may be assumed, when it came to maintaining her standard of living. One may glean something about his relative importance to her in the description of the circumstances of his death in chapter twelve where she simply writes: 'he died in the drawing-room in the midst of the beautiful china and pictures he loved and had collected'.[8]

8 Alicia Adélaïde Needham, 'A Daughter of Music' (unpublished typescript autobiography), p. 67.

FIGURE 8.1: Alice Adélaïde Needham in Red Cross uniform as a volunteer in 1915. Reproduced by kind permission of the Syndics of Cambridge University Library.

Some biographical details of Alicia Needham appear in the autobiography in a romantic and fanciful language, often speaking in allusions and images that are difficult to understand for an outsider. For example, about her birth she writes: 'It happened on a Hallowe'en! On an October morning in the dim past ages a little wisp of a witch arrived in the middle of Ireland near the Royal and Ancient Hill of Tara!'[9] One would have to

9 Needham, 'A Daughter of Music', p. 1.

be from an English-speaking country or otherwise knowledgeable to know that Hallowe'en is 31 October, but she does not mention the year. Nor does she identify the exact place of her birth – the closest localities suggested by the reference to the Hill of Tara were either Tara village or Navan town in Co. Meath. That she was, in fact, born elsewhere in the county (in Oldcastle) is confirmed in a piece by Annie Patterson in the *Weekly Irish Times* of June 1900. Even the annual volumes of the British 'Who's Who?' in which she appeared omit a date of birth and simply indicate the place as 'County Meath'.

About her family she writes: 'My father was of the Montgomerys of Ayrshire (Earl of Eglinton's family) who settled in the County Down in the time of James I.'[10] No explanation is given for the fact that she was born in Oldcastle and not Downpatrick (presumably the old family home), where the family moved in her early childhood. She does not even mention the town name of Downpatrick, instead describing a place in 'in the very shadow of the Mourne Mountains',[11] a town with a 'little old Cathedral, where Cromwell stabled his horses, and in the churchyard is the real authentic grave of St Patrick'.[12] Describing the maternal side of her family, she states that they were 'of French Huguenot descent', had settled in Co. Cavan, and that her mother had been, in her girlhood, a friend of Patrick Burns, one of the last itinerant Irish harpers.[13]

Referring to her early musicianship she reminisces:

> I was a little musician from the age of five, and never tired of music or found any difficulty with it [...] it is no trouble for me to practice through every conceivable kind of scale [...] in every key or through a whole concert programme, and read the newspapers at the same time![14]

With similar ease she seems to have composed her songs, as we shall see below.

Her writings suggest that the social tensions between Protestants and Catholics in the northern counties of Ireland were quite acute, even in those pre-partition years (the late 1860s); as a child, though, she did not feel deeply affected by these. She describes the processions of both congregations on specific days of the year, such as St Patrick's Day (17 March) and 12 July:

> On the 12th July we children would gather all the orange lilies and shove them through this [garden] gate on grateful perspiring participants in the procession. We were not at all bigoted either, and we also

10 Needham, 'A Daughter of Music', p. 3.
11 Needham, 'A Daughter of Music', p. 6.
12 Needham, 'A Daughter of Music', p. 7.
13 Needham, 'A Daughter of Music', p. 4.
14 Needham, 'A Daughter of Music', pp. 8–9.

> would search in the fields to do the same with shamrock for the St Patrick's Day people.

But her childhood chapter is the only part of the autobiography with repeated references to political tensions in Ireland. Later, there is no word whatsoever about the Easter Rising of 1916, nor does the founding of the Irish Free State in December 1922 merit even a footnote.

Her childhood must have been a very happy time for her, which might explain why she wrote so many children's songs; her collections of lullabies became her biggest commercial successes. Recalling these early songs, she says:

> How I used to love writing all these songs, pretending to myself they were children of my heart and sending them reluctantly out into the world, but after so many hundreds I became like the old woman who lived in a shoe, and wrote so many I didn't know what to do.[15]

After her marriage in 1892, and with the encouragement of her first publications from 1896 onwards, she continued writing music in a seemingly unending stream:

> For ten years, I might say twenty years and more, songs, piano soli, quartettes, trios, song cycles, hymns, all flowed from my happy pen. They were so prolific, these years, that I sometimes, if tired, feared to look at a poetry book lest a poem might strike me and set itself instantaneously to music in my head, and I should be inclined to run away and set it down.[16]

Her earliest success was called 'An Irish Lullaby', about which she writes: 'Certainly every teacher taught it, but this took time and a few years. After they were published such extraordinary nice press-notices of my songs appeared that I began to pluck up courage and give vent to my free thoughts in "letting myself go", so to speak.'[17] Another lullaby called 'Husheen' became perhaps her best-known song, made famous by celebrity singers of the time such as Clara Butt, who recorded it in 1930. In published form it became no. 9 in a collection of twelve songs entitled *An Album of Hush Songs* in 1897.

From restrained modesty to (perhaps unintended) arrogance it is a short distance sometimes, and we can sense something of the latter in her description of her successes in the composition contests at the Feis Ceoil: 'For about six years in succession I amused myself sending in songs, quartettes [*sic*] and arrangements of Irish airs to the Irish Musical Festival,

15 Needham, 'A Daughter of Music', p. 13.
16 Needham, 'A Daughter of Music', p. 28.
17 Needham, 'A Daughter of Music', p. 29.

the Feis Ceoil in Dublin, carrying off so many prizes that I thought at last it was time to stop and give way to others.'[18]

There is also a strange mixture of pride and condescension in her identification as an Irishwoman. The condescension shines through in the preceding quotation, but also in describing achievements of her family, where she ends a passage by saying: 'I often think how many extraordinary men are lost among the limitations of little narrow-minded corners in this little ocean-girt isle.'[19] On the other hand, she uses phrases like 'we Celts' and 'my Irish blood' in characterising positive personal attributes, which make clear that she used her Irishness as a way to distinguish herself from others in the English part of the British Isles. Yet, although she never says it explicitly, she was quite aware and proud of coming from a well-to-do family of the Protestant faith with an Ascendancy family background, who boasted seemingly strong ties with high society and steadfast loyalty to the British crown.

One wonders, in fact, how truthful the narrator is when she writes of 'best friends' who included bishops and members of the aristocracy. She even claims that she 'came of the same good old stock' as US president Woodrow Wilson. Her son's godfathers included Sir Dyke Bayliss, Lord Castletown of Upper Ossory and Reverend Canon Carver of Dulwich College; his godmothers were Annie Patterson (the Irish composer and author) and Emma Hardy (wife of the writer Thomas Hardy).

Curiously enough, considering that Needham lacked any family or musical relations to Wales, in 1906 she was made the first woman president of the National Eisteddfod of Wales, along with fellow presidents of distinguished ranks, such as such as the Lord Mayor of London and the Bishop of Bangor. A few years later she was also made a 'Bardess of Wales' under the title 'Harp of Ireland'. She was the first woman to conduct at the Royal Albert Hall. In 1910 she was a VIP at a banquet given in Dublin by Lord Aberdeen, the then Lord Lieutenant of Ireland, to honour 'Irish Women of Letters'.

Without doubt, her married life in London provided her with a secure and prosperous home, a large circle of influential friends, numerous social occasions, the resources to make frequent visits to Ireland – and, not least of all, the freedom to sit down at her piano and 'let music flow out of her pen'. Needham's single biggest competitive success occurred when she won the contest for the Prize Song for the coronation of King Edward VII in 1902. Apparently, more than three hundred composers submitted entries,[20] with Needham walking away with the £100 award for a song that she claims to have dashed off at the last minute while she happened to be staying at Dublin's Shelbourne Hotel. Other famous songs by her

18 Needham, 'A Daughter of Music', p. 30.

19 Needham, 'A Daughter of Music', p. 3.

20 *Every Woman's Encyclopaedia* (London, n.d. [1910]).

include an arrangement of the traditional folk tune 'The Dark Rosaleen' to words by James Clarence Mangan, which, she rather fancifully claims, became something of an Irish national anthem. She further composed original songs in an Irish folk style, such as 'The Donovans' and 'The Exile's Return', most of which were written and published before 1900. She was also known for her song cycle *A Bunch of Shamrocks* (1904), which she performed at a Mangan memorial concert in Dublin in May 1905. Her *Four Songs for Women Suffragists* (1908) reflected her commitment to the early women's emancipation cause,[21] while her *Army and Navy Song Cycle* (1912) was intended for and used extensively in recruiting soldiers for the British Army.

The death of her husband in 1920 caused serious disruption to Needham's life. In those days, without any government pension schemes for widows, she was forced to sell the house and furniture, paintings, books and china, and had to move into a considerably smaller flat in a less fashionable district of the city. She writes: 'my music-room shelves left empty, and four tons of books sent away to storage, all the best things and treasures sold, I only keeping enough for a little flat!'[22] The sales of the house and family possessions may have kept her afloat financially for a few years – but a different kind of decline is clearly visible. She does not seem to have composed anything after 1920; her collection of correspondence ends in 1921; her diaries conclude in 1924; and her autobiography comes to a halt in 1926. She literally withdrew step by step from the public. When she made it into the headlines during this period, it was with rather curious non-musical events such as when, in 1922, she sued the operator of a Turkish baths facility for £30 damages following an injury sustained from slipping on wet stairs.[23]

The 'Joseph Needham Papers' in Cambridge reveal that Needham turned to astrology and occultism; she began believing in the rebirthing of the dead and devoted time to so-called 'spirit photography'.[24] She started interpreting the course of her life in astrological terms, making observations

21 The four songs were titled *Marching On, Daughters of England, Fight On* and *Clipped Wings*; see Elizabeth Crawford, *The Women's Suffrage Movement: A Reference Guide 1866–1928* (London, 1999).

22 Needham, 'A Daughter of Music', pp. 67–8.

23 She claimed negligence as an attendant should have guided her down three marble steps. The judge responded in the trial 'I have been in Turkish baths, but I have never been assisted from the hot to the cooling room by an attendant.'; *The Irish Times*, 25 October 1922, p. 6.

24 Item A.765 of the Joseph Needham Papers is an undated album of 'spirit photographs' – portraits of people purporting to show psychic auras, lights and spirits – that includes her autograph comment: 'The photographer is an amateur. Knows not as yet how to develop or print and only began when she was told by Mediums that she was a Spirit Photographer about two years ago. Nobody is more astounded than herself!'

such as 'with the moon in the 9th house, how could I be other than an insatiable wanderer all my life' or 'Uranus is going to be the death of me'.[25] Notices in *The Irish Times*,[26] and the *British Medical Journal*,[27] of 1933 reveal that by this time she had fallen into serious financial difficulty and suffered health problems. John Smyth Crone, former president of the Irish Literary Society in London, organised a 'testimonial' to her benefit. One of the last public notices about her is a short article revealing that she converted to the Catholic faith in December 1934.[28] The autobiography – which, as shown above, probably dates from around 1935 – may have been another attempt at raising money. In the light of her decline, one wonders about the nature of the relationship with her son. By this time, he was already a distinguished academic at Cambridge.

But whether by 1926 or 1935, Ireland and the United Kingdom had evolved into entities considerably different to how they had been constituted during Needham's time as an active, successful composer, a time that predates the First World War. This is potentially another explanation for her break with composition around 1920. A reason for the silence in her autobiography about anything relating to the Anglo-Irish conflict and Irish independence could have been that she did not realise or accept the extent of the political change that had occurred.[29] In the light of these changes, conditions for publication of her autobiography could not have been worse, quite apart from the formal and stylistic deficiencies of her text outlined above. For an Irish readership, it would have been difficult to understand how, in spite of her identification and pride in being Irish, she failed to mention either the War of Independence or the Home Rule movement that preceded it. Quite obviously, she purposefully excluded any political discussion from her memoir.

In fact, her rather anecdotal typescript is so dependent on currying favour with an audience still adhering to the Anglo-Irish view of the world that the very demise of this world after the Easter Rising, the First World War and subsequent Irish conflict robbed her of her audiences on both sides of the Irish Sea. Recent turmoil in Ireland would likely have reduced the appeal of a potential autobiography about wealthy members

25 Needham, 'A Daughter of Music', p. 1.

26 The notice in *The Irish Times*, 26 June 1933, p. 6, includes the statement that 'Mrs Needham is now in indifferent health, and a number of music-lovers have come forward to show their appreciation of her work by helping her.'

27 *The British Medical Journal*, 14 October 1933, p. 716.

28 'King Edward's Coronation Song Prize-Winner', *The Irish Times*, 21 December 1934, p. 8. This ends with the telling remark, 'Her love of horses drew public attention in the City of London at one time on account of her plan of giving them apples in the streets.'

29 In the literary sphere, Elizabeth Bowen's well-known novel *The Last September* (1929) captures very well that ignorance and unwillingness among Anglo-Irish landowners.

of the Protestant Ascendancy class; for the English, meanwhile, Ireland was no longer simply a constituent of the Union. As early as the 1920s, Needham therefore found herself in a completely changed political and social environment. She may have had difficulties coping with this, in addition to the worries of her deteriorating financial situation. Her world had sunken in the sea changes of these years and left her in a withdrawn state surrounded by occult objects and the spirits of the past.

9

Mary Dickenson-Auner: A Life with the Violin

Margarethe Engelhardt-Krajanek

'A little four-year-old girl was asked: what are you going to be? The quick reply was: "violin virtuoso". Nobody knows where the child got to know this word and what it meant by it. But it was a prophecy.'[1] With these words Mary Dickenson-Auner (1880–1965) – who would grow up to be not just a gifted violinist but a composer too – started her autobiographical notes, written just before her death in Vienna. (For another discussion of a composer who drafted her autobiography see Klein, Chapter 8, this volume.) Talent and determination enabled Dickenson-Auner to overcome the obstacles put in her way as a woman. Her story is that of a performer and composer born in Ireland who built a successful career on the continent in the early twentieth century but remained attached to her Irish identity, often returning to motifs from Irish folk music in her compositions. Despite these achievements, her legacy has since largely been forgotten. This chapter takes steps towards retrieving the musician from obscurity, by using archival sources to trace the main events in her life and career, especially her performance career. Detailed discussion of her compositional catalogue lies beyond the scope of this chapter, but an index of works is provided for readers who wish to pursue further study.

I became aware of the work of Dickenson-Auner in the late twentieth century in Vienna. Her complete musical catalogue – three boxes full of scores, sketches, notes, letters and tapes – was in the possession of her son, Michael Auner, who lived in Klosterneuburg near Vienna. My interest in her work and music led me to approach Michael about cataloguing and exploring the collection, and with his permission I began

1 M. Engelhardt-Krajanek, 'Mary Dickenson-Auner: Violinistin-Pädagogin-Komponistin, Leben und Werk' (Unpublished PhD thesis, Bergische Universität Wuppertal, 1995), p. 10.

this work in the early 1990s. I cataloged the material, created an index of works, checked the composer's personal details and reconstructed her biography. This work became my dissertation at the University of Wuppertal.[2] Upon completion of my dissertation and with the consent of the family, I donated the composer's estate to the University of Music and Performing Arts in Vienna, where it remains today, to ensure the material would be available for other scholars to explore and research the work of Dickenson-Auner.

Early Life and Education

Mary Frances Dorothea Dickenson was born on 24 October 1880 in Lower Baggot Street, Dublin. Her father, Augustus Maximilian Newton Dickenson, descended from English landed gentry on his father's side, but his mother, a Fitzgerald, was Irish. Mary Dickenson's mother, Mary Frances MacDonnell, was the eldest child of Hercules MacDonnell. MacDonnell, who was educated at Trinity College Dublin and made a career as a civil servant, was also known as a music critic for the *Irish Times* and active music enthusiast in nineteenth-century Dublin.[3] He founded the Dublin University Choral Society in November 1836 and was central to the reorganisation of the Irish Academy of Music in 1856 (from 1872, the Royal Irish Academy of Music), where he remained the honorary secretary for twenty years.[4]

In 1883, after the death of Augustus Dickenson, Mary's mother moved with her six children to the German health resort of Wiesbaden. The family was financially secure due to the fortune of the late Dickenson. It was while in Wiesbaden that Dickenson began her music education. As she would later write in her autobiographical notes:

> A big event when I was six years old was when my brother Cecil was going to have violin lessons. I did not leave my mother in peace, I also wanted to have violin lessons and finally, she gave into my passionate insistence.[5]

2 Margarethe Engelhardt-Krajanek, 'Mary Dickenson-Auner'. An abridged version of this dissertation was published in: Kay Dreyfus, Margarethe Engelhardt-Krajanek and Barbara Kühnen, *Die Geige war ihr Leben: Drei Frauen im Portrait* (Strasshof, 2000).

3 Paul Rodmell, 'MacDonnell, Hercules Henry Graves', in Harry White and Barra Boydell (eds), *The Encyclopaedia of Music in Ireland* (Dublin, 2013) vol. 2, p. 613.

4 Richard Pine and Charles Acton, *To Talent Alone: The Royal Irish Academy of Music, 1848–1998* (Dublin, 1997), p. 103.

5 Mary Dickenson-Auner, 'Mein Musikleben', p. 2: Dickenson-Auner wrote her autobiographical notes under the title 'Mein Musikleben' ('My Musical

In 1896, when the aspiring violinist was sixteen years old, her mother Mary Frances uprooted the family for financial reasons and they moved to England to a small town near Croydon, Surrey. Dickenson continued her violin studies at the Croydon Conservatoire of Music where she studied with Samuel Coleridge-Taylor, whom she described as charming and witty.[6] He was eager for her to apply for a scholarship to the Royal Academy of Music in London. However, this was not possible as the family returned to Ireland in 1898.[7]

Irish Intermezzo

> Another move! This time to Ireland, my homeland that I hardly knew because I had left it at the age of three. I was very unhappy because I did not see a chance for appeasing my hunger for music.[8]

Dickenson wrote that her mother was hostile to her attempts to continue her musical studies in Ireland, but that her grandfather, Hercules MacDonnell, noticed her dedication and enthusiasm for music and intervened by paying for her to study at the RIAM with renowned violinist Guido Papini. 'There you go, have a few lessons with Papini.'[9] MacDonnell paid for three lessons, but upon hearing Dickenson play, Papini offered her a position as one of his assistant teachers: she gave lessons to the beginners' group and, in exchange, received lessons from Papini. In her notes, Dickenson credits her time as an assistant teacher for her initiation of chamber music lessons in the RIAM: 'My grandfather MacDonnell and Sir Francis Brady founded the Academy of Music in Dublin', she wrote, and 'I, his granddaughter, started the chamber music class there, which still runs today.'[10]

During her year-long stint in the RIAM, Dickenson was a regular performer in student concerts and recitals; e.g. on 20 October 1898 she participated in 'Mr Robert Dwyer's Second Annual Concert' and on 16 February 1899 she appeared in an afternoon performance at the Academy with the RIAM's Double Quartet. An event at which she performed on

Life') – 'Mein Musikleben' is archived in the Estate of Mary Dickinson-Auner, Library of the University of Music and Performing Arts, Vienna.

6 Two documents from Dickenson's musical life in Croydon are preserved: one concert programme of 4 February 1898 and the Students' Afternoon Concert of 1 April of the same year. Both were performed in the Small Public Hall, Croydon. See Engelhardt-Krajanek, 'Mary Dickenson-Auner', p. 206.

7 Axel Klein, 'Dickenson-Auner, Mary', in Harry White and Barra Boydell (eds), *The Encyclopaedia of Music in Ireland* (Dublin, 2013), vol. 1, p. 297.

8 Dickenson-Auner, 'Mein Musikleben', p. 5.

9 Dickenson-Auner, 'Mein Musikleben', p. 6.

10 Dickenson-Auner, 'Mein Musikleben', p. 5.

24 January 1899 attracted advance press coverage because the 'Amateurs Ladies Concert' promised to be a 'unique' concert in which 'all musicians will be exclusively women'.[11] On 1 May 1899, Dickenson played with the Dublin Glee and Madrigal Union, on a programme that also featured a performance by Hamilton Harty. She was introduced to him and, consequently, invited to perform in a 'Grand Concert' charity event on 24 June 1899, where she played Henryk Wieniawski's *Légende*, Op. 17 and Sarabande and Tambourin by Jean-Marie Leclair under Harty's direction.[12] Despite many performance opportunities, Dickenson was dissatisfied with her progress. Commenting on her lessons with Papini, she recalled: 'I did not really make any progress with playing the violin, the lessons were too irregular and often did not take place at all, so I very often despaired.'[13] Papini's shortcomings for being inconsistent with lessons was well known within the RIAM at this time.[14] Dickenson had not forgotten Coleridge-Taylor's suggestion and still aspired to study at the Royal Academy of Music in London. She confronted her family with her request to move to London and reminisced in her notes, 'I told my mother one day that if the family would not agree I would become a street musician. My mother was greatly shocked and begged my relatives to let me have my own way because I would be capable of following through on this threat.'[15]

As a result, on 21 September 1899 Dickenson completed the entrance examination at the Royal Academy of Music in London. Days later, on 25 September, she was a registered member of Émile Sauret's violin class. Sauret recognised his student's talent but also acknowledged her technical shortcomings. Dickenson thought highly of him as a teacher. She wrote: 'Émile Sauret was a pupil of [Henri] Vieuxtemps and a truly great artist. With Sauret I learnt to wield a smooth bow but the left hand still caused me some trouble.'[16] From autumn 1899 she majored in violin and harmony, and in 1900 added organ and singing to her studies. Her compositions became regular features of the student concerts: on 10 March and 19 May 1900, works by Dickenson were performed by her fellow students Annabel McDonald and Louie Levens. On 14 July 1900,[17]

11 Concert programme, 'Amateur Ladies Concert', 28 January 1899, St Stephens Green, Dublin. See Engelhardt-Krajanek, 'Mary Dickenson-Auner', p. 218.

12 Concert programme, 'Grand Concert (In aid of Dr. Stevens' Hospital Nurses' Home)', 24 June1899, Killarney Wood, Bray. See Engelhardt-Krajanek, 'Mary Dickenson-Auner', p. 219.

13 Dickenson-Auner, 'Mein Musikleben', p. 6.

14 Pine and Acton, *To Talent Alone*, p. 255.

15 Dickenson-Auner, 'Mein Musikleben', p. 6.

16 Dickenson-Auner, 'Mein Musikleben', p. 7.

17 Concert programme, 'Fortnightly Concert', 14 July 1900, Royal Academy of Music, London. For more, see Engelhardt-Krajanek, 'Mary Dickenson-Auner', p. 219.

her two early quartets 'Sleep' and 'Red Poppins' were performed by female students at a concert, while in November 1900, Ethel M. Wood sang two other compositions of Dickenson's, 'Le Poète' and 'La Libelulle', accompanied by the composer.[18] At this point of her career, Dickenson signed scores with her own name but in later years, from 1905 to 1913, she used the pseudonym Frank Donnell.

From London to Prague

In 1903, after four years at the Royal Academy of Music in London, Dickenson made the decision to study in Prague. She noted that: 'after four years of study, I had a bronze and a silver medal for violin playing as well as a major certificate, which actually concluded my studies. I was particularly proud of a bronze medal for sight reading and perfect pitch because it wasn't easy to get.'[19] The move was prompted by her teacher's decision to take up a position in the United States. Dickenson commented that Sauret had wanted to take his best students with him, Maggorie Hayward and Dickenson, but they 'felt that he would not be able to give us a lot more and we both decided to go to Professor Ševcík in Prague'.[20]

During his teaching career in Kiev between 1875 and 1892, Otakar Ševcík had developed a violin technique that attracted attention all over Europe. His masterclass at the conservatoire in Prague was oversubscribed. Dickenson recalled: 'Professor Ševcik received me very kindly and after that, the dressage started. I cannot find another word for it because the most difficult pieces were presented to us, like the Hungarian variations by [Heinrich Wilhelm] Ernst and a lot of Paganini. That meant practice, practice, and once again, practice.'[21] In 1904, Ševcík arranged a concert where one hundred of his 'show pony' students performed. Dickenson wrote: 'We played the G-Minor Fugue by Bach for solo violin all together. That of course, created a sensation! Also the *Moto Perpetuo* by Paganini but only those who knew it by heart were allowed to play it and there was only 20 left.'[22] The 'dressage act' by Ševcík achieved the desired result; after two years of studies Dickenson was invited by conductor Oskar Nedbal to give a concert with the Czech Philharmonic Orchestra. She managed to win over musicians, spectators and critics. The most feared reviewer in Prague, Chavala, wrote about Dickenson in the Prague *Politik*: 'As an accomplished artist – who is firm from a musical point of view and equipped with a reliable technique – she does not know

18 Concert programme, 24 November 1900, Royal Academy of Music, London. For more, see Engelhardt-Krajanek, 'Mary Dickenson-Auner', p. 219.

19 Dickenson-Auner, 'Mein Musikleben', p. 8.

20 Dickenson-Auner, 'Mein Musikleben', p. 8.

21 Dickenson-Auner, 'Mein Musikleben', p. 9.

22 Dickenson-Auner, 'Mein Musikleben', p. 10.

fear, she played the *Symphonie espagnole* for solo violin and orchestra by Lalo, with a charming verve, a fresh sound, smoothly, with a lot of confidence.'[23]

Dickenson celebrated another debut during her years in Prague. The violinist Willy Lang asked her to write a small composition for him that he wanted to play the following evening in the Prague Musik-Klub. She delivered the *Irish Love Song* to him and, as a result, the publisher Mojmir Urbánek signed a contract for it on the same evening.

International Success and the First World War

The Prague debut was Dickenson's breakthrough as a performer. Between 1903 and 1913, she gave concerts in Prague, Vienna, Salzburg, Laibach, Trieste, Düsseldorf, Berlin, London and Dublin. Her tours to London and Dublin between 1911 and 1913 were a tremendous success. Welcomed by the media in London as a 'homecomer', it was not only her 'male energetic way of playing, her perseverance and dignity' that were admired but also the fact that she was, in the eyes of a reviewer for *The Lady*, simply a 'brilliant performer'.[24] By now, Dickenson was thirty-three years old and at the height of her performing career. In 1913, she married the Romanian diplomat Michael Auner, whom she had met in Vienna. However, political instability before the First World War soon cast a shadow over the young couple. Auner was ordered back to Hermannstadt in Transylvania. The married couple 'hastily' returned to Romania.[25] The Romanian city Sibiu, known as Hermannstadt in German, had been on the point of intersection between East and West for centuries. Although there was increased political unrest, the city was hardly touched by the war. Dickenson-Auner brought her violin and an enthusiasm to improve musical life in the town. Her house became the cultural centre of Hermannstadt during this time.

In these years, Dickenson-Auner also took up the role of motherhood. In June 1914, her daughter Moira was born and, on 13 February 1916, she gave birth to a son, Michael. Shortly afterwards, her husband Michael was called up for military service. Dickenson-Auner decided to flee Romania with her two children to stay with her cousin in Holland. Once in Holland, she was forced to earn a living playing in Viennese coffee houses and at marriages and funerals, but her notes also document nine concerts. Two of the latter engagements led her back to the professional stage: she gave a concert with the Amsterdam Symphonic Orchestra led

23 Review, *Politik*, 11 January 1905. For more, see Engelhardt-Krajanek, 'Mary Dickenson-Auner', p. 233.

24 Review, *The Lady*, 11 May 1911. For more, see Engelhardt-Krajanek, 'Mary Dickenson-Auner', p. 239.

25 Dickenson-Auner, 'Mein Musikleben', p. 20.

by conductor Cornelius Dopper in the hall of the local Concertgebouw; there was a further performance under the baton of Jan van Gilse in the Concertgebouw Tivoli, Utrecht, where she played Glazunov's Violin Concerto in A Major, Op. 82.[26]

Although Dickenson-Auner got along rather well with her family in Holland she experienced a profound depression in this period of her life and in her notes she recorded that she 'could not imagine that life could ever be worth living again'.[27] During this period she became involved with theosophy, a religion founded by the Russian immigrant Helena Blavatsky. Her religious beliefs began to influence her compositions heavily at this time: she focused on symbolistic and religious themes in her songs, oratorios and operas. She also authored several essays about theosophy and its teachings and practices.

1920: A Fresh Start in Vienna

In 1920, Dickenson-Auner returned to Vienna with her children to be with her husband once again. The family sought a fresh start and, under the circumstances, established themselves well. The violinist made her official debut in the city on 16 January 1922 at the Vienna Concert Hall: she played Lalo's *Symphonie espagnole*, Reger's Concerto for Violin in A Major, Op. 101, plus her own composition, *Irish Fairy Tale for Violin and Orchestra*.[28] At this point, Dickenson-Auner was eager to extend her repertoire to include more contemporary European music. She recalled:

> From a Hungarian friend, I received the manuscript of Bartók's violin sonata and decided to perform it as a premiere in Vienna. The brilliant pianist Eduard Steuermann agreed to play the piano part. We practised the extremely difficult piece over a period of three weeks, not knowing how an audience would react to it because it was very atonal and made high demands on the audience.[29]

The performance led to Dickenson-Auner inviting Bartók to Vienna to prepare her forthcoming Salzburg International chamber music performances. In an account of their rehearsals, she said: 'Bartók was a sensitive, quiet person who liked to sit in the garden and work. The rehearsals with him were very valuable and his intelligent remarks gave me a lot of food for thought.'[30]

26 Review, *Rotterdamsche Courant*, 17 June 1918. For more, see Engelhardt-Krajanek, 'Mary Dickenson-Auner', p. 247.
27 Dickenson-Auner, 'Mein Musikleben', p. 24.
28 Review, unknown newspaper, 16 January 1922. For more, see Engelhardt-Krajanek, 'Mary Dickenson-Auner', p. 248.
29 Dickenson-Auner, 'Mein Musikleben', p. 26.
30 Dickenson-Auner, 'Mein Musikleben', p. 28.

The Salzburg International Chamber Music Performances

The performances took place 7–10 August 1922, as part of the third Salzburg Festival, under the directorship of Richard Strauss.[31] In the first concert, on 7 August, Dickenson-Auner, accompanied by Bartók, played his Sonata for Violin and Piano. In the third concert on 8 August, she played Willem Pijpers Sonata for Violin and Piano. The programme of seven concerts presented work by Ravel, Debussy and Busoni, Hindemith, Honegger, Webern and Schoenberg.[32] This programme reflected Dickenson-Auner's desire to network with the musical avant-garde in Vienna. She had applied for membership of Arnold Schoenberg's Association for private musical performances too.[33] These took place once a week and were only open to association members. Every work was played several times, in different interpretations. Schoenberg asked Dickenson-Auner to rehearse Busoni's Sonata No. 2 and an unspecified work by Bach. She completed nine rehearsals with Alban Berg, Benno Sachs and Erwin Stein, among others. She noted:

> Every one of them had his own interpretation of the music. I listened to everything, was very interested but in the end, I followed my own instinct. The last rehearsal took place at Schoenberg's place in Mödling where he wanted to change everything completely. For the public performance I played the very nice and wide-ranging opus the way I had imagined, and Schoenberg and the audience nodded approvingly.[34]

Music Education: Dickenson-Auner's 'Listening Lessons'

Apart from her concert activities, Dickenson-Auner felt the wish to 'do something useful for people'.[35] Influenced by her religious beliefs and what she saw of the public school system through her children's experience, she believed there was one thing missing for these school reforms in Vienna in the 1920s: a solid musical education for primary-school pupils. She developed her idea of the 'listening lesson' (*Hörstunden*).[36]

31 <http://www.concertprogrammes.org.uk/html/search/verb/GetRecord/4848/> [accessed 20 August 2021].

32 Concert programme, 7 August 1922, Internationale Kammermusik-Aufführungen, Salzburg. For more, see Engelhardt-Krajanek, 'Mary Dickenson-Auner', p. 225.

33 Dickenson-Auner, 'Mein Musikleben', p. 26.

34 Dickenson-Auner, 'Mein Musikleben', p. 27.

35 Dickenson-Auner, 'Mein Musikleben', p. 32.

36 Freiea Hoffmann, 'Dickenson-Auner, Auner, Mary (Frances Dorothée), geb. Dickenson' (2012) <https://www.sophie-drinker-institut.de/dickenson-auner-mary> [accessed 17 July 2021].

FIGURE 9.1: Mary Dickenson-Auner. Author's private collection.

This programme was initially authorised for one school in Vienna by the municipal supervisory council for education but would expand to seventeen schools by 1938.[37] The concept of the listening lessons was simple: in cooperation with the class teacher, Dickenson-Auner introduced the pupils to the life of one composer each week and performed some of their music. Together with musician friends, she presented a variety of chamber music and explained the structure and theory behind the music.[38]

37 Report, *Die Stunde*, 17 February 1925. For more, see Engelhardt-Krajanek, 'Mary Dickenson-Auner', p. 137, p. 196ff, p. 265ff.

38 Report, *Die Stunde*, 17 February 1925. For more, see Engelhardt-Krajanek,

However, when Austria's ties to Nazi Germany developed, the aural lessons were forbidden due to her British citizenship.[39] Finding herself and her musical colleagues increasingly in conflict with the Nazi regime, Dickenson-Auner decided to withdraw from public life. 'As a foreigner, I was, of course, not allowed to perform publicly but I was not allowed to do private tuition either, which is why I lost all spheres of activity at once.'[40]

Success in Later Life

In Dickenson-Auner's notes she described the following years as the strangest and most interesting stage of her life:

> Several years earlier, an inner voice had said to me: 'You have not fully exploited all the gifts you have received from destiny.' The answer was: 'I know but now I am too old. I cannot start something new at the age of 60.' The inner voice was not going to be right in the end. Because all of a sudden, the way had been paved and prepared for me. Since I did not have anything else to do, the first priority was to write down all the music I had often dreamt of but never hoped to really express. The tones, tunes, themes, work that had been pushed back for so long now virtually broke out like a tidal wave and I could not write it down fast enough.[41]

Between 1938 and 1963, Dickenson-Auner (who had divorced from Auner in 1934) dedicated herself completely to composition: she wrote five symphonies, two oratorios, three operas, and numerous chamber music works and songs. Thirty-five of the seventy-two preserved compositions originated during this period. She returned regularly to two main themes in her compositions – the theosophical doctrine and Celtic Ireland. Thus, of the seventy-two surviving works, eleven reference Ireland in their titles, while another eleven works explore Irish themes either in the music or in the choice of libretto.[42] In the field of sacred music, Dickenson-Auner's idols were Skryabin and Bach. Her 'preference for fugues and variations' reminded 1950s Viennese music critics of Max Reger's compositions.[43]

Between the years 1947 and 1957, twelve chamber concerts featuring works composed by Dickenson-Auner were performed in Vienna. In her seventieth year she persuaded the conductor Felix Prohaska to perform

'Mary Dickenson-Auner', p. 139.

39 Hoffmann, 'Dickenson-Auner, Auner, Mary (Frances Dorothée), geb. Dickenson' (2012) <https://www.sophie-drinker-institut.de/dickenson-auner-mary> [accessed 17 July 2021].

40 Dickenson-Auner, 'Mein Musikleben', p. 43.

41 Dickenson-Auner, 'Mein Musikleben', p. 44.

42 Engelhardt-Krajanek, 'Mary Dickenson-Auner', p. 169ff.

43 Dickenson-Auner, 'Mein Musikleben', p. 53.

her Symphony for String Orchestra, Op. 33. Four of her symphonies were recorded by the Austrian Broadcasting Association. The tape from her Coronation Symphony, which she classified as one of her best works, still exists. The work was recorded in 1959 by the choir and the orchestra of the Austrian Broadcasting Association under the baton of Kurt Richter and broadcast in 1960 on Radio Vienna.[44]

After the Second World War, the composer tried to re-establish contacts with Ireland, with some success. Radio Éireann gave the first broadcast of her Irish Symphony in February 1953.[45] She also caught the interest of the journalist Richard Michael Fox. In a substantial article published by the *Irish Press*, Fox remarked: 'In her orchestration, she tries out new sound effects by letting every instrument speak for itself, according to its character, and without blending it into the others too much. In many of her themes, she has recourse to Irish tunes, the others have *Celtic character*.'[46]

Dickenson-Auner died from heart failure on 25 May 1965 at the age of 85. She left behind a catalogue of seventy-two scores, many of which had been performed and warmly received within her lifetime. Since her death, however, her work had been largely neglected until the discovery of her autobiographical notes and music and the catalogue that followed. One hopes that the future may see performances and increased scholarly interest in her music and her life, both in her native Ireland and Vienna; and that the catalogue and autobiographical notes that form the basis of this chapter will support future studies.

Compositions are archived in: Estate of Mary Dickenson-Auner, Library of the University of Music and Performing Arts, Vienna.

Index of Works

Instrumental works

Piano

Basso Ostinato (1915)
3 Klavierstücke (1918/37)
Capriccio for Piano, Op. 35 (1951)
Prelude and Fugue, Op. 37 (1951)
'Second Thoughts', Op. 39 (1952)
Two Piano Pieces: I. 'Elegie', II. 'Will o'the Wisp', Op. 46 (1955)

44 Archive Austrian Broadcasting cooperation ORF, Vienna, 1960. For more, see Engelhardt-Krajanek, 'Mary Dickenson-Auner', p. 232.

45 The broadcast is advertised in radio listings; see *Irish Independent*, 16 February 1953, p. 5.

46 R.M. Fox, 'This Irishwoman has Won Musical Fame in Vienna', *Irish Press*, 17 April 1958, p. 6.

Strings

'Sleep' String Quartet (1900)
'Red Poppins' String Quartet (1900)
'Irish Love Song' for Violin and Piano (1908)
Canon for 2 Violins No. 1, Op. 9 (1909)
Canon for 2 Violins No. 2, Op. 9 (1910)
Canon for 2 Violins No. 3, Op. 9 (1910)
Canon for 2 Violins No. 4, Op. 9 (1910)
Kadenzen zu Ludwig van Beethovens Violin-Konzert (Variation B) (1910)
'Caoine' (Lament) for Violin and Piano (1910)
'Irish Melody' for Violin and Piano (1911)
'Trischka' (Romanian Shepherd's Flute) for Violin and Piano (1912)
Kadenz zu Ludwig van Beethovens Violinkonzert (Variation B) (1918)
'Träumerei' for Violoncello and Piano (1925)
'Irische Klage' für Violoncello and Piano (1940)
I String Quartet (1941)
II String Quartet (1942)
III String Quartet (Londonderry Air) , Op. 23 (1944)
Suite for Solo Violin, Op. 30 (1949)
IV String Quartet, Op. 31 (1949)
Sonata for Violoncello and Piano, Op. 38 (1952)
'Irische Klage' for Violoncello (undated)
Scherzo (Irischer Tanz) for Cello and Piano (undated)

Chamber music for mixed ensembles

'Trischka' (Romanian Shepherd's Flute) for Clarinet in A (undated)
Quintet for Clarinet, 2 Violins, Viola and Cello, Op. 26 (1949)

Orchestral Works

Variations in D Minor for Violin and Orchestra, Op. (13) 2 (1909)
Romance in D Major for Violin and Orchestra, Op. 10 (1910)
'Caoine' (Lament) for Violin and Orchestra (1911)
'Trischka' (Romanian Shepherds Flute) for Violin and Orchestra (1912)
II Irish Violin Concerto (1914)
Irish Fairy Tale for Violin and Orchestra (1921)
II Concert for Violin and Orchestra (1942)
Variations and Fugue on an Irish Folk Song ('The Ministrel Boy') for Orchestra and Organ, Op. 30 (1943)
Concert for Violoncello and Orchestra, Op. 32 (1943)
Two Small Orchestral Pieces, Op. 46 a I. Elegie, II, Irrlicht (1957)

Symphonies

I Symphony (Irish Symphony), Op. 16 (1941)
'The Shadowy Waters' Symphonische Dichtung, Op. 28 (1948)
II Symphony (1948)
Symphony for String Orchestra, Op. 41 (1950)
III Symphony for Orchestra, Op. 41 (1953)
IV Symphony (Coronation Symphony) for Orchestra and Choir, Op. 44 (1955)
V Symphony (American Symphony), Op. 45 (1957)

Vocal Works

Operatic and Dramatic Works

'The Pain', in 5 Pictures, Op. 9 (1906); libretto: Mary Dickenson-Auner
'Maureen', Symphonic Opera in 3 Acts (1946); libretto: Dickenson-Auner
'The Shadowy Waters', A Musical Dream Play in One Act, Op. 29 (1949); libretto: William Butler Yeats
'The Seven Ravens' Fairy Tale Game in Four Pictures', Op. 42 (1954); libretto: Hans Pero
'Illusions', Musical Drama in One Act with Prologue and Epilogue (1955); libretto: Dickenson-Auner

Choral Works and Oratorios

'Invocation' for Three-Part Women's Choir or Boys' Choir or 3 Solo Voices (2 Soprano, 1 Alto) (1923); libretto: Dickenson-Auner
'Our Father' for Choir, Solo Voices (Soprano, Alto, Tenor, Bass) and Organ (1944)
'From Night to Morning' (*Pacem in Terra*) Oratorio for Solo Voices (2 Soprano, 2 Alto, 2 Tenor, 2 Baritone, Bass) Choir, Orchestra and Organ (1951); libretto: Bhagavad Gita, Percy B. Shelley, Kahhil Gibran, Alexander S. Puschkin, Walt Whitman, Friedrich Nietzsche, Dante Alighieri, William Shakespeare, Laotse, Kalidasa, Johann Wolfgang von Goethe, Francis Bacon
'Lux in Tenebris' Oratorio for Choir, Solo Voices (Soprano, Alto, Tenor, Baritone, Bass) and Orchestra, Op. 49 (1958); libretto: Dickenson-Auner
'Small Thanksgiving Prayer' for Four-Part Boys' Choir; libretto: Dickenson-Auner

Songs

'Le Poète' for soprano and piano (1900)
'La Libelulle' for soprano and piano (1900)

'Sun Rays' for soprano and piano, Op. 8 (1906); text: Dickenson-Auner
'Anxiety Cry' for soprano and piano, Op. 10 (1906); text: Dickenson-Auner
'Before Sunrise' for voice and piano, Op. 12 (1906); text: Friedrich Nietzsche
'Lullaby' for alto and piano, Op.14 (1909); text: Dickenson-Auner
'Current' for soprano and piano (1909); text: Dickenson-Auner
'Storm Song' for voice and piano (1918); text: Dickenson-Auner
'Friendship Songs II' for voice and piano (1921); text: Dickenson-Auner
'Sunrise' for soprano and piano (1933); text: Dickenson-Auner
'Inspiration' for medium voice and orchestra (1942) text: Dickenson-Auner
'Japanese Song' (Yellow Chrysanthemum) for soprano and two flutes, Op. 34 (1951); text: Dickenson-Auner
'Seine Worte' for soprano or tenor with piano accompaniment, Op. 43 (1955) text: Dickenson-Auner
'Dainty Toes' for voice and piano, Op. 50 (1958) text: Fred C. Church
'Oh! Love is a Hunter Boy' for piano and voice (undated)
'Her Hair was like the Beaten Gold' for voice and piano (undated)

10

'Opera Over a Cooking Stove': Gender Dynamics in the Music Career of Joan Trimble

Ruth Stanley

Joan Trimble (1915–2000) was an accomplished composer and performer, whose compositions reveal deft craftsmanship and skilful orchestration for diverse media, including two pianos, brass band, TV opera, orchestra, incidental music and chamber music.[1] Following her education at the Royal Irish Academy of Music and Trinity College, Dublin, she pursued further studies in composition and piano at the Royal College of Music (RCM), London. A student of Howells and Vaughan Williams, her early compositions won prizes at the RCM and Feis Ceoil, Dublin. Trimble's music typically assimilated impressionist techniques, with an idiom deeply rooted in her Irish heritage. Yet, Trimble became self-conscious of the 'Irishness' and lyricism of her music, later writing that 'the growing trend for atonal and serial music was undermining the confidence of many established composers – let alone a small figure like myself'.[2] She was also aware of the limited visibility of female composers, a factor that may account for her reticence to compose without the stimulus of a commission or encouragement from a mentor. Furthermore, both Trimble and her music were subject to gender-based criticism. For example, in press notices advertising the forthcoming broadcast of her TV opera *Blind Raftery* (1957) much was made of Trimble's domestic role, while there was scant reference to her professional musical credentials.

1 Much of the information in this chapter is rooted in the author's original study on Joan Trimble. See Ruth Stanley, 'Joan Trimble (1915–2000) and the Issue of her "Irish" Musical Identity' (Unpublished MA dissertation, University of Limerick, 2003).

2 Joan Trimble, 'Joan Trimble', *Contemporary Music Review*, 11 (1994), 277–84, at p. 281.

With the exception of two commissions in 1969 and 1990, Trimble ceased composing after *Blind Raftery*.

This chapter examines the trajectory of Trimble's music career with reference to the gendered environment noted above, paying particular attention to the ways in which relevant educational and professional infrastructures provided support, or not, to women. The media's role in stereotyping both Trimble and her music stands as a further theme in this chapter, with a critical focus on reception and aesthetics. Trimble's domestic responsibilities as mother and housewife were both real and idealised, and these are further critiqued in relation to media coverage of the composer's TV opera. Trimble's career may be contextualised within wider sociological and cultural debates. Over forty years ago, Angela Carter astutely observed that 'the behavioural modes of masculine and feminine [...] are culturally defined variables translated in the language of common usage to the status of universals'. They are spurious archetypes that 'serve only to confuse the main issue, that relationships between the sexes are determined by history and by the historical fact of the economic dependence of women upon men'.[3] During the 1990s, in a key 'New Musicology' critique grappling with music and gender, Marcia Citron asserted that 'in order to arrive at a just assessment of women's works, other factors must be taken into account: sociological, cultural, historical, economic, political'.[4] Jane Bowers and Judith Tick similarly criticised this gap in scholarly musical discourse. They argued that 'musicologists have paid little attention to the sociology of music, whether this be concerned with the social class and economic status of musicians, stratification in the professions, or access to educational opportunities'.[5] The majority of Trimble's compositional output dates from the first half of the twentieth century, a time that was 'a period of transition between old mores and new freedoms', when 'a more general social and political emancipation for women stabilized a sense of creative possibility that had not really existed earlier'.[6]

3 Angela Carter, *The Sadeian Woman: An Exercise in Cultural History* (London, 1979), p. 7.

4 Marica J. Citron, 'Gender, Professionalism and the Musical Canon', *The Journal of Musicology*, 8 (1990), 102–17, at p. 112.

5 Jane Bowers and Judith Tick (eds), *Women Making Music: The Western Art Tradition, 1150-1951* (London, 1986), p. 3.

6 Judith Tick, Margaret Ericson and Ellen Koskoff, 'Women in Music', *Grove Dictionary of Music and Musicians Online* <www.oxfordmusiconline> [accessed 6 January 2021].

'Irish' Roots and Early Career in a 'Man's World'

Born and raised in Enniskillen, Co. Fermanagh, Trimble's childhood coincided with the First World War, the Irish Civil War and the War of Independence. She was six years old when political partition led to the formation of Northern Ireland, which remained within the United Kingdom. Fermanagh became one of the 'Six Counties' in Northern Ireland. According to Axel Klein, Trimble denied 'having gone "abroad" when she left for London in 1936, since the Irish Free State was still a British dominion and England therefore not a foreign country'.[7] Trimble retained strong familial connections with Dublin through her mother, Marie Dowse. Her bond with Dublin was reinforced by her music studies and relationships forged at the RIAM.[8] Practical reasons determined Trimble's decision to travel to England; she feared she 'might drift' and recognised that Ireland offered little scope for career musicians.[9] Yet she remained passionate about Irish music, culture and heritage throughout her lifetime. To quote Kevin Myers, 'She was at home in independent Ireland; at home in Northern Ireland; at home in London. Her own commitment to Irish culture gave a special sovereignty all of her own.'[10]

Trimble's arrival as an undergraduate student at the Royal College of Music (RCM) in 1936 coincided with a boom in employment opportunities for women composers. As with the Royal Academy of Music (RAM) in London, the RCM had a tradition of admitting large numbers of women and training them to varying standards. Even by the early 1920s, women accounted for approximately 76 per cent of music teachers in England, Scotland and Wales.[11] The music industry was developing rapidly in its technology, through gramophone recordings, film and radio, which further served in creating careers for professional musicians.

7 Axel Klein, 'Irish Composers and Foreign Education: A Study of Influences', in Patrick F. Devine and Harry White (eds), *The Maynooth International Musicological Conference 1995: Irish Musical Studies 4* (Dublin, 1996), pp. 271–84, at p. 274.

8 Joan Trimble, 'Intermezzo: Joan Trimble', in Richard Pine and Charles Acton (eds), *To Talent Alone: The Royal Irish Academy of Music 1848–1998* (Dublin, 1998), pp. 396–9.

9 She was conscious of Hamilton Harty's statement in 1920: 'The Irish student is greatly facile, and still more greatly indolent. He reaches a certain point and then drifts. Ireland offers him no scope; yet as a rule, he is reluctant to leave home.' Quoted in Trimble, 'Joan Trimble', p. 277.

10 Kevin Myers, 'An Irishman's Diary', *The Irish Times*, 12 October 2000 <https://www.irishtimes.com/opinion/an-irishman-s-diary-1.1108484> [accessed 6 January 2021].

11 Jennifer Doctor, 'Intersecting Circles: The Early Years of Elizabeth Maconchy, Elizabeth Lutyens, and Grace Williams', *Women & Music: A Journal of Gender and Culture*, 2 (1998), 90–109 at pp. 90–1.

The generation of British composers who studied and began their careers during the interwar years became the first to enter a professional sphere that revolved around sound technology and media. According to Doctor, an atmosphere developed at the RCM that encouraged young British composers to create serious works and seek performances.[12] Elizabeth Maconchy, Grace Williams and Elisabeth Lutyens were the first female composers to aspire to professional composer status in the traditional sense. Following in their footsteps less than a decade later, Trimble similarly received support and encouragement from staff at the RCM, including Arthur Benjamin, George Dyson, Armstrong Gibbs,[13] Herbert Howells, Gordon Jacob and Vaughan Williams. In particular, she acknowledged the considerable influence of Howells and Benjamin, to whom she owed the starting point for her development as a composer.[14] Her talents were further recognised in the numerous prestigious awards she received at the RCM, including the Cobbett and Sullivan composition prizes (1940).[15]

Regarding women composers, Tick states that 'The extent to which each [...] felt burdened by gender ideology varied considerably, but none of them was indifferent or unaffected, particularly in the reception of their music.'[16] Trimble, herself, declared that 'composition was a man's world'.[17] As a student at the RCM during the 1930s, she knew little of women composers at that time. She recalled, 'There were plenty of ladies who had written songs and ballads for Victorian and Edwardian music-making and I accompanied my father when he sang them – songs, which were as good if not better than those of the men who outnumbered them', including those by Guy D'Hardelot, Liza Lehmann, Poldowski, Maude Valérie White and Régine Wieniawski. Indeed, it was not until later that she learnt that Guy D'Hardelot and Poldowski were male pseudonyms for Régine Wieniawski and Helen Rhodes. She had also assumed that Chaminade was a man, until she discovered that 'C' stood for 'Cécile'.[18] During the 1930s, Trimble was familiar with the names of her contemporaries, Lutyens, Maconchy and Elizabeth Poston. Regarding Lutyens and Maconchy, Trimble later reflected, 'I had heard no music by [them], both ex-RCM students and making their mark on

12 Doctor, 'Intersecting Circles'.

13 Trimble's song 'My Grief on the Sea' (1937) won a prize at Dublin Feis Ceoil in 1938 under the adjudication of Armstrong Gibbs, who subsequently arranged for the piece's publication with Winthrop Rogers.

14 Trimble, 'Joan Trimble', p. 277.

15 Trimble was awarded competitive scholarships, known as Council Exhibitions (1937 and 1938), the Ashton Jonson Exhibition for piano studies (1938), and the Wesley Exhibition for extemporisation (1938).

16 Tick, 'Women in Music'.

17 Trimble, 'Joan Trimble', p. 278.

18 Trimble, 'Joan Trimble', pp. 277–8.

British music, so far as they were given the opportunity to.'[19] Trimble's statement suggests that, as women, they were hindered in a profession that prioritised men. For Trimble, the lack of female role models within the field of Irish composition was even more marked: 'Irish women composers were few and far between.'[20]

Trimble believed that she did not conform with the image of other composition students at the RCM.[21] Although interested in the music of contemporary composers such as Hindemith and Bartók, she was concerned that she was unable to compose using modern techniques. According to Trimble, 'composition came from my head and my fingers together at the piano. A process of extemporisation if you like.'[22] She recalled that 'Howells' insistence that I treat my academic work as composition came to a head when I begged to try some "real" composition. Something new for me – can I have a break from everything else?'[23] Trimble subsequently composed two songs, 'My Grief on the Sea' (1937) and 'Green Rain' (1938). To quote Philip Hammond, her 'gift for composition [...] seems to have appeared Athene-like and fully matured without all the specific background, technical study, exercises and failed, early attempts which are *de rigueur* in the tried and tested methods of academia'.[24] Trimble stated that Howells 'brought out the best in me in my craftsmanship and encouraged me enormously'.[25] He did not attempt to impose his compositional style: 'I was allowed, indeed encouraged to disagree if I wished to.'[26] Likewise, Vaughan Williams advised Trimble to follow her own inclinations towards composition regardless of the current fashions.[27] Notably, Edmund Hunt discerns clear stylistic differences between Irish composers, such as Trimble and Maconchy, who

19 Trimble, 'Joan Trimble', p. 278.

20 Trimble, 'Joan Trimble', p. 283. The gender balance in Irish composition improved considerably in the final quarter of the twentieth century. See Jane O'Leary, 'Contemporary Music in Ireland: Developments in the Past Twenty Years', in Devine and White (eds), *The Maynooth International Musicological Conference 1995*, pp. 285–95. I have not found any evidence to show that contemporaries Ina Boyle or Rhoda Coghill had any influence on Trimble's career. Trimble and Coghill knew each other from attending Feis Ceoil events in their youth.

21 Trimble, 'Joan Trimble', p. 278.

22 Philip Hammond, 'Woman of Parts: Joan Trimble', *Sound Post*, 5 (1984–85), 24–7, at p. 25.

23 Trimble, 'Joan Trimble', p. 278.

24 Hammond, 'Woman of Parts', p. 25.

25 Trimble, 'Joan Trimble', p. 277.

26 Private letter from Trimble to Axel Klein, 3 August 1995.

27 When she composed *Pool Among the Rushes* (1940) for clarinet and piano, he said: 'I'd rather you'd written that than a symphony.' Quoted in Michael Dervan, 'The Reluctant Composer', *The Irish Times*, 2 June 1995.

studied with Vaughan Williams.[28] Klein observes that Trimble followed in the path of Herbert Hughes and Arnold Bax in composing an Irish or 'Celtic' music that was informed by impressionism.[29]

Trimble's two-piano career with her sister, Valerie, was launched in 1938, when they performed *Jamaican Rumba*, a work composed by Benjamin and dedicated to the Trimble sisters. With Benjamin's encouragement, Joan wrote *The Humours of Carrick* and *The Bard of Lisgoole* to perform alongside his rumba in their recital programme. When publisher Leslie Boosey heard Trimble's compositions and accepted them for publication, he asked for another piece that might form a trio. Trimble's hesitation at this unexpected request fired Benjamin to say 'if a publisher actually *asks* you for a work – you write it'.[30] Consequently, Trimble composed *Buttermilk Point*. Benjamin also contacted Kenneth Wright of the BBC; the successful audition of the Trimble's two-piano duo was to lead to many subsequent engagements with the broadcaster.[31] Trimble's response to Boosey established a pattern that would become consistent throughout her composing career; her compositions were invariably written following specific requests or commissions. Indeed, had it not been for Vaughan Williams's insistence that Trimble enter the RCM's Cobbett Competition, she would not have composed her piano trio, *Phantasy Trio* (1940), nor been awarded the Cobbett prize by Dyson.

At the outbreak of the Second World War all public events were cancelled, including concerts, broadcasts and the Trimble sisters' scheduled debut recital at the Wigmore Hall. In support, Dyson proposed a two-piano concert at the RCM and suggested that Joan write a new composition for the occasion. This resulted in her *Sonatina* (1940), a three-movement work for two pianos. Written at a time when she was unsure of the direction in which her compositional aesthetic was leading,

28 Edmund Hunt, '"A National School of Music Such as the World has Never Seen": Re-appropriating the Early Twentieth Century into a Chronology of Irish Composition', in Mark Fitzgerald and John O'Flynn, *Music and Identity in Ireland and Beyond* (Aldershot, 2014), pp. 53–68, at p. 64.

29 Axel Klein, 'Roots and Directions in Twentieth-Century Irish Art Music', in Gareth Cox and Axel Klein (eds), *Irish Musical Studies 7: Irish Music in the Twentieth Century* (Dublin, 2003), pp. 168–82, at p. 173. For a further study of 'Celtic' influences in Trimble's music, see Lisa McCarroll, 'The Celtic Twilight as Reflected in the Two-Piano Works of Joan Trimble (1915–2000)' (unpublished study in partial fulfilment of DMA, University of Houston, 2013).

30 Trimble, 'Joan Trimble', p. 279.

31 Kenneth Wright (1899–1975) was a prominent figure in the BBC, joining the Music Department in 1926. He became a music programme builder for the BBC. He had a profound interest in music, supported contemporary music and was a prolific composer of light music. See Jennifer Doctor, *The BBC and Ultra-Modern Music, 1922–1936: Shaping a Nation's Tastes* (Cambridge, 1999), pp. 409–11.

Trimble attempted to move away from her so-called 'Irish idiom' as she felt that her music was unfashionable. She was conscious that many of her contemporaries were experimenting with new techniques that undermined the traditional tonal-centred music of the past. Adamant that she would not write a work that was branded as 'pleasant to listen to' and 'charming',[32] Trimble sought to compose a work that was 'formalised, dissonant as far as possible, uncompromising'.[33] Despite her efforts to write something 'new', however, she later admitted that 'it did not quite work out that way!'[34] Indeed, a reviewer in the *Musical Times* detected a stylistic consistency in Trimble's *Sonatina,* which retained the 'high standard' of her earlier 'successful essays'.[35] The reviewer further praised Trimble's keyboard writing for its 'resourcefulness and [...] fine sense of colour and spacing'.[36]

However, Trimble's compositions did not escape the epithets of 'charming' and 'pleasing' that she had sought to avoid. Feminist scholarship demonstrates that such language may be viewed within a wider context of gender-linked criticism. Citron writes that the compositions of Chaminade 'were regularly deemed charming and graceful – aesthetically in accord with the sex of their creator'.[37] Such criticism intersects with traditional notions of canon formation and hierarchy of genre, whereby 'large forms hold greater value than the small forms'.[38] This further aligns with historical perceptions of women's music, often styled as 'stereotypically small scale, simple, modest, undemanding, amusing, charming, less serious and "pretty"'.[39] As Halstead argues, the composition of music for small forces does not meet with the stereotypical image of a 'great' composer, who must 'prove his or her position by producing many large-scale compositions'.[40] Thus, the following review of Trimble's *Sonatina* belies a system of criticism 'saturated with cultural meaning':[41]

> The third movement [...] seems misconceived as a conclusion to what is throughout somewhat improvisatory in manner and matter; something

32 Hammond, 'Woman of Parts', p. 26.
33 Trimble, 'Joan Trimble', p. 280.
34 Trimble, 'Joan Trimble', p. 280.
35 Author unknown, 'New Music', *Musical Times*, 83 (1942), 114–15. The 'three successful essays' are almost certainly *Buttermilk Point, The Bard of Lisgoole* and *The Humours of Carrick.*
36 Author unknown, 'New Music'.
37 Citron, 'Gender', p. 109.
38 Citron, 'Gender', p. 109.
39 Jill Halstead, *The Woman Composer: Creativity and the Gendered Politics of Musical Composition* (Aldershot, 1997), p. 174.
40 Halstead, *The Woman Composer*, p. 193.
41 Ruth A. Solie, 'Feminism', *Grove Dictionary of Music and Musicians Online* <www.oxfordmusiconline> [accessed 6 January 2021]. Solie's phrase particularly refers to the traditional understanding of 'absolute music'.

> a little more formal, more four-square even, would pull the pleasing little work to a more decisive conclusion, something rather less like Debussy and more like Mozart, shall we say?[42]

Another dimension to the media coverage was the attention that Joan and Valerie Trimble received as performers, especially in their early career. Following one recital, a reviewer reported that their ruby velvet dresses, 'cut on rather medieval lines', provided highlights for the two dark pianos and dark dado of the hall: 'The audience were very inquiring as to which was which? Which dominated the affair? Which had most responsibility? What were their ages?'[43] To quote Alasdair Jamieson, 'It is doubtful that they would have attracted that sort of attention if they hadn't both been women first of all, also sisters who looked like twins, and then that they came from Ireland. These qualities suggested an other-worldliness that enhanced their "star" persona.'[44]

Patrons, Professions and Prejudice

Dating from 1939 and spanning three decades, the Trimble sisters' regular engagements with the BBC brought wide exposure to their performance ensemble and an opportunity for audiences to hear repertory either composed or arranged by Joan Trimble. Furthermore, the BBC commissioned Trimble to compose for diverse media: fifteen *Ulster Airs* (1939–40) arranged for orchestra; a march-rhapsody for brass band, *Érin go Bragh* (1943); a television film score, *The Voice of Ulster* (1948); duets for voice and piano, *The Milkmaid* and *The Lamb* (1953); and a television opera, *Blind Raftery* (1957). The BBC's attitude towards female employees was largely progressive for the times. As early as 1926 the broadcaster's managing director John Reith asserted that 'we have been wrong in our attitude to the women on our staff in nearly all situations [...] they should be as eligible as men for promotion'.[45] A BBC memorandum in 1928 stated that single and married women, including mothers, should work with equal status, declaring 'it is not only against public policy, it is also illogical to rule that motherhood entails discharge'.[46] (See Beausang (Chapter 1) and Watson (Chapter 11), this volume, for discussion of Radio Éireann's contrasting reluctance to employ women during this time.) This

42 National Gallery Concert, *The Times*, 6 May 1941, p. 6, cited in Alasdair Jamieson, *Music in Northern Ireland: Two Major Figures: Havelock Nelson (1917–1996) and Joan Trimble (1915–2000)*, (Claygate, 2017), p. 148.

43 'A Two-Piano Recital', unreferenced cutting in Joan Trimble, *Scrapbook*, cited in Jamieson, *Music in Northern Ireland*, p. 99.

44 Jamieson, *Music in Northern Ireland*, p. 99.

45 John Reith, 'Women in the BBC', BBC Written Archives Centre C124, 30 April 1926.

46 A.C. to D.G. (full names unknown), November 1928, BBC WAC C124.

enlightened policy changed as a result of the Depression and an official marriage bar was introduced in 1933.[47] With the onset of the Second World War, the BBC was forced to alter its policy once again; the marriage bar was no longer rigidly enforced owing to the recruitment of men and single women to the armed forces. The timing of the policy change was certainly fortuitous for the Trimble sisters, who both married during the war years.

The Trimble sisters joined the Society of Women Musicians (SWM) in 1943. Tick notes that the SWM was one of a number 'all-female professional societies [...] formed in reaction to discrimination'.[48] Established in 1911 with Lehmann as its first president, the society was a counter-response to the Society of British Composers (1905), which had failed to include women in its membership. The SWM's main objectives were 'to act as a representative body where the interests of women in music are concerned. Works by Members, which have been approved by the Composers' Committee, are included in these programmes, and composers and executants are brought into touch with each other.'[49] Trimble was an active member of the SWM until its disbandment in 1972. She was afforded performing opportunities, including recitals of piano duets by Hindemith, Lambert and Mozart. The SWM archives also reveal programmes of her vocal and piano compositions.

Throughout the 1940s and 1950s, the SWM campaigned to have female examiners on the Associated Board of the Royal Schools of Music. David Wright records how the heads of the RAM and RCM, Stanley Marchant and George Dyson, refused to appoint women and 'maintained their obduracy despite a post-war crisis in which the Board found itself swamped by a significant increase in the number of candidates and an acute shortage of male examiners'.[50] It was not until 1956 that the first female practical examiners were nominated, opening up yet another stream of income and professional activity for Trimble. To quote Wright:

> It is difficult not to conclude that, in their prejudice against women examiners, Dyson and Marchant were more prepared to damage the Board than to concede the gender issue. The injustice had considerable economic significance, because the Board was effectively disenfranchising women from a significant element of professional musical activity.[51]

47 BBC WAC C124.

48 Tick, 'Women in Music'.

49 Annual Report, RCM, SWM/No. 175 Box 4.

50 David C.H. Wright, *The Associated Board of the Royal Schools of Music: A Social and Cultural History* (Woodbridge, 2013), p. 11.

51 Wright, *The Associated Board of the Royal Schools of Music*, pp. 11–12.

It is fascinating to view Dyson's role in this controversy, especially given his encouragement towards Trimble. However, no amount of mentorship can mask the pervasive and injurious nature of systemic prejudice. What Wright accurately describes as 'a quite remarkable act of institutional misogyny' was not unique within the profession. Yet, the reprehensibility of leadership in discriminating against women for so long was certainly conspicuous, when 'the distinction of women performers in British musical life had already been recognized in all sorts of ways, not least by the employment of women on the staffs of the Royal Schools themselves'.[52] Trimble's appointment as Professor of Accompaniment and General Musicianship at the RCM in 1959 is situated within the extraordinary social changes that occurred in the twentieth century, helping to 'overcome some of the ideologies about women's artistic place', especially 'the entrance of women into the paid labor force at progressively higher professional levels'.[53]

Reception and the 'Happy Housewife Heroine'

The gendered media coverage of Trimble's TV opera *Blind Raftery* was especially striking in two articles entitled 'Opera Over a Cooking Stove' and 'Mum Writes an Opera'.[54] Both pieces focused on the musician's domestic role, while failing to mention her established profile as a composer. Furthermore, there is no reference to her commissions from Radio Éireann and the BBC, her training with Herbert Howells and Vaughan Williams, nor to the Cobbet and Sullivan prizes she was awarded in composition.[55] The attention to Trimble's private life subverts her professional status and reinforces a traditional stereotype of women, ranking the achievements of marriage and motherhood above talent and career. Moreover, such critiques fail to acknowledge the wider social structure that frames the creative output of women. To quote musicologist Ruth Solie:

> The activist slogan 'the personal is political' means to underscore the conviction that the representation of personal achievement or lack thereof in terms of individual personalities and private lives obscures

52 Wright, *The Associated Board of the Royal Schools of Music*, pp. 141–2.

53 Bowers and Tick, *Women Making Music*, p. 9.

54 'Opera Over a Cooking Stove' was written by Daphne Pollard and 'Mum Writes an Opera' by Roger Hill. The original sources are unknown; both reviews are contained in a box of newspaper cuttings at the RIAM. I am grateful to Philip Shiels, RIAM librarian, for bringing these to my attention.

55 *Suite for Strings* (1953) in four movements for string orchestra was commissioned by Arthur Duff at Radio Éireann.

> the systemic nature of the gendered framework within which all men and women must operate and from which power and authority derive.[56]

It is also worth pausing to reflect on the period in which the earlier-mentioned articles were written. The year was 1957; the 1950s became synonymous with the word 'housewife' as a descriptor for the middle-class married woman. Indeed, Trimble was styled by one interviewer as 'one of the busiest housewives in Britain'. Reportedly, she 'was cooking a stew and at the same time, mentally composing one of her arias for her opera', before sitting down with the interviewer to talk about 'her hectic life' as they 'sipped coffee in the sitting-room of her London suburban house'.[57] Feminist author Betty Friedan critiqued the 1950s image of the 'Happy Housewife Heroine' as typified by 'the suburban housewife with an up-and-coming husband and a station wagon full of children'.[58] According to Friedan, this image was 'created by women's magazines, by advertisements, television, movies, novels, columns and books', and was responsible for shaping modern women's lives and mirroring their dreams.[59] Friedan coined the phrase 'the feminine mystique', to reflect the notion that women should commit to 'the fulfilment of their own femininity'. However, she understood that the 'mystique' was a restatement of the old image: 'occupation: housewife' and that 'beneath the sophisticated trappings, it simply makes certain concrete, finite, domestic aspects of feminine existence [...] into a religion, a pattern by which all women must now live or deny their femininity'.[60] Trimble, herself, was quick to dispel any myth around the challenges of balancing her domestic and professional responsibilities, saying, 'It's not the least bit romantic just plain hard work.'[61]

For all their problematic gender stereotyping, these articles reveal much about Trimble's tenacious working methods. In the past, Trimble claimed, she 'always had to have peace and quiet when [...] composing'.[62] This reflects Virginia Woolf's famously 'prosaic conclusion – that it is necessary to have five hundred a year and a room with a lock on the door if you are to write fiction or poetry'.[63] However, Trimble was forced to completely reorganise her way of working when composing her TV opera in 1957. At this stage, she was mother to three children (between six and twelve), maintaining a large house (with every room in use), working as

56 Solie, 'Feminism'.

57 Pollard, 'Opera Over a Cooking Stove'.

58 Betty Friedan, *The Feminine Mystique* (London, 2010), p. 21. While Friedan was writing about American women, similar patterns were evident in the UK.

59 Friedan, *The Feminine Mystique*, p. 21.

60 Friedan, *The Feminine Mystique*, p. 29.

61 Pollard, 'Opera Over a Cooking Stove'.

62 Pollard, 'Opera Over a Cooking Stove'.

63 Virginia Woolf, *A Room of One's Own* (London, 1945), p. 103.

secretary for her husband's GP surgery, and practising piano to meet the demands of her busy performing career. 'I have simply got to be able to work at any time', Trimble declared, 'whatever is going on around me, wherever I happen to be'.[64]

Conclusion

In the words of Halstead, it is evident that 'the social status and domestic role of women as a group, compared with men as a group, raises many issues which cannot be ignored when examining the cause of inequalities between male and female musical creation and contribution'.[65] Like Clara Schumann, Trimble found that balancing a professional performing career and raising a family left virtually no time for composition. After *Blind Raftery*, Trimble all but abandoned composing,[66] having decided that if one is to be successful at anything, one must devote oneself entirely to it.[67] This fits a rather depressing pattern of women's psychological attitudes towards their creative output. Bowers and Tick affirm that 'the cumulative testimony of primary sources [...] demonstrates women's crippling internalization of their culturally determined marginality'.[68]

There is also the tentative question of whether Trimble's music may be classified within a middlebrow aesthetic, and the degree to which her music bridged domestic and public spheres through the media of radio and television. Notably, the BBC refused to air Trimble's song-cycle *The County Mayo* (1949), deeming the work unsuitable for both the 'Third programme (too light?)' and 'the Home Service (too heavy?)'.[69] Paradoxically, perhaps, Kenneth Wright (BBC Head of Productions for

64 Pollard, 'Opera Over a Cooking Stove'.

65 Halstead, *The Woman Composer*, p. 67.

66 In 1977 Trimble retired from music life in London, where she had retained a busy career in performing, teaching and examining. She returned to Enniskillen to become managing director of the family newspaper, *The Impartial Reporter*. Her music experienced a renaissance during the 1980s, leading to concerts, interviews, recordings and broadcasts. A commission from the Arts Council of Northern Ireland resulted in her wind quintet, *Wind Diversions* (1990). Other original works not mentioned in the main text are: 'Girl's Song' (1937) for mezzo soprano and piano; *The Pool Among the Rushes* (1940) for clarinet and piano; *The Green Bough* (1941) for two pianos; *In Glenade* (1942) for string orchestra; *Puck Fair* (1951) for two pianos; *Pastorale – Hommage à F. Poulenc* (1943) for two pianos; and *Introduction and Air for Two Harps* (1969).

67 For a discussion of the difficulties faced by Trimble and other Irish women composers, see Jane O'Leary, 'Outside the Pale of Musical Civilisation', *The Irish Composer* (1988), 24–6, archived online: <https://www.aicnewmusicjournal.com/articles/archives-women-composers-outside-pale-musical-civilisation> [accessed 11 July 2022].

68 Bowers and Tick, *Women Making Music*, p. 11.

69 Trimble, 'Joan Trimble, p. 281. It was later revived and aired on BBC Radio 3.

Television) commissioned Trimble to compose *Blind Raftery* in the belief that she could produce the kind of music that a fringe audience, unused to opera and its traditions, might find accessible and pleasing to the ear: 'The Irish "idiom" is universally liked; I decided that Joan Trimble's music was genuinely Irish; that her earlier works promised a development she had never fulfilled, nor would unless stimulated by a commission of this sort.'[70] Such pronouncements on nationality relate to questions of identity that 'have prolonged debates regarding schools of composition and their place within the history of music in Ireland', and which are all the more pertinent owing to 'the tendency among some twentieth-century commentators to marginalize emigrant and Anglo-Irish composers'.[71] While this chapter has explored the impact of gender dynamics in Trimble's music career, it also exposes 'the existence of other systems working in concert with the gender system',[72] which lead to further tantalising questions about class, identity and post-colonial concerns.

70 BBC correspondence signed by Wright, p. 2, *c*.1957. As the first page is missing, the date and intended recipient(s) are unknown. RIAM BR/BBC.

71 Hunt, '"A National School of Music Such as the World has Never Seen"', pp. 66–7.

72 Solie, 'Feminism'.

11

Rhoda Coghill and the Gender Politics of Piano Performance

Laura Watson

> I walked across quickly, like a shadow, without looking at the audience, I sat down with my eyes lowered and placed my hands on the keyboard [...] I realised, first, that I should start and, second, that she was the singer and I was the accompanist, that this concert was her concert, not 'ours', as she used to say, that the glory was for her.[1]

The protagonist of Nina Berberova's 1936 novella *The Accompanist* is a young pianist, Sonechka Antonovskaya. She is a recent conservatory graduate, hired by a glamorous, wealthy soprano to rehearse at her home and accompany her on stage in concert tours. The round-the-clock nature of the young musician's employment soon necessitates a move into the singer's apartment. As Sonechka narrates: 'I became a member of the family, I was Maria Nikolaevna's principal audience and at the same time – her servant.'[2] The pianist finds herself catering to her employer's domestic and emotional needs, as well as tending to their artistic collaboration. The story begins in St Petersburg in 1919 but the account of the pianist's life resonates beyond those historical and geographic boundaries and transcends fiction. Sonechka's initial plan to support herself by teaching piano, just as her mother and grandmother had, alludes to how such labour was perceived as 'women's work' across Russia, Europe and the United States by the early 1900s. In Berberova's novel, references to the narrator's practice routines, the partnership with the star soloist

1 Nina Berberova, *The Accompanist*, trans. Marian Schwartz (New York, 1988), pp. 36–7. *The Accompanist* is briefly mentioned in James Parakilas, Mark Tucker and Michael Chanan, '1920s to 2000: New Voices from the Old Impersonator', in James Parakilas (ed.) *Piano Roles: A New History of the Piano* (New Haven and London, 2002), pp. 288–320, at p. 290.

2 Berberova, *The Accompanist*, pp. 48–9.

and audience perceptions of the pianist's role show that the author was sensitive to the realities of the accompanist's profession. Berberova's book is fiction, but by drawing attention to the feminisation of the accompanist's role – highlighting the expectation that the young female pianist should act as a caring, domestic figure and presenting her as a musician of secondary importance to the soloist – the author creates a world that resonates with the gendered, biased environment encountered by at least one Irish twentieth-century woman musician.

In this chapter I discuss Rhoda Coghill's multifaceted career and reception history as a pianist. Coghill (1903–2000) published a handful of scores (including arrangements), saw one major composition of her own performed (the 1923 rhapsody *Out of the Cradle Endlessly Rocking*, for solo tenor, chorus and orchestra), and, beyond the world of music, authored two acclaimed poetry collections.[3] Almost a century after its composition, the 1923 rhapsody has yet to be published or commercially recorded. No commercial recordings of any Coghill scores were available until 2021, when Deborah Grimmett released a CD that features her performance of the 1939 *Saoirdhréacht Gaedhealach* (*Gaelic Fantasy*) for piano.[4] Coghill's public profile is largely associated with her post as Station Accompanist at the state broadcaster Radio Éireann (later, RTÉ: Raidió Teilifís Éireann). She was appointed in 1939 and only left upon reaching retirement age in 1968. In addition, she regularly worked as a concerto soloist throughout the 1940s and was in demand as an accompanist all her life. Coghill's career trajectory and reception history are inseparable from the societal attitudes and policies that prevailed in Ireland throughout much of the twentieth century. She contended with systemic biases – from pernicious gendered commentary in critical writings (or omission from such texts altogether) to discriminatory employment legislation, such as the 1924 and 1956 Civil Service Regulation Acts that required women to resign from posts upon marriage. Coghill worked in a society that scrutinised male and female musicians according to sharply differentiated ideologies. I examine the impact of those insidious cultural and social pressures on her activities and status as a performer.

For over three decades now, scholars such as Marcia Citron, Susan McClary and many others have demonstrated how gender ideologies have shaped art music and its discourses. Perceived binaries have traditionally delineated a masculine-coded public world from a feminine-coded private domain, distinguishing the historically male environment

3 For discussion of the artistic connections between Coghill's different careers, see Laura Watson, 'Epitaph for a Musician: Rhoda Coghill as Pianist, Composer, and Poet', *Journal of the Society for Musicology in Ireland*, 11 (2016), 3–23.

4 *Lineage: Tracing Influence*, with Deborah Grimmett, New Classics Records, 2021.

of the concert stage from the female-run salon, differentiating the professional male instrumentalist from the female amateur, and so on. Yet, one instrument threatens the stability of these binaries and exposes their constructedness. James Parakilas asserts that 'the piano has always exhibited a unique power to act as a cultural go-between', for it inhabits 'both sides of all the social boundaries that it has itself helped to define'.[5] Those boundaries are demarcated by public/private lines; within these, as Parakilas's discussion subtly reminds us, there exists another pianistic dichotomy: solo performance and accompaniment. Coghill migrated between these different spheres, switching between the high-profile world of the concert virtuoso and the lower-key setting of the accompanist.

She negotiated these divides as a woman at a time when prejudice towards female pianists and anxieties about feminine-coded performance aesthetics endured. This chapter is in four parts: I begin with contextual commentary on earlier European and North American discourses about women pianists; subsequently, I explore how these might have influenced critical attitudes towards Coghill. Following this, I address her work and status in relation to mid-twentieth-century Irish cultural values. Finally, I consider how her presence on the national airwaves complicates notions of gendered private and public musical spaces.

Critical Attitudes Towards Female Pianists in the Nineteenth and Twentieth Centuries

When Coghill came to public attention at the age of fifteen female pianists were not a rarity:[6] individuals such as Clara Schumann, Cécile Chaminade and Amy Beach had toured Europe and the United States.[7] Despite apparent strides towards acceptance, though, the qualification 'woman pianist' became a trope in early twentieth-century North American musical discourse.[8] By this point women also outnumbered men as piano teachers in what Judith Tick has ranked as one of 'the most highly "feminized" professional occupations in the United States'.[9] Dieter Hildebrandt painted a bleak picture of an international 'musical

5 Parakilas, 'Introduction', in Parakilas (ed.) *Piano Roles*, p. 4.

6 The first reference to a public appearance by Coghill appears in an *Irish Times* advertisement on 4 May 1918, p. 4. Coghill, then fourteen years old, was billed as 'the child pianist' and one of the attractions at a forthcoming concert in the Theatre Royal, Dublin.

7 These three women were composer-pianists, as was Coghill, although her only work for solo piano was the *Saoirdhréacht Gaedhealach* (*Gaelic Fantasy*) (1939). Later she arranged it for piano and orchestra, playing the solo part in a broadcast with the RTÉ Light Orchestra on 15 March 1972.

8 See Judith Tick, *Ruth Crawford Seeger: A Composer's Search for American Music* (New York and Oxford, 1997), pp. 16–21.

9 Tick, *Ruth Crawford Seeger*, p. 16.

proletariat' in this era – the 'failed pianists, unmarried ladies, impoverished widows' who faced 'lifelong servitude as a piano teacher'.[10] In Britain, the piano was the instrument most closely associated with girls and women, and the one most likely to feature in a domestic setting.[11] The situation in early twentieth-century Ireland mirrored those across the Atlantic and Irish Sea. Girls and young women were well represented at the prestigious annual Feis Ceoil piano competitions. Furthermore, ever since the mid-nineteenth century, Dublin had been home to renowned women educators such as Royal Irish Academy of Music piano pedagogue Fanny Robinson and Feis Ceoil founder Annie Patterson.[12] Continuing this tradition, Patricia Read led a piano school in her name, where Coghill studied for fifteen years before being appointed to the teaching staff.[13]

Yet the increasing visibility of women in Irish music education did not automatically translate into recognition for professional female pianists. Critical indifference to Coghill as she grew older exemplifies this reticence, the tendency to minimise her accomplishments on grounds that implicate interconnected gender and age bias. To understand the mixed messages that circulated around Coghill's status as a performer, it is instructive to consider the historical European context. In nineteenth-century Paris, as Katharine Ellis has documented, concert audiences were confronted with an unsettling paradox, 'women's public display of that most appropriate female domestic accomplishment: playing the piano'.[14] These professional performers challenged 'traditional ideas about the meaning of pianistic virtuosity' and assumptions that women 'should play different repertory from their male counterparts'.[15] Their bodies were objectified by French reviewers who scrutinised 'the physicality of women's playing' but remained silent about men in this regard, apart from 'comments related to power'. Reference to finger technique became a coded way for critics to highlight a performer's femininity.[16] The views espoused by these critics reflected educational practices at the Paris

10 Dieter Hildebrandt, *Pianoforte: A Social History of the Piano*, trans. Harriet Goodman (New York, 1988), p. 126.

11 Paula Gillett, *Musical Women in England, 1870–1914: Encroaching on All Man's Privileges* (New York, 2000), p. 3.

12 For more on Robinson and Patterson, see Jennifer O'Connor, 'The Role of Women in Music in Nineteenth-Century Dublin' (Unpublished PhD thesis, Maynooth University, 2010).

13 The details of Coghill's association with the Read Pianoforte School (part of the Leinster School of Music) are stated in a letter from E.M. Clark to the *Irish Times*, 9 January 1939, p. 7.

14 Katharine Ellis, 'Female Pianists and Their Male Critics in Nineteenth-Century Paris', *Journal of the American Musicological Society*, 50 (1997), 353–85, at p. 355.

15 Ellis, 'Female Pianists', 355, 363.

16 Ellis, 'Female Pianists', 367.

Conservatoire. At this elite institution, the annual piano competitions were segregated by sex and by associated gender-appropriate repertoire. Thus, the women's test pieces, for example, never featured Beethoven but always included Chopin.[17] Some of these attitudes inflected twentieth-century Irish musical discourse.

As discussed below, Coghill, too, faced gender-coded critiques of her public performances, particularly in relation to the female physique and its perceived expressive limitations. One might expect that the invisibility afforded by radio granted some reprieve from gendered culture policing. However, on the contrary, Coghill's right to pursue a broadcasting career at all was contingent upon compliance with employment regulations that discriminated against women. Radio Éireann was part of the civil service, which meant that its female employees were subject to the marriage bar until 1973, years after Coghill had retired. Coghill's predecessor at the station was Kitty O'Doherty, who later became Kitty O'Callaghan and one of the rare exceptions to the rule against employing married women. In 1932 the station faced government objections to their plan to retain O'Callaghan in her role; the government eventually relented in this case but, in general, they opposed the employment of married women musicians at the station.[18] (See Beausang, Chapter 1, this volume.)

Coghill, hired seven years later when she was in her mid-thirties, never married. Her status as a single woman (or spinster, in the language of the time) meant that in mid-twentieth-century Catholic Ireland there would have existed an unspoken public understanding that she remained celibate. As the ethnomusicologist Ellen Koskoff has observed about female instrumentalists, 'women who play often do so in contexts of social and sexual marginality'.[19] Common to many societies, she explains, is a greater tolerance of female instrumentalists who remain on the social peripheries. Koskoff writes:

> Young unmarried, uninitiated girls and older women are thought of in many societies as existing in a marginal state. Premenstrual women, who are not yet settled in their adult status, and postmenopausal women, who are no longer believed to be sexually active, cannot be threatening to the social and sexual order. Frequently, restrictions regarding instrumental performance are lifted for these females.[20]

The trajectory of Coghill's career stretched from adolescent to pensioner and went uninterrupted by marriage. Her life, therefore, gave the

17 Ellis, 'Female Pianists', 363.

18 For details of government objections to the recruitment of women, see Richard Pine, *Music and Broadcasting in Ireland* (Dublin, 2005), pp. 66–7.

19 Ellen Koskoff, *A Feminist Ethnomusicology: Writings on Music and Gender* (Urbana, Chicago and Springfield, 2014), p. 122.

20 Koskoff, *A Feminist Ethnomusicology*, p. 131.

consistent appearance of existing within the unthreatening 'marginal' states that Koskoff describes. This condition is arguably what enabled her to operate in mid-twentieth-century Irish society as a 'respectable' professional musician.

FIGURE 11.1: Rhoda Coghill at the piano in the radio studio, Henry Street, Dublin 1. Courtesy RTÉ Archives.

Critical Attitudes Towards Coghill at the Start and End of her Career

In response to her early public appearances, Coghill was praised as a fundamentally cerebral performer. 'Her study of the modern composers has been thorough', an *Irish Times* critic noted in 1920 about the seventeen-year-old's interpretation of Debussy.[21] Five years later Coghill was identified as 'the clever Dublin pianist',[22] and as a musician with 'a highly analytical type of mind' who made 'carefully calculated' gestures.[23] Other reviews underlined her brilliance and formidable record of achievement. Not only did critics approve of her intellectual approach to music but they were also struck by her cool stage demeanour. 'She is a remarkably undemonstrative player', one wrote in 1928, 'and in many a keen contest her *sang-froid* has enabled her to snatch victory'.[24] Here, Coghill is implicitly praised for the suppression of stereotypically feminine attributes such as heightened emotional expression.

By her late twenties, following a Dublin concerto debut playing Tchaikovsky's Piano Concerto No. 1, a successful recital in London, and a summer course with Arthur Schnabel in Germany, Coghill was lauded as one of the nation's finest pianists. Her London performance and sojourn in Germany signalled nascent ambitions to develop a career beyond Ireland. Although these ambitions never progressed, Coghill achieved a measure of wider fame. During the 1920s she featured in reports from Dublin that were published in the British *Musical Times*. Meanwhile, she was touted at home as a cultural ambassador to international visitors. One such instance of this occurred in September 1929, when the conductor Sir Thomas Beecham arrived in the capital for a weekend of concert engagements and to promote his vision for opera.[25] It promised to be a highlight of that year's musical calendar. Beecham was formally greeted at Dún Laoghaire pier by a party of local dignitaries, including the twenty-five-year-old Coghill and her former teacher Patricia Read.[26] The following day Coghill appeared as soloist in the first of two concerts led by Beecham at the Theatre Royal. These were also relayed across the airwaves. Under Beecham's baton, on Saturday 14 September Coghill reprised the first movement of the Tchaikovsky Piano Concerto that

21 'Miss Coghill's Pianoforte Recital', *Irish Times*, 23 February 1920, p. 3.

22 'Miss Rhoda Coghill's Recital', *Irish Times*, 20 March 1925, p. 3.

23 'Pianoforte Recital: Miss Rhoda Coghill', *Irish Times*, 21 November 1925, p. 9.

24 'An Irishman's Diary', *Irish Times*, 27 January 1928, p. 4.

25 The visit had been organised by the Dublin Committee of the League of Opera; they had previously welcomed Beecham to Dublin for meetings about his opera plans. See 'Eminent Musician to Visit Dublin', *Irish Times*, 13 July 1929, p. 6.

26 'Sir Thomas Beecham in Dublin: To-Day's Orchestral Concert', *Irish Times*, 14 September 1929, p. 5.

had sealed her reputation in 1927. Her performance that day exhibited a 'high degree of technical and interpretative ability'.[27] Garnering her share of column inches alongside Beecham, Coghill was an undisputed star of the Dublin music scene. Years later, however, there was bafflingly little acknowledgement of this past or her many concerto appearances throughout the 1940s. Instead, she was typically regarded as an accompanist rather than as a soloist.

From the 1950s, despite her ongoing service to the state broadcaster and other performance engagements, Coghill's name receded from the foreground of discourse about music in Ireland. Reports surrounding an event in 1970 indicate the extent to which her virtuoso reputation had already faded from public memory. In December 1970, two years after her retirement from RTÉ, Coghill was recognised with a Jacob's Radio and Television Award. An *Irish Times* correspondent at the ceremony remarked that 'very few [...] remembered Miss Coghill's contribution to Irish music as a concerto pianist'.[28] Hers was the sole Jacob's Award granted to a woman in 1970; moreover, it came with gendered connotations. The *Irish Independent* reported that Coghill was honoured for her 'long and distinguished service to music on radio over the years as accompanist and advisor and the special help she has given young musicians'.[29] An *Irish Press* journalist echoed this assessment by repeating the view of an unnamed person in attendance: 'Rhoda was a great deal more than [an accompanist], because her opinions, taste and judgment were always sought and were of the greatest values to the authorities. Her life-long dedications and her kindness to young musicians must also be remembered.'[30] The cumulative sense of these three national press accounts is that Coghill was, first and foremost, an accompanist, and that this occupation was 'lacking' in some way. Whereas her mid-century activity as a concert soloist – the public performance of canonic European works – was retrospectively highly valued in 1970 as a 'contribution to Irish music', her long career as 'station accompanist' was accorded less respect and regarded as insufficient on its own terms.

The devaluation of accompaniment is linked to Coghill's status as a woman in the music profession. During the 1930s and 1940s, as a Feis Ceoil adjudicator and accompanist, she monitored and advised on the development of young performers. These roles, enacted by a woman in a conservative society, would have lent Coghill a nurturing identity. In the workplace environment of the radio station, it is apparent that

27 'Fugato', 'A Vocal Interlude', *Sunday Independent*, 15 September 1929, p. 9.

28 'An Irishman's Diary', *Irish Times*, 12 December 1970, p. 11.

29 'Girls from Jacobs Picket Award Winners Banquet', *Irish Independent*, 11 December 1970, p. 13.

30 Sheila Walsh and Noel Conway, 'Press Diary: Two Smashing Parties', *Irish Press*, 11 December 1970, p. 13.

Figure 11.2: Rhoda Coghill receiving the Jacob's Award in 1970. Courtesy RTÉ Archives.

senior figures there also linked Coghill's accompanist role to a stereotypically feminine nurturing function. Here, let us recall the protagonist of Berberova's novel, the accompanist who felt pressured to fulfil extra domestic duties. We can see parallels with the additional, gendered expectations that Radio Éireann/RTÉ colleagues placed upon Coghill. The extent to which she was expected to mentor inexperienced musicians is hinted at in the wording of the 1970 award. Further evidence that she was relied upon to 'help out' at the station in a nurturing role is indicated in an *Irish Times* report from 1955 on Peadar Ó Dubhda's children's programmes:

> Rhoda Coghill, the Radio Éireann accompanist, has been a great help to him in his children's programmes. She has her own music for his songs, and he tells me that she is also assisting him with his song book for schools, which the Department of Education has now taken up, and hopes to have published during the coming year.[31]

The expectation that the accompanist would assist with background tasks seems to have been a hazard of the job. In that respect the 1970 award acknowledges her range of station duties but minimises Coghill's credentials as a performer. She was a versatile pianist who had frequently performed as a soloist on radio and in concert, as well as accompanying. To the station's further benefit, she had collaborated with world-renowned instrumentalists such as Léon Goosens, Evelyn Barbirolli and Josef Suk when they made guest appearances.[32]

'Music is a Virile Art': Coghill's Status in Mid-Twentieth-Century Ireland

To understand the shift in public perceptions of Coghill, from soloist to background figure, we turn to her mid-century career and critical reception. The marginalisation of women and girls in the sphere of Irish art music during these decades was insidious. So pervasive was it that, as we see below, even Coghill internalised some misogynistic ideologies, which served to undermine her. The landmark essay collection *Music in Ireland* (1952), edited by Aloys Fleischmann, is symptomatic of the cultural suspicion that existed towards female musicians. In particular, Charles Lynch's chapter 'The Concert Pianist in Ireland' warrants scrutiny. Almost immediately, Lynch ranks 'pianist' as a separate occupation to 'accompanist':

31 'Quidnunc', 'An Irishman's Diary', *Irish Times*, 5 January 1955, p. 6.

32 A list of prominent musicians she accompanied is provided in Pine, *Music and Broadcasting*, p. 92.

> To the first question which arises, namely whether it is possible for the professional pianist in Ireland to live entirely by his art, the answer must be 'No'. The only whole-time position which a pianist in Ireland can fill is that of accompanist at either of the two radio stations, Radio Éireann or the BBC, Belfast. But the concert pianist and concert accompanist serve two separate branches of music, nor does the pianist normally accept engagements as an accompanist.[33]

The message is clear: to work as an accompanist, even for a national broadcaster, was beneath the calling of a concert performer.

Describing recent high-profile performances by pianists in Dublin, Lynch continued:

> For its broadcasts of serious music from the studio given by solo piano or by chamber music combinations involving piano, Radio Éireann engages for the most part Irish artists [...] Apart from studio recitals the pianist may be engaged to play with the Radio Éireann Symphony Orchestra. During the Second World War Irish pianists were regularly engaged for the series of symphony concerts given for a period of two years at the Mansion House, and later for a further five years at the [...] Capitol Theatre. During the whole of this period the orchestra also gave its usual broadcasts from the Henry Street studio, and many works which were well received by the audiences at the Mansion House and Capitol Theatre were repeated in the studio with the same conductor and soloist.[34]

Lynch's overview is curiously disconnected from concrete detail. Remarkably, Coghill is entirely absent from his account. To be fair, Lynch does not identify other pianists nor explicitly trump his own achievements either. By 1952, however, Coghill had been a fixture at Radio Éireann for thirteen years, a fact that surely merited acknowledgement. Furthermore, with reference to the concerts given in the studio and at city concert venues, Lynch omits to mention that Coghill had starred as the concerto soloist in a dozen of these events during the 1940s. Having been hired along with Coghill for the 1942 season, he would have been aware of this legacy.[35] Table 11.1 lists Coghill's concerti performances:[36]

33 Charles Lynch, 'The Concert Pianist in Ireland', in Aloys Fleischmann (ed.) *Music in Ireland: A Symposium* (Cork, 1952), pp. 177–84, at p. 177.

34 Lynch, 'The Concert Pianist', pp. 178–9.

35 See 'Symphony Concerts', *Irish Times*, 24 September 1942, p. 3.

36 All these performances are mentioned or reviewed over the years in the *Irish Times*. Additional details of performance locations are provided in Patrick Joseph Kehoe, 'The Evolution of the Radio Éireann Symphony Orchestra, 1926–41' (Unpublished PhD thesis, Technological University Dublin, 2017), Appendix A.

TABLE 11.1: Coghill's concerto performances with the Radio Éireann Symphony Orchestra during the 1940s.

Brahms no. 2	13 May 1941	Mansion House
Beethoven no. 5	15 October 1942	Mansion House
Grieg	28 November 1943	Capitol Theatre
Beethoven no. 5	21 May 1944	Capitol Theatre
R. Schumann	14 January 1945	Capitol Theatre
Rachmaninov no. 2	28 June 1946	Studio
Beethoven no. 4	8 December 1946	Capitol Theatre
Grieg	17 January 1947	Studio
Franck, Symphonic Variations for Piano and Orchestra	17 June 1947	Studio
Rachmaninov no. 2	18 May 1948	Phoenix Hall
Mozart no. 23	30 November 1948	Phoenix Hall
Mozart no. 23	28 June 1949	Phoenix Hall

As indicated by the catalogue of performances shown in Table 11.1, in 1952 when *Music in Ireland* was published, Coghill was one of Ireland's most eminent pianists. It is very difficult to justify her absence from Lynch's chapter. Elsewhere in the book, her name appears only three times – under listings of teachers, station accompanists, and musicians who had played at the Royal Dublin Society recitals. As we will see from the qualities that Lynch valued, the only plausible explanation for Coghill's exclusion from this account is that a performer who reached her professional prime as a middle-aged woman did not accord with his vision of who a pianist ought to be.

Coghill may have internalised some ideas that Lynch espoused, such as that of the soloist and accompanist serving 'two separate branches' of music. She was sensitive to the different expectations associated with these two categories. For example, in 1993, she spoke of accompaniment as an exercise in diplomacy:

> You mustn't want to dominate or over-assert yourself. At the same time, you must be able to perform your own part of the music so that together with the soloist or with a chamber music group [...] you must combine with them so that all the elements of the music are equally important.[37]

Coghill suggested that the accompanist should practise restraint and accommodate the needs of others – a characterisation that is distinctly feminised, especially when contrasted with Lynch's vision of a soloist.

37 *Rhoda Coghill Talks to Ray Lynott About Her Career*, RTÉ FM3, 14 October 1993.

Basing his observations on performances he had witnessed at the Feis Ceoil, he critiqued the standard of Irish pianism using gender-coded rhetoric:

> it is clear that piano-playing here suffers from a certain lack of inner intensity or excitement – lack of spiritual throb in the music. After all, music is a virile art, and big climaxes marked up to *fff* should be given with all the power and *excitement* of which an artist is capable, provided of course that he always keeps within the bounds of beautiful tone.[38]

Lynch aspired to hear pianists who measured up to conventionally masculine ideals. His ideal pianist could therefore not be embodied in the figure of a reserved, middle-aged woman such as Coghill. Lynch's commentary is rife with anxieties that originated in nineteenth-century discourses about girls and women at the piano. Like the Parisian critics, he construed male physicality as a source of pianistic power. His rhetorical strategy also echoes the mental gymnastics practised by pedagogues such as Czerny in response to the vexed issue of the piano's association with amateur female players. As Parakilas observes, Czerny's manual *Letters to a Young Lady* exemplifies his reliance 'on artificial gender distinctions to maintain the power of men in a field that otherwise would soon have been dominated by women'.[39] Consciously or not, Lynch borrowed from an entrenched tradition of gendered aesthetics, a tradition that could only exclude Coghill from the highest ranks of the pianist's profession.

Those standards had partly informed how critics judged Coghill. Anticipating her first concerto appearance, one critic advised that 'the soloist should dominate the performance'.[40] In the 1940s Coghill frequently ventured into masculine-coded canonic territory with works such as Beethoven concerti. According to most reports published in the *Irish Times* (the main source of music reviews in the period), she surpassed expectations. Her 1944 performance of Beethoven's Piano Concerto No. 5 was judged outstanding: she had 'never played with more brilliance or artistry' and 'her fluent, polished technique was quickly evident in the opening runs'.[41] Gendered aesthetics, at the very least, coloured a couple of reviews in subsequent years. Coghill's interpretation of the Schumann concerto in 1945 was characterised as 'beautifully sensitive' and 'exquisitely shaped' in the 'more tranquil parts' but needing a 'more vigorous treatment of the bravura passage in the opening section'.[42] In

38 Lynch, 'The Concert Pianist', p. 183.

39 Parakilas et al., 'The Piano Lesson', in Parakilas (ed.), *Piano Roles*, pp. 110–49, at p. 121.

40 'Obligato', 'Tchaikovsky's Piano Concerto: His Use of Russian Themes', *Irish Times*, 24 October 1927, p. 4.

41 'Symphony Concert', *Irish Times*, 22 May 1944, p. 3.

42 'Symphony Concert', *Irish Times*, 15 January 1945, p. 2.

1946 her reading of Beethoven's Piano Concerto No. 4 was praised as 'finely balanced' and graced with a 'light and fluent technique' but the same critic also drew attention to her 'delicate touch' and faulted her tone in the second movement as 'not very penetrating'.[43]

Awareness and anxieties about the feminisation of piano performance sometimes concerned women as well as men. Coghill's remarks on how to navigate accompaniment testify to this, as do comments she made in the 1940s about the Feis Ceoil. It was a widely culturally ingrained paradox that 'boys were trespassing into a female realm when they learnt to play piano [...] whereas girls were trespassing into a male realm when they got too good at it'.[44] Authorities such as Czerny had circumvented this by promoting the highest echelons of pianism as male territory. Similarly, as a Feis Ceoil adjudicator, Coghill strongly encouraged boys to participate in Ireland's most elite piano competitions. The annual syllabus contained reports from adjudicators on the previous year's contest. In the 1945 edition, Coghill wrote that 'a most encouraging feature [in 1944] was the large number of boys who competed, all of whom showed themselves mostly keenly interested'.[45] Her remarks were also paraphrased in the press while the 1944 competitions were in progress.[46]

Radio Silence?

It was rare to encounter Coghill's voice in print, or on radio for that matter – the 1993 RTÉ radio interview marking her ninetieth birthday appears to be unique. This is no small irony considering she had broadcasted for over forty years. In the early twenty-first century, when women remain under-represented on Irish radio, we might ask what kind of 'voice' did Coghill project on the airwaves? She was a guest performer from the earliest days of 2RN when, as Pine has shown, the government treated radio as a 'vehicle for nation-building' and, therefore, as an essential public utility.[47] The station was founded in 1926; Coghill made her first appearance in 1927. Her debut radio recital exclusively comprised dances by Chopin. This is a programming decision, which, by bringing a Chopin recital into the intimate space of a listener's home, verges on a reconstruction of the highly feminised nineteenth-century salon culture.[48] From 1939 Coghill was permanently employed with the station, playing

43 'Radio Éireann Orchestra', *Irish Times*, 9 December 1946, p. 5.

44 Parakilas, 'The Piano Lesson', pp. 119–20.

45 Feis Ceoil Syllabus (1945), p. 51. Archived in the Feis Ceoil Association Records, MS Collection List 92, National Library of Ireland. MS 40228/6.

46 'Feis Ceoil Awards', *Irish Times*, 10 May 1944, p. 3.

47 Pine, *Music and Broadcasting*, p. 3.

48 Details of the programme are listed in 'Broadcasting Today', *Irish Times*, 4 April 1927, p. 3.

everything from art-music repertoire in solo and ensemble settings to traditional folk arrangements. Self-evidently, radio's sound source is invisible – and when the broadcaster's remit is instrumental performance, as opposed to speech or song, the human voice is inaudible too. The only potential marker of a gendered body is silenced. While it is tempting, therefore, to hypothesise that radio rendered Coghill's identity as a woman irrelevant, the culture of radio itself had become so gendered in the first half of the twentieth century that this scenario is unlikely.

Radio is a liminal medium between the outside world and inner sanctum: programmes are produced for the public but predominantly consumed in the intimate setting of the home. Through Radio Éireann, Coghill's work as a performer was easily accessible to casual listeners, whether enjoyed as part of a relaxing evening routine or as distraction from domestic drudgery. Crucially, audiences would have primarily encountered Coghill's performance within the home environment. The relationship between Coghill, the airwaves and home is significant because, as scholars such as Maggie Andrews have shown, the radio had become associated with domesticity, and hence femininity, by the early 1930s. Andrews's exploration of British broadcasting in the interwar years traces how the radio became 'both a soundscape to domestic life and [...] a signifier of domestic tranquillity, entwined in fantasies of home for listeners'.[49] At the same time, 'the consequent assumption of a high proportion of woman listeners evoked much anxiety',[50] and became a factor in 'contributing to the low status of broadcast media in the ensuing years'.[51] Andrews's analysis of radio during the interwar years and beyond is applicable to Ireland insofar as the ideal of 'domestic tranquillity' influenced much Radio Éireann programming of this period; e.g. the station soothed listeners with performances of familiar traditional and classical repertoires. Lynch's bifurcation of pianist and accompanist, therefore, was likely influenced by (and reinscribed) the social construction of radio as a feminine sphere. That gendering of the airwaves extended in Ireland to how the profession of radio accompanist was perceived. Since the inception of 2RN in 1926, 'Station Accompanist' had been a post solely held by women: Kitty O'Doherty, then Coghill. As Citron wrote about the lesser attention granted to female musicians in the private sphere, 'the public arena has been privileged, and its activities have been chronicled, preserved, and praised'.[52] During the twentieth century, performance on Irish radio was valued less than that which occurred in a visible, public

49 Maggie Andrews, *Domesticating the Airwaves: Broadcasting, Domesticity and Femininity* (London and New York, 2012), p. 25.

50 Andrews, *Domesticating the Airwaves*, p. 4.

51 Andrews, *Domesticating the Airwaves*, p. ix.

52 Marcia Citron, *Gender and the Musical Canon* (Cambridge, New York and Melbourne, 1993), p. 102

venue. The insufficient recognition of Coghill's contribution to Irish music can partly be attributed to the domestic function and consumption of her radio pianism. If, as Hildebrandt implies, the pianist's power resides to some degree in capitalising on the visuals of performance – 'there is nothing more exciting than the sight of a grand piano open on a concert stage in a hushed and expectant auditorium'– this is a further reason that Coghill has been under-acknowledged.[53]

In conclusion, Coghill's career as a performer resisted easy classification. It confronted the dichotomies outlined at the start of this chapter. The role of Station Accompanist was more complex than the official title implied; it gave Coghill scope to perform solo recitals and concerti too, but by the same token she was also expected to assist with other tasks at the station. Radio Éireann was the interface between her worlds of the public stage and concealed studio; for example, she played with the station orchestra in concerti during the 1940s. Her career trajectory exposed the limits of opposing ideological constructs such as masculine and feminine musical domains, public and private performance – and, for the pianist, accompaniment versus solo performance. The breadth of Coghill's activities breached gender norms for mid-twentieth-century Irish society and sometimes confounded critics. Since 2016, events such as the National Concert Hall's 'Composing the Island Festival' have contributed to a reassessment of twentieth-century Irish music history. Coghill's *Out of the Cradle Endlessly Rocking* was one of the 'forgotten' works spotlighted during this festival. As well as these much-needed revisionist projects, it is essential to appraise historical narratives of performance and to recognise how gender discrimination has marginalised the impact of vital musicians such as Coghill.

53 Hildebrandt, *Pianoforte*, p. 4.

Part IV

Situating Discourses of Women, Gender and Music in the Twenty-First Century

12

Women and Composition: Fifty Years of Progress?[1]

Nicola LeFanu

As the twenty-first century progresses, can those of us invested in the professional study and practice of music be confident that women working in music will finally gain an equality of opportunity and recognition? If we are not confident, what can we do about it? I have been active in the music profession for over fifty years, and have begun to reflect on that period to see what has been achieved, and what has not and what lessons may be learnt, so that as we look forward, we can see how to bring about change that is enduring, not transient. As I am a composer, I focus on composers, but I think you will find that much of what I say is applicable to other disciplines. Classical music is my field, but it is not a special case. When I talk to colleagues who are conductors or songwriters, or who work in jazz or folk music, they too believe that there are still glaring anomalies in the ways that male and female artists are treated.

One of the most striking things of the last fifty years has been the rediscovery of creative women in music, art and literature; it is a process that is continuing, as illustrated by the Women and Music in Ireland conferences, and, indeed, by this volume. In English-speaking countries, this rediscovery has been particularly evident in literature. In 1973, the Australian publisher, writer and critic Carmen Callil, who spent much of her career in Britain, founded the London publishing house Virago Press.

1 This chapter originated as a keynote address for the third Women and Music in Ireland conference in 2014. Nicola LeFanu delivered a presentation informed by her fifty years of experience as a composer and her position as the daughter of another composer – Dame Elizabeth Maconchy, who identified as Irish and received her early musical training in Dublin. The editors have added notes where appropriate to indicate developments in the Irish music world since 2014 (new editions of scores, premiere performances, recordings and so on), which are of significance to composers in this field.

Through Virago, a wealth of anglophone women writers – Irish, English, Australasian, North American – became available again and new texts were published, many of which became best-sellers.

Meanwhile, the curators of art galleries who had previously only hung 'old masters' began to re-evaluate the work of their female contemporaries. Welsh painter Gwen John became valued above her brother Augustus John, while in Ireland, there was appropriate recognition for her early to mid-twentieth-century peers Mainie Jellett and Evie Hone.[2] This rediscovery of the past in art and literature did not come at the expense of the present: women-only prizes such as the Women's Prize for Fiction were founded to support new work, and the scholarship that underpinned the rediscoveries extended into studies of living artists. When Germaine Greer published *The Obstacle Race* in 1979, she was ostensibly dealing only with women artists up to the mid-twentieth century, but she used her analysis of the problems that women artists had encountered to illuminate the issues still facing her contemporaries.[3]

In music, the scholars who began in the 1970s to unearth 'forgotten' women composers were mainly based in the United States. They were diligent musicologists, inspired by the American women's movement of second-wave feminism, who sought to redress the balance of the representation, in the curriculum at least, of male and female musicians. Through their work, the ubiquitous *Source Readings in Music History*, which relate only to the work of male composers, became balanced by the availability of texts such as Carol Neuls-Bates's *Women in Music Source Readings* (1982).[4] For the first time, we could read letters from Francesca Caccini that give a vivid picture of a composer at work, and extracts from the diaries of Fanny Hensel and Clara Schumann.

Since those early days of the 'new musicology' there has been an exponential growth in scholarship enabling us to find out all about women composers, past and present. It is no longer 'new' or 'news'. What has been achieved? How much of this music has been established in the repertoire so that we are familiar with it? Hildegard of Bingen seems to have regained her rightful place. But how easy is it, for example, for singers to obtain lieder by German composers such as Corona Schröter, Louise Reichardt, Emilie Zumsteeg or Fanny Hensel? Take the fine symphonic poem *Irlande* by Augusta Holmès: is that familiar to the audiences who appreciate comparable music of that era by César Franck

2 Jellett's *A Composition* is the cover image of this volume.

3 Germaine Greer, *The Obstacle Race: The Fortunes of Women Painters and Their Works* (New York, 1979).

4 Oliver Strunk, *Source Readings in Music History* (London, 1952); Carol Neuls-Bates, *Women in Music: An Anthology of Source Readings from the Middle Ages to the Present* (New York, 1982).

and Camille Saint-Saëns? There was a programmed dedicated to Holmès on Lyric FM a few years ago, but how well known has *Irlande* become?[5]

Music exists to be performed, to be heard. So, easy access to performing materials is a priority. The advent of digital music processing has made life much easier for today's composer. She can make her own copy and distribute it in print or online. Some composers are very entrepreneurial; some are very good at self-promotion and harness the power of new technology to that end. Others are by nature more self-effacing and only become noticed if, perhaps, a well-known performer champions their work, or a prize in a competition leads to further performances. That is a traditional way of establishing a career and many composers still aspire to that route.[6] They hope to secure a contract with a major publisher, with thc promotional power to obtain them plenty of commissions. Yet music publishers are a dying breed, their livelihood threatened by the free availability of music online.

When I look ahead half a century, I speculate as to whether the commonly accepted notion of a musical canon will have been dissolved or whether the instant availability of music online will have intensified it? In fifty years, what will be known of such fine composers as Gráinne Mulvey, Deirdre Gribben, Jennifer Walshe, Judith Ring? Will they be household names? And if so, will that come about through being established in a canonic repertoire, via concert halls and broadcasting? Or will they become established primarily through online presence?

Each chapter in this volume highlights the work of remarkable women who should not have been forgotten or marginalised. What can we learn that will help ensure the present generation of Irish composers do not follow the same path? Let us explore the work of one composer as a case study of music history and representation in the past fifty years: Ina Boyle

5 'Women of Note' episode on Augusta Holmès, *The Lyric Feature*, Lyric FM, 7 September 2012.

6 In the last two decades, many Irish composers have developed their careers through formal associations with artistic organisations. Elaine Agnew was appointed the inaugural RTÉ Lyric FM Composer in Residence in 2008. She was succeeded by Linda Buckley in 2011 and Sebastian Adams in 2016. Composers have also been appointed to prestigious international residencies: e.g. Jennifer Walshe was appointed to a DAAD Artist-in-Berlin residency (2005); Amanda Feery was hosted by the Centre Culturel Irlandais, Paris (2019); Ann Cleare received the Ernst von Siemens Music Foundation Composers' Prize (2019). The founding of Irish National Opera (INO) in 2018 has created more opportunities to commission Ireland-based composers, e.g. Evangelia Rigaki's installation opera *This Hostel Life* premiered in 2019; Feery's *A Thing I Cannot Name*, filmed in June 2021, streamed as part of the West Cork Literary Festival in July 2021; Finola Merrivale's 'virtual reality community opera' *Out of the Ordinary* will be presented in locations around the country in 2022. See <https://www.irishnationalopera.ie/whats-on/current-upcoming-productions> [accessed 2 July 2021].

(1889–1967). She was little known in her lifetime; and from her death in 1967 until *c.*2010 her music was virtually never performed. Now, there is a steady stream of performances and broadcasts in Dublin, Belfast, London and further afield in the United States and Canada. How has this come about? Much of the credit must go to a group of dedicated scholars and performers who have invested substantial time and energy in researching and promoting Boyle's work.[7] They have lobbied performers and broadcasters; their fundraising campaigns have had major impact.[8]

What were the reasons for the neglect of her work, in her lifetime and ever since? Apart from infrequent visits to London for composition lessons with Vaughan Williams she lived in seclusion in the family home, Bushey Park, Enniskerry, Co. Wicklow. Her friend Elizabeth Maconchy wrote: 'But living out of the world, though it suited her temperamentally, had the disadvantage that she made very few musical contacts and that her music remained little known and unperformed.'[9] Boyle was not the only Irish woman composer of the twentieth century whose work has been neglected, but she was certainly one of the most prolific. Over sixty years she produced a steady stream of orchestral, choral and vocal compositions, three symphonies, a violin concerto, an opera, ballet music, most of which was never performed during her lifetime. She produced her scores to professional standards, kept in touch with performers, and stayed abreast of new musical idioms, even though she did not adopt them. Although retiring by nature, she was tireless in promoting her music and circulating scores to conductors, choir directors, performers

7 Key figures in the promotion of Boyle's music include: Katie Rowan, relative of the Boyle family; Roy Stanley, TCD Music Librarian; Jonathan Grimes, Head of Information CMC; Kerry Houston, Director of the Research Foundation for Music in Ireland; Ita Beausang, co-author of *Ina Boyle 1889–1967: A Composer's Life* (Cork, 2018); Aylish Kerrigan, mezzo-soprano; and individuals who have edited her scores. Edited works include: String Quartet in E Minor, *Still Falls the Rain* and *No Coward Soul is Mine* (ed. David Byers); 'Glencree' Symphony (ed. Sarah Burn, with funds from the Ambache Trust); *A Sea Poem* and Violin Concerto (ed. Colin Clout); *Elegy* and *Psalm* (ed. Emma O'Keeffe); various songs (eds Orla Shannon, Iain Burnside, David Scott, David Rhodes, Roy Holmes). Most of the information on Boyle here is sourced from the Beausang and de Barra book.

8 In 2017 Katie Rowan's crowdfunder campaign generated funds to support the first commercial recording of Boyle's orchestral works. Recorded by the BBC Concert Orchestra, conducted by Ronald Corp, and featuring the soloists Benjamin Baker (violin) and Nadège Rochat (cello), the CD was released by Dutton Vocalion in 2018. See <https://www.crowdfunder.co.uk/discovering-ina-boyle> [accessed 2 July 2021]. The CD *Ina Boyle Songs* (Delphian, 2021) was recorded in the Wigmore Hall by Iain Burnside (piano), with singers Paula Murrihy, Robin Tritschler and Ben McAteer.

9 Elizabeth Maconchy *Ina Boyle: An Appreciation, with a Select List of her Music* (Dublin, 1974), p. 3.

and publishers. She even financed the publication of a few of her choral works.[10] She did not seek anonymity or relish her lack of recognition: she said of the performance of her oratorio *Soldiers at Peace* that it was the happiest evening of her life. Was the neglect due to location or domestic duties? That too played a part. She was the daughter of elderly parents, responsible for their care and running the household. Nowadays, Bushey Park, in Enniskerry, Co. Wicklow looks like a classic Georgian 'big house' as it has been beautifully restored, but in Boyle's day it was dilapidated, with no money for repairs.

There is no doubt that the Second World War severely affected her life. It curtailed her visits to London at an important stage in her career and severed many musical and social connections. When the war ended, she was a middle-aged woman from another era. Sombre texts and archaic themes did not appeal to the post-war generation. After her death, the handwritten scores were presented to the Manuscripts and Archives Research Library, Trinity College Dublin, where researchers and performers may access them, but many scores and parts have yet to be typeset and edited for performance.

These reasons for neglect – politics, fashion, location – bedevil all composers but they can impact particularly on women, as has been well documented. Another phenomenon must be kept in mind. A glance at the history of women's activities in music shows cyclic patterns of recognition and neglect. For example, in London in 1911, the Society of Women Musicians was founded. By then, women had been permitted access to conservatoire training across Europe for one or two generations, yet they were not gaining a foothold in the profession. Just over sixty years later, the society closed, believing that their objectives had been met. At the time, I would have agreed; my female contemporaries and I had marvellous opportunities throughout the 1960s and 1970s. Yet a mere fifteen years on, we realised that the next generation were not having the same recognition as we enjoyed. In 1987, a London festival celebrating women composers was called *The Hidden Sounds* because music by women had all but vanished from concert programmes. Following the festival a new campaigning organisation was formed, Women in Music (WiM), whose members represent a range of genres: classical, film, jazz, folk and popular music.[11]

The dates of these organisations are revealing: 1911, the height of the English campaign for women's suffrage; 1987, when Thatcher and her Conservative government were rolling back the social reforms of the

10 For example, Boyle paid £11 7s to Novello to publish the vocal score of *Soldiers at Peace* (1916); she also financed the Oxford University Press publication of *Thinke Then My Soul* (1938).

11 For more on WiM, see <http://www.womeninmusic.org.uk/history.htm> [accessed 1 July 2021].

1960s. I used to have a wall chart with the names of women composers from the time of Hildegard to the present. It demonstrated graphically the link between times offering women opportunities for achievement and blank eras when, like 'Trespassers will be prosecuted', women were unwelcome as music makers. The chart was a visual guide to the shifting customs and practices of European dynasties. It was easier to be an Italian female composer in the seventeenth century than in the eighteenth century. For highly trained women musicians in nineteenth-century Europe, it was more acceptable to be a performer than a composer. The recognition earned by Irish and English female novelists from the late eighteenth century could not have been dreamt of by their musical contemporaries.

The link between women's achievements in music and their social and economic status is clear. Progress made in gender equality makes it hard to believe that recent years would show serious remaining problems. However, the composer Jennifer Fowler has analysed the programmes of the annual BBC Proms from 1989 to 2010 and the statistics are dreadful. Of the sixty or so concerts each year within this period, it was rare that more than one woman appeared as a conductor, or that among roughly twenty-five living composers featured annually more than one was a woman.[12] In 1996 and 2006, there were no women composers programmed at all. Since 2010 there has been improvement, with increased representation of women composers and conductors.[13]

The only country I know where statistics show a better deal for women composers is New Zealand. Women there have achieved high office in many fields, holding posts such as Governor General, Prime Minister, Chief Justice and Arts Council Director, and women in that country were the first in the world to win the right to vote. I am sure there is a correlation between this more balanced culture and the success in Australasia of scholar Jenny Macleod, composer Eve de Castro-Robinson, and one of New Zealand's inaugural Artist Laureates, the composer Gillian Whitehead.

Right now, in both Ireland and England, there are many women composers of all ages whose music is being widely performed. The advent of so many young women arriving on the scene and achieving a high profile might make it look as though there is no longer any need to campaign for a better deal for women. I disagree: this positive cycle could pass. I think we need to work at breaking the cyclic pattern. Everyone can make a difference by how they approach their programming and performances; for example, look at the work of Jane O'Leary. She founded and

12 For statistics, see <http://www.womeninmusic.org.uk/proms10.htm> [accessed 1 July 2021].

13 Notably, Marin Alsop was the first woman to conduct the Last Night of the Proms, in 2013.

directs the Concorde Contemporary Music Ensemble, which has always been even-handed in its choice of composers. O'Leary and Concorde have helped develop the careers of so many of Ireland's composers, as well as introducing Irish audiences to work from overseas. Think too of what the Contemporary Music Centre has achieved with the production and distribution of CDs, which from the first featured women prominently.

Nowadays, women musicians have every chance to receive advanced training. (See Beausang, Chapter 1, this volume, regarding recent compositional and conducting opportunities.) Yet there are still talented young women who are afraid to take an authoritative role as conductor or composer. I am disheartened by how few young women come to the Irish composition summer school each year, since there is no lack of role models for them: Ireland has such a high tally of fine women composers. We cannot take for granted that the works of today's successful women will be remembered. At the outset of *The Obstacle Race*, Greer points out how a 1976 exhibition of women artists was hailed as a pioneering event – yet a similar event had occurred seventy years earlier, in 1906, from which most of the work was lost and forgotten.

In the twenty-first century, we still live in an age of transition. Each of us needs to give the women of the coming generations the confidence to succeed in their musical careers. We need to lobby musical establishments on their behalf; we need to be alert to what happens when composers are no longer glamorous young things. We need to be supportive of the new ways that composers' careers may develop through unfamiliar avenues. If the progress of the last fifty years is not to be wasted, then all of us, as musicians, teachers, researchers and listeners must champion the music being composed by women in Ireland. We must make sure it is heard, and break the cycle of neglect, forever.

Select recordings of composers mentioned are listed in the Recording and Broadcast Media sections of the Bibliography.

13

Transcending Conventional Habits: Music and the Collaborative Process in Joint Works

Rhona Clarke

This chapter develops ideas first presented at the Women in Music in Ireland conference in 2012. It focuses on the collaborative process, which forms part of my own compositional practice with reference to my works for installation in art galleries. The process of realising joint works with visual artist Marie Hanlon is discussed here; the chapter teases out the differences between this and the more solitary approach usually required in writing for a concert audience, with or without a visual element. After an initial overview of the collaboration and its origins, there follows a more detailed consideration of three works composed in 2014: *Everything we see…*, an installation based on a painting by René Magritte; *The Small Hours*, a piece for live accordion with video; and *Cornerspace*, a video with sound. I attempt to ascertain how the relationship between the sound and the visual elements evolved and developed; I also wish to examine the interdependence between the two disciplines. Finally, the question is broached as to whether this collaborative experience has informed my current practice in writing abstract concert music.

Overview of the Collaboration

Having discussed for many years the possibility of working together, visual artist Marie Hanlon and I started our first collaborative piece in 2009. Several years later, our most recent joint work, *Behind Closed Doors* (2016), for seven percussion players with accompanying video, was premiered by a Royal Irish Academy of Music ensemble, directed by Richard O'Donnell, at Tambourimba Percussion Festival Cali, Colombia on 24 June 2016.

The impetus for our first project began with a call for proposals from the Contemporary Music Centre and the Galway Music Residency's Ensemble in Residence, the RTÉ ConTempo Quartet. The awarding of this commission marked the beginning of our collaboration. It involved the composition of a piece with an accompanying visual slideshow. Titled *Pas de Quatre*, the work was premiered at Solstice Arts Centre, Navan, Co. Meath in 2009. Later that year we produced our second joint work; this was a short film based on the Burren landscape of north Co. Clare, entitled *Relic*. The piece was shown at the Burren College Art Gallery and formed part of what developed into our first collaborative exhibition. In addition to the film, we combined three short sound works with a set of drawings. The audio was accessed via headphones placed on listening posts adjacent to the wall display. These sound pieces grew out of percussion sound samples captured during two sessions with Richard O'Donnell and were gathered initially with only the film work in mind; the potential for expanding the work into a full exhibition suggested itself as we went along. Titled *Between the Lines*, this exhibition was presented by the gallery as the Burren Annual 2011. The edited samples became the main sound material and to a large extent determined the outcome of the music. Deciding which samples were chosen and how they should be manipulated and combined was what constituted the act of composing in this instance. However, the first decision in creating the work was a jointly agreed one: that the music would consist of percussion sounds that we both felt were expressive of the rocky Burren terrain and appropiate to the visual material. Although for the most part we worked on the separate disciplines independently, there are correlations between the sound and visual elements. For instance, the drawings are monochromatic – black and white, while the similarly reductive sound work concentrates on the timbral elements of skins, metal or wood.

In our second joint exhibition *DIC TAT*, shown at Draíocht Centre for the Arts, Dublin (2014), a metronome acted as an impetus for the creation of line drawings and of sound works. A video titled 'Dic-Tat' formed one of the elements of the exhibition. Presented as a synchronised video on two monitors, one monitor showed a metronome playing a sequence of beats from slow to fast, while the other screened a hand drawing in real time at the dictate of the given beat. The immediacy and simplicity of the resulting drawings inspired short sound pieces, also linear in nature, which were installed in pairs at three separate listening posts. The six pieces emerged from the idea of working with or against a regular pulse. 'Canon', 'Forethought' and 'Afterthought' started as improvisations that I created via a controller keyboard, to click tracks of different tempi, inputted to a sequencing programme. These are short, impulsive pieces, each lasting no longer than three minutes, produced at speed and without the necessity of painstaking, time-consuming notation. The resulting improvisations were then further developed to form a more coherent structure. Using the digital audio workstation Pro Tools, virtual instruments were selected. For example, 'Forethought' uses a virtual grand piano – probably the most conventional timbral choice. While virtual instruments seem to me perfectly acceptable for sound installations, this is not an option I would choose for a concert hall situation as a substitute for real, acoustic instruments. Virtual instruments, played back via sequencing software, have quite a mechanical sound. This is partly because they lack the sympathetic tones created from the harmonic series common to all acoustic instruments. In 'Forethought', the mechanical quality was intentional as it was in keeping with the idea of exact, regular pulse. Several of the short pieces layer different sounds to form a collage. In the piece called 'Stiletto', metronome samples mirror Hanlon's video 'Dic-Tat'. Tongue-clicks in the foreground alternate with wood-block sounds in the background, using spacial distance between the samples. Electronic sounds taken from the software are also featured in the piece. The method is one of selection and placing of material, but also of 'drawing' with sound.

In most cases, improvisation is the starting point in our individual practices; however, in this project, where we both consciously tried to counter learnt and accustomed processes, spontaneity and improvisation assumed greater importance and became central to our ways of working. There is no doubt, though, that the material resulting from this improvisation emerges consciously or unconsciously from learnt and practised techniques. In discussing this 'moment to moment non-stop flow' Stephen Nachmanovic says:

> When we are totally faithful to our own individuality, we are actually following a very intricate design [...] We carry around the rules inherent in our organism, as living, patterned beings, we are incapable of producing anything random [...] In our playing, drawing or dancing, the inner, unconscious logic of our being unfolds and begins to mould the material.[1]

With this in mind, it is not surprising that in her essay on Hanlon's work, having discussed *DIC TAT* as 'a new departure', Rowan Sexton notes that: 'Paradoxically, these new pieces have an aesthetic affinity congruent with Hanlon's established works.'[2] The same could be said of these six electronic pieces in relation to my own previous works, including those composed for acoustic instruments; although the process of producing them is different, there is a continuum. Essentially, we always make work

1 S. Nachmanovich, *Free Play: Improvisation in Life and Arts* (New York, 1990), pp. 19, 23.

2 Rowan Sexton, 'tête-à-tête' <https://www.mariehanlon.com/words/tete-a-tete/> [11 July 2022].

out of who we are and out of our cumulative experiences; this claim is borne out by research in psychology and music. In his article 'Pedagogical Applications of Cognitive Research on Musical Improvisation', Michele Biasutti states that: 'improvisation is a complex, multidimensional act that involves creative and performance behaviours in real-time in addition to processes such as sensory and perceptual encoding, motor control, performance monitoring, and memory storage and recall'.[3]

I should perhaps at this stage explain what I mean by my 'conventional' creative habits. Apart from a few works using electronic processes from the early 1990s and prior to the collaborations with Hanlon, my compositions normally started with a musical idea or ideas, which were notated and then developed. Even where an initial impetus arose through improvisation, either vocally or at the piano, its continuation was, and indeed still is, slowed down by the process of notation, the standard means of registering music as a score. Conventions, such as motivic development, pitch relationships, imitation and every kind of learnt technique are drawn upon consciously in order to develop the musical material. This may result in music that is successfully achieved and pleasing to hear, but it can also produce music that feels stilted or conservative; that initial energy and enthusiasm is so easily lost through the laborious demands of notation. Thinking back to the very first work I composed using analogue tape techniques, *Whaling Afloat and Ashore* made in 1990 to accompany a short silent film, the physical processes involved were akin to those of children at play or to that of an experienced cook combining ingredients for a delicious dessert. I gathered material, recorded samples, selected existing samples from a sound generator and built sounds from a sinewave base; intuition guided the construction.

Three Works Composed in 2014

The three works I wish to consider in more detail here all date from 2014. In the course of producing each, the dialogue between aural and visual elements was worked out in different ways. With *Cornerspace* the visuals came first, or did they? Some of the music featured in the final creation was, in fact, adapted from an existing piece, but essentially the set of photographic stills had been selected and organised into a moving sequence before I even thought about the music. For *The Small Hours*, after initial discussion, it was agreed that the music would be composed first, with the visual part following, based on the music. But with both works, as with other joint projects, no element is finished until everything is

3 Michele Biasutti, 'Pedagogical Applications of Cognitive Research on Musical Improvisation', *Frontiers in Psychology*, 6 (2015) <https://www.frontiersin.org/articles/10.3389/fpsyg.2015.00614/full> [accessed 22 August 2017].

finished. Visual and sound worlds are tweaked and edited with each of us having an input into the whole work.

Everything we see... is an installation with sound, first shown at Solstice Arts Centre, Navan in 2014. The new work was inspired by René Magritte's surrealist painting *The Month of the Grape Harvest* (1959). In the painting a group of bowler-hatted men stand outside an open window. Massed together and uniformly dressed, they gaze into an empty room. In our work, Hanlon and I transform this group into a virtual choir, which, to the sound of a pre-recorded choral background, speaks Magritte's own words. The text draws on quotations from a radio interview in 1965 with Jean Neyens, in which Magritte discusses another of his paintings, *The Son of Man*:[4]

> At least it hides the face partly well, so you have the apparent face, the apple, hiding the visible but hidden, the face of the person. It's something that happens constantly. Everything we see hides another thing, we always want to see what is hidden by what we see. There is an interest in that which is hidden and which the visible does not show us. This interest can take the form of a quite intense feeling, a sort of conflict, one might say, between the visible that is hidden and the visible that is present.[5]

In *The Month of the Grape Harvest*, a certain dichotomy arises through the conflicting ways in which the painting might be read. The anonymous bowler-hatted men seem individually slight, passive, expressionless and unthreatening, yet as a massed group they assume a somewhat sinister aspect. Only two rows of figures are clearly visible; a third row is glimpsed, while the tips of further bowler hats give the impression of many more behind them. Our installation features a large double-sided window, opening on to what might be the outdoors, but in this case is the projection space, which shows a film of a bowler-hatted group. As in the painting, the figures stand outside looking into what is now the gallery space, i.e. the viewer's space (see Figure 13.1). Ambiguity is at the heart of the film in both its visual and sound elements. The choir is not a choir – these figures are not singing; everything seen and heard is called into question. Unlike in Magritte's painting, the bowler-hatted group in the installation comprised women as well as men. While some of the sounds are real, based on samples taken from a single female voice and a single male voice, others were generated using a virtual instrument. Electronics were not part of the original plan: we had applied for funding to employ a professional choir, who would sing a fully scored acoustic piece, the performance of which would be filmed. The funding application

4 *The Son of Man* (1964). In this later work, a prominent foreground figure stands in the centre of the picture with an apple partly hiding his face.

5 H. Torczyner, *Magritte: Ideas and Images* (New York, 1979), p. 172.

FIGURE 13.1: Installation shot of *Everything we see…* at Solstice Arts Centre, Navan. Photo credit: Marie Hanlon.

failed, rendering this option unviable, so we decided instead to make an electronic sound file using the resources at our disposal. At a later stage, student volunteers were filmed miming to the sound file under my direction. This phase led to some outcomes not envisaged initially, such as a deep male sound seeming to emanate from a female 'chorister' and the sound of words spoken by a figure not visible on screen, all of which add to the ambiguous nature of the piece. Although the idea for this work originated with Hanlon, at every stage there was collaboration in fleshing out the sound and visual elements.

The first concrete step in the creative process was to gather sound samples, which were edited and sequenced using Pro Tools. Essentially, I worked on the music alone, but Hanlon listened in and provided feedback at various stages. Together we purchased items for the costumes (shirts, ties and bowler hats) and borrowed overcoats for the 'choir'. Hanlon constructed and painted the set for the installation, comprising an open window with shutters. She also painted the backdrop used for the film of the 'choir', a group of student volunteers. There were two rehearsals with the students, which I directed, instructing them to mime to the sound file, alternately as soloists and as a group. The 'performance' was then filmed by a professional camera operator with both Hanlon and me acting as co-directors. The sound file was then applied to the film using Final Cut Pro, with both elements (sound and film) edited separately before the final version was agreed. Installing the work at Solstice in Navan involved Hanlon working closely with the venue's technician, with my role at this point limited to sound checks.

Had the funding materialised, the musical outcome would have been completely different; furthermore, a mature professional choir would have produced a very different 'look' for the installation. Yet there were unpredictable advantages in realising the project as we did; for instance, the young faces of the students dressed in costume conveyed a sense of strangeness and intrigue, matched by the haunting nature of the electronic vocal sound.

The Small Hours (2014), a work for music with video, was commissioned by the contemporary music ensemble Concorde for their *Up Close with Music* series. Premiered at the Royal Hibernian Academy (RHA) Gallery, Dublin, a subsequent performance took place later in 2014 at Dublin City Gallery, The Hugh Lane. In discussing the commission, Hanlon and I initially decided on a fast, energetic work based on the tango, but then produced something very different in character. Only one decision made at that early stage remained in place: a solo accordion as our instrument of choice. The music was composed first in the conventional manner, using notation software to produce the score. At various stages of the composition, MIDI sound file versions were sent to Hanlon to assist the collaboration. Initially her approval was sought for the slow, sutained cluster-chords that first emerged and on which the music is mostly based. The visual images of interiors both real and contrived from studio props, although filmed in colour, are projected as black and white. Strong contrasts of light and dark, together with an underlying geometry, give the video a formal coherence. A sense of searching pervades the imagery, its fragmented sequences requiring the viewer to find points of connection. This mirrors the sections in the musical structure, which begins using the treble register and follows with a section of low bass clusters. Eventually the piece soars to the highest notes of the instrument, with some abrupt gestures providing necessary bursts of energy towards the end. In my mind, the use of these different registers generates a defined linear shape, such that the structure of the piece has affinities with a visual motif. The title, given when the work was completed, denotes a time associated with the hours before dawn; 'the small hours', can also refer to the daydreaming of our waking hours, those moments when the mind is free of immediate and urgent concerns and wanders, making new connections, associations and discoveries. At such moments, the mind can piece together disparate things to find solutions that previously eluded it, or it can simply find some respite from the constant demands of consciousness.

In the final 2014 work to be discussed, *Cornerspace*, the visual element is slow paced and the imagery spare with each frame dissolving into the next. Once again, perception and deception are central concerns of the piece. Images of corners and corner spaces mix fictitious constructs, made of studio props, with real places. Scale is skewed, uncertainty abounds; there is a constant interplay between spatial illusion, shape, colour and light. Electronic sounds help to engage the visual imagination, prompting the viewer to make connections between images, perhaps at times even suggesting that which is not visible. What is suggested is as much part of the piece as that which is perceptible. The sounds were selected and developed on the basis of their ability to create texture, space and mystery; to some extent, too, they narrate the visual aspect. These were derived from a short electronic work I had originally composed for the exhibition *Between the Lines*, but not used then. That work lent itself to adaptation and development for this project, as it seemed to suit the defined lines of the corners and the idea of echo. The music mirrors the way the visuals are paced, moving slowly, leaving space for associations to surface. While working on the music, at least as many sounds were deleted as exist in the final version.

So, how has collaboration with Hanlon – a process that began in 2009 – affected my compositions, when film or pictorial elements are not involved? Though difficult to state objectively whether it has impacted the music itself, there is no doubt that the collaboration has affected how I approach the process of composition; furthermore, it is the reason for my return to using electronic methods. This effect on my compositional process is borne out in certain works, as the following discussion shows.

Con coro (2011), for violin, cello and tape, was a commission from Concorde for their *Up Close with Music* series of concerts performed in gallery spaces. The commission brief asked that the space itself, in this case the Rubicon Gallery in Dublin, exert some influence on the outcome. In order to negate the surrounding visual and to 'blur' some of the sound expectations, especially as the pre-recorded element contained adapted cello samples amongst other sounds, I suggested that the audience should be blindfolded or at least offered blindfolds. It might seem that the act of closing one's eyes would achieve the same effect, but this was not so. The blindfolds negated the visual, in favour of heightening other senses without the distracting effect of maintaining closed eyes. In photos taken at the first performance, the audience with black blindfolds added a surreal visual dimension, appropriate to the gallery setting. The choice of pre-recorded tape was a very definite outcome of the return to using electronic processes, which had been set in train by the collaboration.

In composing *SHIFT* (2013), commissioned by the RTÉ National Symphony Orchestra, certain sections in which percussion instruments dominate were realised by improvising into a sequencer via a controller keyboard (using a virtual instrument) and then by modifying and developing the result to produce a score. Here, too, the influence of the previous collaborations is apparent. In a later work, *smiling like that...* (2016), composed for mezzo soprano Aylish Kerrigan with tape, the live vocal part was derived from my own improvisation above the pre-recorded element, an improvisation that I then developed and notated. Finally, *A Different Game*, Piano Trio No. 4 (2016), uses the short sound work 'Forethought', mentioned earlier, as the basis for its third movement, where the original material remains in the piano, and lines for violin and cello are created as a kind of duet above this.

Conclusion

These examples demonstrate that the collaborative process of working with a visual artist has had some effect on my approach to writing works for a concert audience; that effect is evident in at least one such work, *SHIFT*, which was composed solely for acoustic instruments. As to the music itself, although it is beyond the scope of this chapter to appraise the compositions, there is perhaps something bolder and more visceral about works such as *A Different Game* and *smiling like that...* Is this due to the collaborations or is it a matter of becoming older, more experienced and more free? I believe that many factors combine to achieve this seemingly new departure.

14

Surveying the Scene: Current Thoughts on Women and Electroacoustic Music in Ireland

Barbara Jillian Dignam

To be a woman composer of electroacoustic music is to straddle two worlds, both gendered male.[1]

Background

At the 2010 Women and Music in Ireland conference, I presented a paper on women and electroacoustic music, a topic rarely discussed by musicologists at the time. This was unsurprising given that the term 'electroacoustic' was neither frequently employed in mainstream musicological discourse, nor was its definition clear.[2] However, while this explains why most of the literature on the subject has been produced by composers, it does not elucidate why the contributions of women have been largely overlooked.[3] Recent research by female musicians has

1 Andra McCartney, 'Inventing Images and Contesting Gender in Thinking about Electroacoustic Music', *Leonardo Music Journal*, 5 (1995), 57–66, at p. 57.

2 This study considers 'electroacoustic' in its broadest sense, encompassing creative output that moves beyond purely acoustic forces, thereby utilising some electronic means for its generation, production and/or performance. It includes sound art that is not formally defined as 'electroacoustic', but may employ electroacoustic techniques or practices.

3 One only need consider a small selection of well-known literature on electroacoustic music to see consistency of male authors/editors, for example: Simon Emmerson and Denis Smalley, 'Electro-Acoustic Music' in Grove Music Online <http://www.oxfordmusiconline.com>; Thom Holmes, *Electronic and Experimental Music: Pioneers in Technology and Composition*, 6th edn (London, 2020); Simon Emmerson and Leigh Landy (eds), *Expanding the Horizon of Electroacoustic Music Analysis* (Cambridge, 2016); Peter Manning, *Electronic and Computer Music*, 4th edn (Oxford, 2013); Leigh Landy, *Understanding the Art of Sound Organization* (Cambridge, Mass., 2007); Timothy D. Taylor, *Strange Sounds: Music, Technology & Culture* (New York, 2001); Simon Emmerson, *The Language of Electroacoustic Music* (New York, 1986). A more balanced example

attempted to close this gap, supported by online communities (Audible Women, Female:Pressure, DONNE, Women in Music) providing promotion opportunities, networking databases and a digital encyclopaedia of European living women in music.[4] In Ireland, efforts to encourage balanced discourse around women in contemporary music have been re-energised since the launch of the advocacy collective Sounding the Feminists in 2017.[5] Yet, little concentrated research exists on women's creative practices in the electroacoustic arena, with the notable exception of several texts on Jennifer Walshe, who has garnered much international attention owing to her innovative auteur-inspired aesthetic.[6] It seems timely, then, to resurvey the scene, placing the genre in context and reviewing the current status of women in electroacoustic music in Ireland as evidenced through the opinions and experiences of creative artists.[7] Various issues are considered and suggestions for the future presented.

---

is Nick Collins and Julio d'Escriván (eds), *The Cambridge Companion to Electronic Music*, 2nd edn (Cambridge, 2017); here, five of the fifteen chapters are authored by women composers, and one co-authored.

4 Examples include: Christine Eyene (ed.), *Sounds Like Her: Gender, Sound Art & Sonic Cultures* (Nottingham, 2019); Tara Rodgers, *Pink Noises: Women on Electronic Music and Sound* (London, 2010); Andra McCartney, 'Gender, Genre, and Electroacoustic Soundmaking Practices', *Intersections Canadian Journal of Music*, 26 (2006), 20–48; Elizabeth Hinkle-Turner, *Women Composers and Music Technology in the United States: Crossing the Line* (Abingdon, 2006); Helen Metzelaar, '"Women and 'Kraakgeluiden": The Participation of Women Improvisers in the Dutch Electronic Music Scene', *Organised Sound*, 9 (2004), 199–206. Also see <https://www.audiblewomen.com/>; <http://www.female-pressure.net/>; <https://donne-uk.org/> [accessed 11 July 2022]; and the recent documentary by Lisa Rovner, *Sisters with Transistors*, narrated by Laurie Anderson (Modern Films UK, 2020).

5 For more on Sounding the Feminists, see <https://www.soundingthefeminists.com/> [accessed 11 July 2022].

6 For example: Franziska Kloos, *Jennifer Walshe: Spiel mit Indentitäten* (Hofheim, 2017); James Saunders, 'Interview with Jennifer Walshe', in James Saunders (ed.), *The Ashgate Research Companion to Experimental Music* (London, 2017), pp. 343–51; Barbara Jillian Dignam, 'Chasing Sonic Threads: Disentangling the Electroacoustic Tapestry of Ireland', *TEMPO*, 71: 281 (2017), 5–26; Max Erwin, 'Wet Hot Kranichstein Summer: Darmstadt 2016', *TEMPO*, 71: 279 (2017) 87–91; Lauren Redhead, '"New Music" as Patriarchal Category', in Catherine Haworth and Lisa Colton (eds), *Gender, Age and Musical Creativity* (Abingdon, 2015) pp. 171–84.

7 This study has constraints stemming from limited data on gender denominations, namely 'male' and 'female', as per pronouns interpreted from research sources; no data on non-binary or other genders was supplied by, or obtainable from, any source at the time of conducting this study, with the exception of one non-binary designation found on a composer's personal webpage.

The Irish Electroacoustic Context

In 2003, Paschall de Paor concluded his discussion of the early development of electroacoustic music in Ireland thus:

> From slow and gradual beginnings, this genre is currently enjoying an energetic developmental period. Many international fora now recognise the work of our composers and researchers, and, given current educational initiatives, the future is promising.[8]

His positivity was not unfounded: Ireland was flourishing amid the Celtic Tiger years; government spending on education, art and culture was high and many technology-driven programmes were in receipt of support from the European Union. De Paor notes that electroacoustic music proper emerged relatively late despite early explorations on par with international developments; he posits that, had Brian Boydell – the pre-eminent advocate for new music in Ireland, who undertook early experiments with tape recorders *c*.1950 – considered electroacoustic music a legitimate musical genre, as opposed to a 'fascinating game', Ireland may well have made its mark sooner.[9] De Paor traces historical developments beginning with Gerard Victory's *The Orphans* (1957, electronic effects), concluding with a historical timeline of works up to 1989.[10] Nevertheless, he fails to make any reference to women. A cursory exploration of the archive of the Contemporary Music Centre (CMC) uncovers an early work by Bernadette Comac (*b*.1960): *A Homage to Mary* for voice, mixed choir and live electronics (1989). Comac's omission from the timeline is puzzling, considering that she was arguably as established in the discipline as her male peer Fergus Johnston, whose Study No. 1 for electronics (1989) is included. If indeed, as de Paor asserts, international fora were taking note, why did musicologists and others in Ireland not follow suit, especially with respect to the work of female electroacoustic composers?

However under-documented, the supposedly unique figure of the 'female' composer in Ireland remains as enigmatic today as it was in 1998 when Jane O'Leary asked: 'Why should the first question to a composer

8 Paschall de Paor, 'The Development of Electroacoustic Music in Ireland', in Gareth Cox and Axel Klein (eds), *Irish Music in the Twentieth Century* (Dublin, 2003), pp. 29–38, at p. 38. On later developments in electroacoustic music in Ireland, see Barbara Jillian Dignam, 'Electroacoustic Music', in Harry White and Barra Boydell (eds), *Encyclopaedia of Music in Ireland*, vol. 1 (Dublin, 2013) and Dignam, 'Chasing Sonic Threads'.

9 De Paor's quote from personal correspondence with Boydell, 'The Development of Electroacoustic Music in Ireland', p. 30.

10 Victory was commissioned to write *The Orphans* as the Irish entry for the Prix Italia (drama section) in 1957. For a recording, see the Prix Italia Archive <http://www.archive.prixitalia.rai.it/>.

on a panel discussion at an Irish festival of contemporary music be '"How does it feel to be a woman composer?"'[11] In her article 'Women Composers in Ireland: A Changing Profile' (1996), O'Leary describes Ireland as 'a small country with an exceptionally large reputation for some of its cultural representatives'.[12] She presents figures for female composers who were invited to become members of Aosdána alongside those represented by the CMC.[13] A revision of her initial exploration is found below, with the addition of figures for the Association of Irish Composers (AIC) and the Irish Composers Collective (ICC).[14]

The total membership of Aosdána currently stands at the maximum 250.[15] Musicians account for 13 per cent of the membership with thirty-two composers representing the discipline, only eight of whom are women. Until 1996, when Éibhlís Farrell was elected, O'Leary was the only woman, later joined by Rhona Clarke, Siobhán Cleary, Gráinne Mulvey, Elaine Agnew, Jennifer Walshe and, most recently, Linda Buckley in 2021. The 3:1 ratio in favour of male composers is approximately twice the ratio of men to women across all the artistic disciplines Aosdána represents. Music is thus the most gender-imbalanced discipline. Perhaps more significant is the breakdown of *cnuas* recipients, with 50 per cent of female composers currently receiving this supplementary income as opposed to 43 per cent of male composers. This speaks to the higher earning capabilities of men in composition, given that, to receive the annuity, artists must not earn more than €25,770 per year.

It is important to assess discipline-specific organisations to determine if gender disparities are indeed widespread. As the main body for contemporary art music composers in Ireland, the CMC has expanded its representation from eighty individuals in 1996 to more than three times that figure in 2021, presently representing 250 living composers.[16]

11 Jane O'Leary, 'Women Composers: Outside the Pale of Musical Civilisation', *The Irish Composer 1*, 'Essays on Contemporary Music' (1988) <http://aicnewmusicjournal.com/articles/archives-women-composers-outside-pale-musical-civilisation> [last accessed 10 June 2021].

12 Jane O'Leary, 'Women Composers in Ireland: A Changing Profile', *IAWM International Alliance for Women in Music Journal* (1996) <https://iawm.org/iawm-journal> [accessed 14 July 2018].

13 Aosdána, founded in 1981 and supported by the Arts Council, is an elite association of Irish artists.

14 For other analysis of gender make-ups of these organisations, see Mark Fitzgerald, 'Composing Equality', *Enclave Review*, 16, <http://enclavereview.org/composing-equality/> (2018). Also see Benjamin Dwyer, *Different Voices: Irish Music and Music in Ireland* (Hofheim, 2014).

15 Membership of Aosdána is by peer nomination and election, which takes place at the annual General Assembly. Figures correct as of January 2022. See <http://aosdana.artscouncil.ie/members/>.

16 With thanks to Susan Brodigan, library coordinator at the CMC, 24 May 2021. For a list of composers represented, see <https://www.cmc.ie/composers>.

Between 1996 and 2021, the percentage of female composers decreased from 25 per cent to 20 per cent, although the raw figures increased from twenty to fifty. While these statistics signal growth in the number of women composers, a glaring gender imbalance still exists, as illustrated by the male:female ratio of 4:1. These figures by no means deflect from the CMC's efforts to support and promote contemporary composers of all genders, emerging composers as well as more established artists.[17]

The AIC, as a 'democratic organisation' that aims to 'strengthen the voice of contemporary composers', makes clear its policy of positive discrimination, intending to programme a minimum of 30 per cent female composers. Progress to date is encouraging, with a 29.4 per cent representation at events reported in 2016.[18] Its membership gender ratio is 2.22:1, with the highest concentration of women out of the organisations discussed here (32 women; total membership 103). This may be explained partially by the AIC's position as the Irish delegate for the International Society for Contemporary Music (ISCM), which provides opportunities for performance at ISCM World Music Days and the soundSCAPE artist residency.[19] The ICC, a professional networking community, has the smallest membership of forty-nine, but is on a par with the AIC figures at 30.6 per cent women; in addition, three of the past eight ICC chairpersons were women, as is the current AIC chairperson.[20]

Initial consideration of these figures suggests a healthy landscape and it may be posited that any increase in composer numbers signals the evolution of a younger generation. This may be true; however, further inspection exposes widespread disparities that inevitably impact disproportionately on women, thereby limiting possibilities for emerging composers to gain a foothold in the discipline and restricting opportunities for more experienced artists to stand as creative role models.

17 The CMC does not request gender information from prospective applicants; composers voluntarily supply biographical detail for the website. For more on the CMC's events, *Amplify* podcast, and *new music::new Ireland* CD series, see <https://www.cmc.ie>.

18 Figure extracted from Fitzgerald, 'Composing Equality'. For more on AIC's mission statement and policies, see <http://www.composers.ie/about>. Curation of programmes is undertaken by the organisation itself.

19 The AIC is also partnered with the Irish Music Rights Organisation (IMRO), so can advocate for artists' rights, copyright, commission fees, etc. Figures have been calculated from pronouns provided on composer webpages and from CMC data.

20 With the exception of Aosdána, for each of the aforementioned organisations the individual composer must actively approach these bodies for membership. In the case of the CMC, AIC and ICC, composers submit applications, with the AIC and ICC also requiring members to contribute annual subscription fees. While membership of the CMC and AIC has steadily increased since 2010, the opposite is the case for the ICC with a drop of thirteen composer-members between 2018 and 2021. All figures correct as of June 2021.

2016 as Turning Point?

According to Gráinne Mulvey, 'The status of the female composer, while still highly regarded [...] by peers, seems to have changed globally, noticeably over the last decade [with] declining opportunities and outlets available to flourish, and the ongoing struggle to attain equality.'[21] The *Composing the Island* festival presented as part of Ireland's centenary year set out to celebrate Irish art music produced between 1916 and 2016. In the introductory pages of the programme brochure, Heather Humphreys, minister for regional development, rural affairs, arts and the Gaeltacht, described the festival as important 'not just historically, but also in terms of presenting the music of our time and telling us something about what to expect in the future'.[22] Unfortunately, as the programme was unveiled, it became apparent that the voices of women in contemporary music were marginalised compared to those of their male peers – a state of affairs that provoked renewed discussion around gender balance in new music programmes, funding processes and governance structures, in addition to the re-evaluation of the status of the living female composer in Ireland. A concert of piano music by female composers was bolted on to the original programme following objections to the gender imbalance. However welcome, this eleventh-hour gesture may be considered tokenistic appeasement. The festival offered no serious concentration on electroacoustic musics. In fact, a cautionary disclaimer concluded the piano concert press release: 'Please note the works by Karen Power, Anna Murray and Linda Buckley all feature electronics with piano.'[23] Audiences were denied an introduction to the works of emerging composers, many of whom work across media as a norm and will inevitably become the sonic artists shaping the future to which Humphreys referred. In planning for this future, the current environment demands critical reflection: what follows is a summation of composers' current thoughts around the main issues faced by women in new music in Ireland, including electroacoustic music. These findings and proposals to address the gender imbalance are based on survey responses.[24]

21 Gráinne Mulvey, composer survey correspondence with author, 29 August 2017.

22 Composing the Island festival brochure (2016) <https://issuu.com/rtenationalsymphonyorchestra/docs/composing_island_brochure_final_pri> [accessed 11 July 2022].

23 Concert press release, 27 July 2016. Jennifer Walshe was interviewed for a book published to coincide with the festival, yet her innovative music did not appear on the official programme; *becher* (2008) was added to the supplementary piano concert performed by Isabelle O'Connell on 21 September 2016. The book is Michael Dervan (ed.), *The Invisible Art: A Century of Music in Ireland 1916–2016* (Dublin, 2016).

24 Unless otherwise stated, all quoted material and references to responses are extracted from the 2017–18 survey.

Surveying the Scene

In preparing for the 2010 Women and Music in Ireland conference, I conducted a survey between 2009 and 2010, garnering information from female composers. The survey was not intended as an exhaustive national case study, yet it needed to accurately represent a cross-section of different generations of female artists. Selecting who to contact was determined by two criteria: authority, i.e. the extent to which electroacoustic music formed a significant part of a composer's output at the time of the survey; and compositional experience. Composers were thereby categorised as 'emerging' or 'established', with the latter split into mid-career and later-career. Contact was initiated with eleven composers, five of whom were classified as emerging, with the remaining six noted as established; 46 per cent of those contacted participated in the survey: two later-career composers, one mid-career and two from the emerging category.

To present a slightly broader analysis of composer experiences in the more recent electroacoustic and contemporary music context, without imposing scientifically controlled parameters relating to gender, the survey cohort was expanded in 2017–18 to account for the next generation of emerging and more established female composers alongside a limited number of male peers, utilising the same selection criteria. Survey participants from 2009 to 2010 were also contacted with the explicit intention of building upon their original responses. In total, twenty-three composers were invited to participate, seventeen women and six men. Nine female composers responded to the survey, four of whom had contributed to the first study, and five male composers; 71 per cent of participants were mid-career, with the remainder being later-career.

The updated survey featured questions on topics such as the status of the female composer in the Irish contemporary context; the reception of their creative output in Ireland and abroad over the decade up to 2017–18; and the provision of opportunities for (young) women to engage in music technology, sound art, digital medias, etc. More personal questions investigated whether composers had witnessed or experienced instances of gender bias, gender discrimination, gendered language or labelling involving women, and if such experiences impacted their or another composer's sense of creative identity. All participants received the same survey questions irrespective of gender. Some participant responses focused more on contemporary and/or experimental musics than explicitly electroacoustic output, but to request that composers compartmentalise experiences would have instigated a binary approach, not conducive to a fruitful discussion around gender balance. Responses speak to the condition of contemporary music in Ireland at the time of survey, which includes electroacoustic music as a subgenre. Given that all respondents utilise electroacoustic elements to varying extents, their comments are all relevant.

In the words of Karen Power, 'there clearly is an issue, it goes across all music'.[25] While all artists surveyed concur that Irish female composers are well-received nationally and internationally, some express doubt about how their professional status is valued in Ireland. For others, little has changed in attitudes and supports for the artistic practices of women in the discipline. Interestingly, differing opinions arise on the place of electroacoustic music. Comments expose persistent underlying issues around gender inequality in the art form.

In 2009, Mulvey was optimistic about the growing status of the female composer in Ireland, maintaining that women were 'equally on a par with their male counterparts', although she noted that fewer women were choosing composition as a career. More recently, she observed that women composers are becoming increasingly proactive in garnering opportunities for performances in and outside Ireland alongside participation in conferences, courses and residencies. That said, Judith Ring, Jane O'Leary and Karen Power maintain that acquiring opportunities to present work consistently proves problematic for women, especially, as Power states, for composers with unique voices working in more exploratory areas:

> In terms of female composers making groundbreaking work, it's very, very positive. What's not positive is that these females are not being appreciated at home. So, they're being performed and they're getting work outside of Ireland, and that's healthy. We're a very small country; but there should be at least some opportunities at home.[26]

Further to this, Mulvey expresses concern about the value ascribed to works, referring to an underrating of both the high standard and volume of music produced by women, advising that significant work remains to be done in promoting women's creative output. While Rhona Clarke acknowledges the continually low numbers of female composers in the profession, O'Leary asserts that improvements in educational opportunities have led to more professionally trained composers of both genders, attributing women's confident involvement in electroacoustic music to educational role models who have encouraged more women to pursue careers in composition. Educational opportunities have certainly improved with increased options for university study and independent institutions now providing professional practice-based courses.[27] Even so, consideration of cross-institutional figures reveals a worrying trend where enrolment numbers for female students on music technology and sonic arts programmes have remained low in recent years, with

25 Karen Power in conversation with the author, 8 September 2017.

26 Power in conversation with the author, 8 September 2017.

27 The latest offering is the MA in Experimental Sound Practice at University College Cork. See <https://www.ucc.ie/en/cke78/> [accessed 11 July 2022].

most female students discontinuing further study following their undergraduate degrees.[28] A national study is required to ascertain why women are not being enticed into electroacoustic music and creative technologies, and to question whether gender inequalities exist within educational programmes.[29]

Increased exposure to new technologies has had a positive impact on the status of the female composer working in the electroacoustic domain, as Cleary and Ring suggest. Cleary speaks of 'a new generation of very tech savvy composers', some of whom are particularly acclaimed for their use of technology. Bernadette Comac concurs, emphasising that women are quite comfortable in this field, 'lead[ing] from the front in many respects as [...] both the creators and performers of their own works'. Although Power believes that much of what happens in electroacoustic music in Ireland could be termed mainstream, driven internally by academic institutions, she acknowledges 'society's engagement with technology' as a positive step, where 'more artists are just getting their hands dirty even if they may not have the training'. She refers here to an emerging DIY aesthetic that aligns with international trends of the past decade, with pop-up events, improvisation groups, experimental music collectives, and intermedia festivals providing avenues for collaborative and creative expression.[30]

Kerry Hagan cites positive developments occurring in Irish sound art circles where women are 'more prevalent and successful', many frequently and directly engaging with gender in their work. *Sonic Vigil*, a sound art and free improvisation event hosted in Cork, and the *Sonic Dreams* festival curated by Sonic Arts Waterford, provide spaces and opportunities for Irish artists such as Katie O'Looney and Irene Murphy to present work and collaborate with international artists in more experimental sound art fields.[31] Successes aside, some female composers express the opinion that electroacoustic music continues to be marginalised within an already small-scale national art form. Rachel Ní Chuinn offers an interesting hypothesis for this esotericism where women have conceivably been forced to adapt to the limitations of their creative environment: 'There is a wealth of female composers working with

28 Of the forty-nine intakes of new students onto post-graduate programmes in music technology, computer music and creative arts between 2009 and 2016, 29 per cent did not include any female registrations.

29 A similar study was conducted in the UK by Born and Devine. See Georgina Born and Kyle Devine, 'Gender, Creativity and Education in Digital Musics and Sound Art', *Contemporary Music Review*, 35 (2016), 1–20.

30 For discussion of this new aesthetic, see Dignam, 'Chasing Sonic Threads'.

31 See <https://www.facebook.com/SonicVigil8/?ref=page_internal> and <https:/facebook.com/Sonic-Arts-Waterford-827639897318042/> [accessed 11 July 2022]. *Sonic Vigil* has particularly featured the works of Karen Power, Irene Murphy and Katie O'Looney.

electroacoustic music [...] perhaps because they have felt cut out from other forms of composition that require more resources [...] many of the opportunities women have are not well-funded or even well-respected.'

Coupled with this, as Clarke and Mulvey explain, electroacoustic performances tend to take place in smaller venues and are infrequently programmed at major festivals.[32] Such pieces are more often scored for smaller ensembles as opposed to large-scale instrumental and orchestral works that require the resources alluded to by Ní Chuinn. Another marginalising factor Ní Chuinn raises relates to the dissemination of works using unconventionally scored materials. She finds this can often subject a work to more scrutiny and attitudes that invalidate the composition and its composer. All these comments reveal wider issues around the provision of sufficient supports for women in music in Ireland, and as Power highlights, such uncertainty can significantly impact on women's private lives, including making decisions about raising a family.

Both Enda Bates and David Bremner provide male perspectives on the female composer's status in Ireland. Bates acknowledges the absence of fair representation of his female peers at festivals but perceives a change in attitudes, however slow. He is less positive about the general status of contemporary composers in Ireland, especially that of electroacoustic artists. Bremner reinforces the words of Andra McCartney quoted above, summing up the female composer's dilemma:

> My sense is that composers who are female are disadvantaged in terms of high-profile opportunities awarded [...] and electroacoustic music can be subject to bias for other reasons. So, a composer that falls into both categories might be doubly disadvantaged, as their work might not be accorded the status in Ireland that it is abroad. It could be that some subcategories of electroacoustic music are particularly prone to this. In Ireland it seems as if the most visible performance platforms still have not accommodated electroacoustic music, so work in this medium can be overlooked.[33]

Cleary's thoughts on the perception and reception of female composers are telling:

> It seems to be a strange time for female composers. On the one hand, we are now having conversations and speaking openly about issues

32 The National Concert Hall (NCH) programmes do not, as O'Leary contends, cater for the presentation of electroacoustic work, leaving it to DIY collectives and individual composers to curate and present works in smaller, cheaper, and sometimes less accessible or appropriate venues. Furthermore, Enda Bates argues that when deliberations around more high-profile events occur, groups such as the AIC are rarely consulted.

33 David Bremner, composer survey correspondence with author, 7 January 2018.

> regarding gender-balanced programmes and equal commissioning opportunities. On the other hand, these conversations are as a result of continuing neglect by our national institutions. We are speaking out, but as yet, nothing is happening.[34]

Her comments reflect the main issues to have emerged from composer responses: they centre on the programming, commissioning and promotion of creative work by women composers in Ireland, albeit discussion points are markedly more focused on programming issues. Cleary, like many of her female peers, intuits that opportunities were more straightforward in the past: when she embarked on her career, the creative environment seemed less polarised. She alludes to an underlying binarist division, a 'them and us' as she calls it, ascribing this separation to the onset of a transitional period where people are now beginning to acknowledge a male-oriented bias across the discipline. Unfortunately, as Cleary and Power disclose, some women have experienced resistance to discussions of parity, with several individuals refusing to concede that a problem exists. However, both appreciate the support shown by younger male peers, acknowledging that their awareness and positive attitudes towards fellow composers will aid efforts in effecting behavioural and structural changes. Sensitivity to what female composers experience is evident, for example, in Enda Bates's comments: he understands that being asked what it's like to be a 'female' composer 'must be deeply frustrating and ... meaningless'. Bremner makes the important point that 'when there is actual discrimination against women composers ... a woman composer is obliged to think of herself as such, in response to bias'. It is interesting to note that none of the respondents were comfortable with the concept of labelling, by gender, style or genre.

Notwithstanding the above supportive comments, the overriding perception of women composers is that an androcentric monopoly of the governance of organisations and the promotion of contemporary music in Ireland still exists, one that endorses male privilege and inequality. Women's feelings of exclusion in the field of contemporary composition only serve to further highlight ingrained behaviours, practices and viewpoints that stem from a tradition of patriarchy experienced across the arts sector. Patterns of interaction create norms and expectations that may impact on an artistic identity that is both generated and reinforced from within its own network.[35] Inequalities in accessing funding, securing curatorial posts, and receiving appropriate performance spaces and supports all place obstacles in the way of the female composer's artistic

34 Siobhán Cleary, composer survey correspondence with author, 25 August 2017.

35 Paul McClean, 'Culture from Networks: The Network Genesis of Culture', in *Culture in Networks* (Cambridge, 2017), pp. 89–110, at p. 89.

freedom, leaving skills and talents unexploited.[36] An unsupported creative identity becomes compromised, therefore all within the arts community in Ireland have a duty to ensure the equitable recognition and exposure of female artists. Sustained patriarchal ideologies are not only damaging and restrictive for composers and their oeuvre, but also for performers, audiences, the wider economy and historical collection of artworks.[37]

So, what does this mean for women creating electroacoustic works that identify with a niche subculture within the wider arts and culture context? Exposure is an important factor in the promotion of any artwork; unfortunately, opportunities for engaging with technologies do not always result in performances (Cleary) and, if such an occasion arises, as Ní Chuinn reflects, it may be unpaid, low status, last-minute and unsupported. The under-representation of women's music at major festivals and male-dominated organisational structures (adjudication panels and curators) are considered by female composers to be a consequence of unaddressed male privilege.[38] This has led to a general mistrust of networks, organisations and, perhaps, individuals. The frustration is palpable:

> There has never been a female composer as the main feature in a New Music Dublin or its predecessor Living Music festival. There has never been a female artistic director for any of these festivals. It has been pointed out, time and time again, but nothing ever seems to change. (Cleary)[39]

> The monopoly men have on governing boards of high-profile institutions […] in these positions, their first instinct is to programme male curators at festivals. (Comac)

> Marginalisation creates division and conflict and is very unhealthy […] More needs to be done to reach parity. (Mulvey)

36 These are just some of the findings of an EU-commissioned report, 'European Key Changes for Women in Music and Performing Arts', Patricia Adkins Chiti (ed.) (Brussels, 2014) <https://issuu.com/donnemusica/docs/european-key-changes-for-women-in-m> [accessed 11 July 2022].

37 For more on this, see McClean, 'Culture From Networks', and Chiti (ed.), 'European Key Changes'.

38 Some composers noted that, in general, men on these panels are also white and middle class.

39 Since the survey, some inroads have been made, with the New Music Dublin festival increasing its programming of works by women. The 2021 festival included two orchestral premieres by Irish female composers and a small selection of electroacoustic works, some by women. That said, electroacoustic music does not tend to be programmed as part of the larger evening concerts and works are never presented in the main concert spaces.

In discussing challenges in 'defining what "Irish" music might or might not be' (including identity, immigration and diaspora, and religious affiliation), Benjamin Dwyer acknowledges the increase in women composers in Ireland since the 1970s, noting 'a fraternity that traditionally held little or no place for women as professionals'.[40] O'Leary, however, suggests the problem stems from 'lazy programming', calling for more curiosity on the part of organisers and promoters when it comes to searching for music to perform or composers to commission. Ring concurs, suggesting clever programming supplemented by a proactive, creative marketing scheme that does not pander to audience stereotypes. While Rhona Clarke believes that gender biases are subconscious, as people will always commission or programme those within their creative circle, Rachel Ní Chuinn contends that by standing by their biases and appealing to their own sensibilities, these men are missing out on 'a wealth of different ways of making and listening to music'. Bias is inherent to all humans, but as Power indicates, acknowledgement is key: by admitting bias and examining why and how certain decisions are made, the first steps to genuine gender equality can be taken.

The demise of the popular 'Nova' programme hosted by Bernard Clarke on RTÉ Lyric FM has signalled a disquieting trend in the national broadcaster's attitude towards art music in Ireland. 'Nova' was the foremost radio outlet for promoting new music, with electroacoustic and experimental works receiving particular attention. Ní Chuinn places this decision in context, stating that there is now 'no nationally supported outlet for electroacoustic music and I think this impacts disproportionately on women composers'. Mulvey agrees: 'In the light of losing the Nova programme [...] the future for contemporary music is becoming much bleaker. This was one programme that didn't discriminate and was gender balanced.'

Exposure becomes increasingly difficult the further one moves outside of the capital, particularly when seeking an appropriate venue to present music (unless it is a specialised venue such as SARC (Sonic Arts Research Centre) in Belfast). O'Leary identifies the need for more suitable venues in which to promote electroacoustic music and feels 'it is largely up to individuals with a passion for this music to promote it'. Without adequate support structures and a nationwide mechanism for promoting concerts, however, this is unsustainable; consequently, audiences will remain small and the genre will not gain sufficient traction to win government supports. If works of electroacoustic music cannot be disseminated, how can new audiences become aware of them, or potential students and composers become incentivised to study and emulate them?

40 Dwyer, *Different Voices*, pp. 9–15, at p. 10.

Solutions

Musicologist Axel Klein argues that information is vital, education a prerequisite, and appreciation a necessity to evaluate contemporary developments in music.[41] Increased dissemination, education, discourse and critical literature are key to opening lines of conversation, addressing biases and bringing about what Comac calls 'change through innovation'.[42] She feels it is 'paramount that women take control of "historical" facts'. Power agrees: 'We need something set in stone, we need something to be catalogued.'

This points to a need for critical literature that creates a concrete and balanced awareness of what living electroacoustic musics and practices are, as opposed to what they are perceived to be. As Ring contends: 'The more people understand the music, the more appreciated it will be in the concert setting.' O'Leary agrees that audiences need to 'see that composers are "alive" and often very interesting people!' A balance must be sought: on the one hand, smaller-scale educational workshops and listening groups, discussion fora, studio internships and residencies can help introduce engaged groups to the experimental music of women, in addition to providing opportunities for younger women to build confidence as artists and performers. On the other hand, larger-scale balanced performances that more fully represent the genre should be presented to a wider audience and supported by national bodies. All of this requires intuitive programming underpinned by transparent and equality-driven processes for more diverse representation. This could transpire through blind submissions as O'Leary suggests, through equal gender representation on adjudication panels, and the introduction of female curators of new music programmes. Although Mulvey and Cleary support positive discrimination towards women, Ní Chuinn warns against tokenisms:

> I don't think 'women only' events are necessarily helpful [...] performances and dissemination of works should not ghettoise women [...] the exotification of women composers [...] does nothing to assist women in developing their practice [...] There is a current positive trend in supporting women's composition, but I fear it is also being adopted in a fashionable way and I worry that unless there are real resources put into including women on music curricula and investing in supporting women and other marginalised groups [like electroacoustic artists], it will quickly revert to the same [...] traditional networks.

41 Axel Klein, 'Roots and Directions in Twentieth-Century Irish Art Music', in Gareth Cox and Axel Klein (eds), *Irish Musical Studies 7: Irish Music in the Twentieth Century* (Dublin, 2003) pp. 168–82, at p. 170.

42 Bernadette Comac, composer survey correspondence with author, April 2010.

For this to happen, there must be a concerted and collaborative effort made by the art music community to engage in productive consultations without binarist agendas. In addition to groups like Sounding the Feminists, educational pathways and the active promotion of programmes could be examined on a national scale to ensure perceptions, curricula and practices are balanced. In the words of Maya Angelou: 'All great achievements require time.'

15

We Buried the Heteropatriarchy and Danced on its Grave: Towards a Liberation Movement for Irish Traditional Music[1]

Tes Slominski

In 2010, when the first Women and Music in Ireland conference was held at Maynooth University, the study of Irish women musicians, composers and intellectuals was not new. But it was sparse enough within both the academy and in the various performance scenes that comprise 'Irish music' that an historiography of the topic would have felt unsatisfying – enraging, even. My indignant rage about the marginalisation of women in Irish traditional music impelled me to embark on the archival research that I brought to the first Women and Music in Ireland conference. I suspect my fellow authors in this volume recognise this kind of rage – it is, after all, a rage that has fuelled women's history in a dizzying array of contexts. I believe that this rage is one of the reasons that women's history has so often been damned as 'merely recuperative': as a feeling, rage is one motivation among many that directly challenges the fallacy of 'objectivity' in historical research.

The feelings I bring to this piece are more complicated than mere rage, though. Today, I have different theoretical and personal investments in the idea of 'woman' than I had in 2010. As the feminist adage goes, 'the personal is political' – but the 'personal' is (ideally) never static, and thus neither is the 'political'. When I wrote my paper for the 2010 conference, I had been out of the closet as a lesbian for six years, but still passed as straight and relatively gender normative. Over the past decade or so – years that also mark transitions from graduate student to tenure-track professor and then to post-academic – my gender presentation has shifted along with my identity from lesbian to queer.[2] The political is also

1 This title plays on the name of a well-known jig, 'I Buried My Wife and Danced on Her Grave'.

2 Rather than proclaiming a particular set of sexual proclivities (as do 'gay'

personal, and for me, embracing a queer identity is one means of resisting both homonormativity and heteronormativity – of resisting a late capitalist biopolitics that privileges nuclear families (whether heterosexual or same-sex) in its economies, social structures and imaginations, making it very difficult for anyone to live outside this fever dream of two-ness. It is this concern with the unliveability of existing epistemologies and social structures that leads me to call for a liberation movement within Irish traditional music. Such a movement would acknowledge the inequalities and violences within the transnational scene and, vitally, in the societies that surround it – and actively address and eventually eliminate practices and institutions that oppress women, LGBTQ+ musicians, musicians of colour and others marginalised in the current status quo.

In this chapter, I use two classic feminist texts – Adrienne Rich's 'Compulsory Heterosexuality and Lesbian Experience' and Gayle Rubin's 'The Traffic in Women' – to explicate ways that the Irish traditional music scene maintains heteropatriarchal oppressions.[3] I build my arguments from an intersectional critique of both sexism and heterosexism to demonstrate that many of the forces that marginalise LGBTQ+ people are also problems for straight and gender normative women. These forces are also white supremacist, although this chapter is too brief to fully explicate that connection. I conclude by asserting that feminist activist efforts must take other oppressions into account, and I offer several practical suggestions for addressing white supremacist heteropatriarchy in the Irish traditional music scene.

Theorising Practice

Recent work has expanded our knowledge of women musicians and reframed traditional music performance positively as 'women's work' (Granville, Ní Shíocháin); it has traced the hypersexualisation of women (Cusack); and it has exposed the devastating effects of sexism and sexual harassment on women traditional musicians (Monaghan, O'Shea).[4] Work on women in Irish traditional music uses a range of methodologies –

or 'lesbian'), queer people often identify as such to resist the confines of normative, often binary ideas about gender and sexuality.

3 Adrienne Rich, 'Compulsory Heterosexuality and Lesbian Experience', *Signs*, 5 (1980), 631–60; Gayle Rubin, 'The Traffic in Women: Notes on the "Political Economy" of Sex', in Joan Wallach Scott (ed.) *Feminism and History* (New York, 1996), pp. 105–51.

4 The landmark special issue of *Ethnomusicology Ireland* in 2021 (ed. Verena Commins, Síle Denvir, Úna Monaghan and Méabh Ní Fhuartháin) and the Women in Traditional/Folk Music conference at the National University of Ireland, Galway (NUIG) in 2019 that inspired it represent a watershed moment in scholarship about women in Irish traditional music. The bibliography contains full citations of the authors mentioned here.

archival detective work, close reading of written and recorded texts, and ethnography/oral history – to build knowledge about women's experiences and historical roles in the genre. The study of gender in Irish traditional music is still quite new, and the number of women scholars of Irish traditional music has increased dramatically over the past decade. In this new area of study, work has focused on bringing the experiences of women into print, and thus into collective musical/historical consciousness. The sheer impact of sharing stories – as Úna Monaghan's respondents in '121 Stories' and the contributors to the #MiseFosta movement demonstrate – is tremendous: without such stories, we would have no sense of the breadth or depth of the problems of gender inequality in Irish traditional music.[5] To most effectively dismantle oppressive systems, however, we must also engage deeply with cultural theoretical frameworks that can help us better understand the experiences of marginalised musicians.

While it is untenable to force practice to fit within cultural/social/political theory (hereafter, 'theory'), theory can illuminate practice. In general, Irish traditional music scholarship has taken an anti-theory stance, in part because it sits uncomfortably between the subdisciplines of historical musicology and ethnomusicology. This discomfort is understandable: dismissed by the former as too 'simple', and confounded by the particular ways in which US and continental musicology have understood the role of nationalism, Irish traditional music scholarship also offers fundamental challenges to ethnomusicological paradigms that privilege the study of so-called 'non-Western' musics.[6] This disciplinary uneasiness reinforces a populist anti-intellectualism that holds that traditional music must provide a respite from incisive social commentary (a respite for whom?). These wider antipathies have engendered a noteworthy aversion to the use of theory in the study of Irish traditional music.[7] I do not insist that theory take precedence over practice, but demonstrate how theory – including well-established theory – can help

5 Úna Monaghan, '121 Stories: The Impact of Gender on Participation in Irish Traditional Music', *Ethnomusicology Ireland*, 7 (2021), 17–32.

6 Ireland's position in relation to British imperialism and the outsized role of the US academy may explain some reluctance towards theory, and methodologies from outside Ireland can prove hegemonic, homophobic and counter-productive to research on Irish traditional music and dance, as Nic Gareiss and Aileen Dillane discuss in 'The Lion, the Witch, and the Closet: Heteronormative Institutional Research and the Queering of "Traditions"', in Gregory Barz and William Cheng (eds), *Queering the Field* (New York, 2020), pp. 235–56.

7 A recent example of antipathy towards cultural theory in the study of Irish traditional music appears in Martin Dowling's review of Jessie Cawley's book in *The Journal of Music*, 10 August 2021 <https://journalofmusic.com/focus/ways-talking-and-thinking-about-irish-traditional-music> [accessed 10 September 2021].

us better understand lived experience and identify gaps in scholarship and activism.

By now, the concept of intersectionality has gained wide currency in critical race studies and gender studies, as well as in some corners of music and sound studies, but is seldom used as a framework for considering Irish traditional music. As introduced by Black legal scholar Kimberlé Crenshaw, the concept of intersectionality holds that categories of identity are interdependent, and that exclusions and violences accumulate for those who inhabit multiple marginalised categories of race, sexuality, gender, disability, etc.[8] Considering Irish traditional music intersectionally can expose realms of Irish musicking that most Irish music scholarship and practice have long rendered invisible. After all, the Irish traditional music's centre of gravity has historically been understood as white, male, heterosexual, cisgendered, ethnically Irish, settled and (in the past century) functionally middle class.[9] A commitment to intersectional analysis and practice requires that any work towards women's equality must also consider the oppressions of LGBTQ+, BIPOC (Black, indigenous and people of colour), Travellers, disabled people, those with tenuous immigration status, etc.

Irish traditional music can, should and does engage a diverse set of players, listeners and thinkers – and this engagement calls for theoretical understanding to ground both scholarship and activism. In this chapter, I continue my previous work on gender, sexuality and race by considering the effects of Adrienne Rich's concept of 'compulsory heterosexuality' and Gayle Rubin's 'the traffic in women' on all marginalised participants in Irish traditional music, including heterosexual and cisgendered white women. I use theory to show aspects of the Irish traditional music scene that have gone largely unexamined – and by using older theory (both articles were published in the 1970s), I demonstrate that (a) problems identified decades ago are not yet completely solved; and (b) that an aversion to cultural/social/political theory in the study of Irish traditional music means that we have missed opportunities over the past fifty years to adapt feminist, queer and other genres of theory to understand inequities in Irish music making.

Both Rich and Rubin illuminate the economic imperatives and the social norms that shape women's experience in sex/gender systems that rely on metaphors and realities of reproduction to shape or control social behaviour. Irish traditional music is one such system.[10] Embedded in an

8 Kimberlé Crenshaw, 'Demarginalizing the Intersection of Race and Sex: A Black Feminist Critique of Antidiscrimination Doctrine, Feminist Theory and Antiracist Politics', *University of Chicago Legal Forum*, 1, (1989), 139–67.

9 'Cisgender' describes an individual whose gender matches the one assigned at birth.

10 I discuss reproductive metaphors in Irish traditional music in 'Taming

intensely patriarchal society, historically tied to ethnic nationalism, and built on oral/aural transmission (often from older to younger generations), Irish traditional music has historically been a male-identified setting in which the activities of women have been prescribed, proscribed or erased. 'Gender trouble' persists in Irish traditional music, as pushback against individuals, research projects and organisations demonstrates.[11] As theorists whose work led women's studies to address gender more broadly, Rich and Rubin are apt choices to invoke now, when the moment is right – or perhaps a bit overdue – to consider gender in Irish music rather than just the activities of women.[12]

Compulsory Heterosexuality, or, Piping Was Never So Gay

In 'Compulsory Heterosexuality and Lesbian Experience', Rich calls for the examination of heterosexuality as a political institution – a 'beachhead of male dominance'.[13] She argues that the erasure or marginalisation of lesbian experience obscures the social, political and economic forces that constrain all women. Furthermore, theories that understand women's heterosexuality as 'natural' conceal intricate and powerful patriarchal and capitalist structures designed to uphold male dominance. Rich cites cross-cultural attempts to control or remove women who resist or find themselves outside normative heterosexual arrangements – spinsters, widows and women who engage in unsanctioned sexual relationships who, for example, have been the targets of various witch-hunts over the centuries.[14] By the same token, describing lesbian experience as a mere 'lifestyle' trivialises the effort required to resist compulsory heterosexuality in a context that pours its governmental, cultural and affective resources into maintaining binary and reproductively heterosexual social structures.[15]

"the Tradition Bear": Reflections on Gender, Sexuality, and Race in the Transmission of Irish Traditional Music', *Ethnomusicology Ireland,* 7 (2021), 8–16.

11 Monaghan ('121 Stories', pp. 28–9) quotes several extremely negative survey responses from men.

12 Work on masculinities in Irish traditional music and dance is currently limited, though notable exceptions include Sean Williams and Lillis Ó Laoire's *Bright Star of the West: Joe Heaney, Irish Song-Man* (New York, 2016) and Nic Gareiss's 'Light in My Loafers: Thoughts on Queer Irish Dancestry', *Our Steps* (2020). See also Helen Lawlor, Chapter 5, this volume.

13 Rich, 'Compulsory Heterosexuality', p. 633.

14 Rich, 'Compulsory Heterosexuality', p. 633.

15 Rich, 'Compulsory Heterosexuality', p. 652. While important, legislation in favor of same-sex marriage nonetheless maintains normative social structures. For a more expansive representation of queer liberation beyond

In the Irish traditional music scene, the almost complete absence of lesbians and other non-male-identified people who engage solely in sexual relationships with each other is not a strange accident.[16] It is the result of a sex/gender system that privileges male contributions while channelling all participants' expression of gender and sexuality into a handful of 'acceptable' modes. These two forces work together, as the increasing presence of white, cisgendered and openly gay men in the scene demonstrates. Although gay men in the scene have endured harassment because of their sexuality, they remain intelligible in the scene as cisgendered men. Because they tend to conform to accepted modes of masculinity in their body language, sartorial choices and adherence to social codes, they enjoy the privilege of masculinity (and whiteness) despite resisting compulsory heterosexuality. For men in Irish traditional music in the 2020s, gender and its performance appear to outweigh sexuality in determining inclusion in or exclusion from the scene's centre.[17] An anecdote from flute player Augie Fairchild, a transgender American man, supports this conclusion: he describes the contrast between the harassment he endured as a butch lesbian before transition and the male privilege he now enjoys, even though he is in a relationship with another man.[18]

Although more work on masculinities in Irish traditional music (especially in instrumental music) is needed, my aim is to investigate the ways gender normativity constrains women and gender-nonconforming people of all sexualities through discourse and practice. In the following paragraphs, I trace how gender norms manifest in the Irish traditional music scene, and then outline some of their implications for women, nonbinary and gender nonconforming people. For those who adhere to them relatively easily, social norms are understood as 'natural' and even 'timeless' rather than as structures defined by time, place and personnel that contain experience and limit possibilities. In *Trad Nation*, I wrote about how the nationalist movement of the early twentieth century shaped norms of 'appropriate' behaviour for women and made space for

homonormative marriage, see Ryan Conrad (ed.), *Against Marriage: Queer Revolution, Not Mere Inclusion* (Oakland, CA, 2014).

16 Rich's article reflects the terminology of the 1970s, when 'lesbian' may have felt more expansive in the absence of other words to describe the nuances of gender and sexuality. 'Lesbian' is now one identity among many, and in some circles connotes an anti-queer, anti-trans orientation. Here, I attempt to balance current understandings of 'lesbian' with Rich's original use of the word, which I also retain partly to reflect a more general lack of awareness around nonbinary and gender nonconforming identities: in the policing of gender, how one is read is how one is policed.

17 Judith Butler's *Gender Trouble: Feminism and the Subversion of Identity* (New York, 1989) is the foundational text on gender performativity.

18 Augie Fairchild, LGBTQ+ Panel Discussion, 18 June 2021, Celtic Junction Arts Centre, St Paul, MN.

women traditional musicians to perform publicly.[19] These opportunities for women arose in part because women were symbolically linked with the Irish nation through gendered personifications of Ireland, including Erin, Hibernia and Mother Ireland. Women were also responsible for reproducing the Irish population – for bearing ethnically Irish children and then teaching them the songs, music, dances and handicrafts that distinguished Ireland from other nations culturally. Once Ireland won its independence, women's public performance no longer needed to broadcast Ireland's cultural distinction. Instead, the Irish Constitution of 1937 stated that women's place was in the home – still bearing Irish children and sometimes teaching them music and dance, but usually outside the public eye.

Although larger social, religious and political forces dictate many of the norms that shape the Irish traditional music scene, the scene itself maintains social norms that establish it as overwhelmingly heteronormative and beholden to rigid gender binaries. For example, tune titles reflect the male gaze and reinforce the categories established by pre-independence personifications of Ireland as a woman. In tune titles as well as in nationalist and Catholic ideologies, women must be either maidens, wives or mothers – all subject positions understood in relation to men. This connection is not surprising: many of the tunes at the centre of the repertoire were collected and published in the early twentieth century. In a genre that privileges its connections with the past, naming conventions for newer tunes also draw from these collections.[20] Tune names that reflect other ways of being a woman have little chance of overtaking tune titles such as 'Maid at the Spinning Wheel', 'London Lasses', 'The Pretty Girls of the Village', 'The Mother and Child Reel', etc. The few tune names that gesture towards alternative femininities or arrangements that resist compulsory reproductive heterosexuality are negative, including 'I Won't Be a Nun!', 'The Growling Old Woman' and 'Hag with the Money'.[21]

The male gaze is inescapable: who is meant to 'cherish the ladies' or to find Peg, Maggie Morrissey, the girls of Mayo, Kate or Anne 'pretty' or 'bonny'? I am quite certain that these women – and the women musicians who play these tunes – are not meant to be appreciating each other![22]

19 Tes Slominski, *Trad Nation: Gender, Sexuality, and Race in Irish Traditional Music* (Middletown, CT, 2020).

20 Francis O'Neill's early twentieth-century collections remain the gold-standard source for tunes.

21 This theme also emerges in the '121 Stories' Úna Monaghan has collected (see especially pp. 21 and 24), where women report the use of 'belligerent' and 'battle-axe' to describe confident, assertive women.

22 Lesbian sexuality seems to still be unspeakable in Irish traditional music contexts: even Karan Casey's article in *Ethnomusicology Ireland,* which discusses her song 'Down in the Glen', does not identify early twentieth-century

Judging from the sneering laughter that frequently arises at mention of 'The Choice Wife' – also known as 'An Phís Fhliuch' and, famously, 'The Wet Quim' – female sexuality is both dirty and exists solely for men's consumption rather than for women's pleasure.[23] As someone who believes that people should enjoy as much consensual sex (of whatever configuration) as they and their partner(s) wish, my critique here is not against talking about or having sex. Instead, it is about the male control of sexual discourse and agency within the Irish traditional music scene and the larger culture. The ways male musicians talk about tunes are not inconsequential: they are a means of exerting control, as are retorts such as 'It's just a joke!' But for whom is a joke funny? Jokes illuminate foundational cultural inequities, and research demonstrates that 'disparagement humour' contributes to higher social tolerance for discrimination against members of groups targeted by such humour.[24] In other words, sexist jokes normalise sexism.

The proliferation of 'wife' tunes and the striking absence of 'husband' tunes simultaneously enforces heterosexual union while ensuring that all agency remains with men.[25] Common tune pairings also foreground binary heterosexuality, including 'The Duke of Leinster', which is almost always played with 'The Duke of Leinster's Wife' ('The Ladies' Pantalettes'). As with other sets Michael Coleman recorded, these two tunes appear together frequently in sessions – but seldom as 'The Duke of Leinster'/'The Ladies' Pantalettes', which could suggest a different set of possibilities for our dear duke! Though less commonly recorded, 'Man of the House' and 'Woman of the House', and 'If There Weren't Any Women in the World' and 'If There Weren't Any Men in the World', also sometimes turn up together in sessions. These pairings are notable because they are based less on musical flow than on their titles. While

revolutionaries Julia Grenan and Elizabeth O'Farrell as devoted and passionate lovers. The song lyrics do not shy away from the two women's relationship but, oddly, the journal article does.

23 The Chieftains recorded the tune as 'The Wet Quim' on *Chieftains 2* (1969). Discussion on the Chiff and Fipple online forum replicates the joking that happens frequently in sessions (Chiff and Fipple, 'O'Farrell's Welcome to Limerick'.

24 Thomas E. Ford et al., 'Effects of Exposure to Sexist Humor on Perceptions of Normative Tolerance of Sexism', *European Journal of Social Psychology,* 31 (2001), 677–91. For more on 'disparagement humour' and social norms, see Ford, 'Psychology Behind the Unfunny Consequences of Jokes that Denigrate', *The Conversation,* 6 September 2016 <https://theconversation.com/psychology-behind-the-unfunny-consequences-of-jokes-that-denigrate-63855> [accessed 10 September 2021].

25 See Alan Ng's extensive database of Irish tunes at www.irishtune.info. While tunes generally shy away from overt violence against women, they are not entirely absent from the repertoire, as with the tune/song 'Kitty Lie Over'.

this handful of heteronormative tune sets is relatively inconsequential, it reinforces a pattern of compulsory heterosexuality. This pattern emerges much more visibly in the prevalence of heterosexual couples in the Irish traditional music scene and in the enduring terminology (and policing) of 'gents' and 'ladies' in set and céilí dancing.

The social validation of heterosexual couples is even more powerful than discourse in establishing and maintaining norms of compulsory heterosexuality within the Irish traditional music scene. These norms also surface in the immense value placed on the generational (parent-to-child) transfer of knowledge and the enduring expectation that all women must aspire to motherhood. In a heteropatriarchal system that continues to assign childcare duties to women, this expectation also perpetuates what fiddler Bernadette McCarthy calls 'the disappearing act' – the tendency of women to leave the scene either temporarily or permanently when they have children. Ironically, the children of women musicians who have curtailed their own musical participation sometimes appear on 'next generation' stages at festivals – stages that showcase normative heterosexuality alongside the enticing fantasy of hereditary talent, whatever the gender, sexuality or family circumstances of the children and teenagers on stage.

In considering the power of normative social structures, it is useful to dissociate behaviour – for example, sexuality – from the institutions and social practices that structure the expression of that behaviour. Here, I am not interested in policing the behaviour of heterosexual couples or suggesting that heterosexual relationships are solely instruments of negative control. After all, the proliferation of musical couples is one result of increased access for women and enables more women access to the scene. And as an often all-consuming hobby, participation in the scene provides opportunities for dating and marriage that potentially allow both partners to continue playing. Indeed, many LGBTQ+ musicians wish for more dating options within the scene – but while the number of cisgendered gay men appears to be increasing in Irish traditional music, the number of woman-identified, trans and non-binary/gender-nonconforming musicians in the scene remains strikingly low. An informal tally suggests that the traditional music scene includes proportionally fewer LGBTQ+ musicians than the presence of LGBTQ+ people in the general population of either Ireland or the United States would lead us to expect.

The near-absence of openly LGBTQ+ musicians in the Irish traditional music scene demonstrates the power of compulsory heterosexuality and indicates that despite claims of 'tolerance' and several welcoming local scenes, the Irish traditional music scene as a whole has not yet established itself as an entirely accepting or safe place for non-normative musicians.[26]

26 See Tes Slominski, 'Queer as Trad: LGBTQ Performers and Irish Traditional

LGBTQ+ people (like women and musicians of colour) still must attempt to gauge the safety of any new context – a thought process that can be exhausting and ontologically damaging, and which may partially account for the low numbers of LGBTQ+ and/or BIPOC musicians in the scene. Even in more tolerant or even accepting local environments, the safety of women, LGBTQ+ musicians and musicians of colour is never guaranteed in an entrenched white supremacist heteropatriarchy. Here, I share part of my own story to illustrate the potential costs of having to choose between participation and having one's identity accepted.

As a young musician bouncing between Ireland and the East Coast of the United States in the 1990s and early 2000s, I determined that it was not safe to come out in the Irish music scene. I feared that coming out would jeopardise my ability to participate in a genre I was passionately attached to, and decided that being accepted in the traditional music scene was far more important than exploring my queer sexuality. How did I come to these conclusions? Over a decade of musical experiences in Ireland and the United States, I had witnessed (and, I confess, occasionally participated in) countless jokes at the expense of actual or suspected gay people. I had seen the repeated enactment of stereotypical gay gestures at tune names like 'Strike the Gay Harp' and 'Never Was Piping So Gay'. I had heard rumours about women seen too often in each other's company and had witnessed the great lengths men went to in order to try to establish that they were not gay. Most of all, I could not find any openly LGBTQ+ adult role models in the Irish traditional music community to demonstrate that it would be safe to come out. When I did come out around 2005, it was with much trepidation and a strong support network outside the traditional music scene. While I hoped to be able to continue to participate, I was prepared to walk away. Fortunately, most (but not all) of the musicians I came out to responded with support. Perhaps not surprisingly, though, the worst sexual harassment I have experienced in the trad scene happened in Ireland after I came out, from a male musician I had come out to. This harassment, which felt like an attempt to 'correct' my sexual orientation and return me to my 'proper' place in the sex/gender system, simultaneously connected me with countless heterosexual women who have experienced sexual harassment in the scene and demonstrated the danger of openly violating the norms of compulsory heterosexuality.[27]

Music in the United States', in Fred Maus and Sheila Whiteley (eds), *The Oxford Handbook of Music and Queerness* (New York, 2021) and *Trad Nation.*

27 Bisexual invisibility remains an issue in the Irish traditional music scene. In a world without compulsory heterosexuality, bisexual people might be more visible instead of hidden in heterosexual relationships.

The Traffic in Women: A Crooked Road to Gender Equality?

Compulsory heterosexuality is one result of a sex/gender system that implicitly views women as objects of exchange between men. In 'The Traffic in Women', feminist anthropologist Gayle Rubin describes the ways that patriarchal societies cast women as objects of exchange between men. For example, the custom of a father giving away his daughter in marriage is one manifestation of a system of exchange that goes much deeper. By identifying common structural features in social customs (including marriage) cross-culturally, Rubin exposes the gender imbalances that characterise heteropatriarchies. In a heteropatriarchal system, the women with the greatest exchange value are women of childbearing age who exemplify cultural ideals (including beauty/appearance, 'proper' behaviour, wealth, etc.) – women who seem best positioned to reproduce and uphold the system. In such a system, a woman's exchange value decreases over time, no matter what her other qualities.

This description of the exchange of women in heteropatriarchal societies may seem shocking or outdated at first. Women in both Ireland and the United States do enjoy a great deal more agency than they did in 1975 when Rubin wrote this essay. But again, I encourage us to think about social structures and the ways they shape individual action. Specifically, how does the 'traffic in women' continue to affect women and queer musicians in the Irish trad scene? Monaghan's groundbreaking work provides considerable evidence that, unlike male musicians, women musicians' access to the scene and experiences within it are often contingent on their relationships (or lack thereof) with men:

> Respondents reported that relationship status matters for women in Irish traditional music: 'the woman in a band or duo *must* be 'the girlfriend' (#89). Other examples included being consistently described in relation to their musician boyfriend rather than in their own right, or being accepted or welcomed into a group at first because of their relationship with a male musician.[28]

During the years I dated men, I had similar experiences. One memorable instance demonstrates vividly the operation of 'the traffic in women'. While I was living in Ireland in the early 2000s, a male musician very badly wanted me to date him but did not know I was seeing someone else. He was gentlemanly but relentless in his attempts until the man I was dating pulled him aside to tell him I was not 'on the market'. All my attempts to stave off his attentions were irrelevant – what mattered was that I already 'belonged' to another man. Having a father (or brother) in the trad scene may also convey benefits, including increased access and some protection from harassment (see Kearney, Chapter 6, this

[28] Monaghan, '121 Stories', p. 26.

volume, on Josephine Keegan).[29] The existence of such benefits reinforces the idea that women only have a place in the traditional music scene because of their relationships with men. The 1985 album *Fathers and Daughters* illustrates this point: the album's concept relies primarily on women's positions as daughters rather than recognising them for their independent skill as musicians.[30]

In contrast, women without male connections have often been sidelined. In *Trad Nation*, I tell the story of Mary Kilcar, an unmarried middle-aged flute player in rural Galway in the early twentieth century. The only reason we know anything about her is because the fiddle player Lucy Farr cites her as an influence. In an interview, Lucy related a conversation in which Mary pointed out how lucky Lucy was to be a member of a musical family whose father held house parties. Mary felt that she would not be welcome at musical gatherings as a single woman. In the 1920s and 1930s, pubs had not yet become places for playing trad, but even if they had been, Mary would have been similarly excluded: in some places in rural Ireland, women were strongly discouraged from entering pubs as late as the 1980s. Thus, women like Mary Kilcar who did not participate in the 'traffic in women' have tended to disappear from the historical record of Irish traditional music. Would even a woman musician of Julia Clifford's stature be as well known if she had not been Denis Murphy's sister or Pádraig O'Keeffe's student?[31]

The patriarchal exchange of women affects women musicians in very clear ways, but what about queer musicians? For women and nonbinary musicians who excuse ourselves from the 'traffic in women', our 'exchange value' in the sex/gender system of heteropatriarchy is either confusing or nonexistent. This refusal can lead to exclusion or harassment in some situations and a sense of freedom in others. I hesitate to speak for gay and queer men, but extrapolating from Rubin's theoretical framework (and based on my own observations), men's value does not derive from exchange – it is seen as intrinsic and the result of a man's actions, skills and accomplishments. Therefore, gay male traditional musicians do not 'lose value' in removing themselves from the traffic in women. Instead, they sometimes seem to lose the connection and camaraderie among men that is a byproduct of participating in heterosexual dating, marriage and other ways that straight men bond. In a scene where musical sound is just one part of the social glue, this loss can be profound.

29 Monaghan, '121 Stories', p. 22. Jessie Cawley writes more extensively about the role of family interactions in 'Musical Development in Irish Traditional Music: An Exploration of Family Influences', *Ethnomusicology Ireland*, 2 (2013), 95–111.

30 *Fathers and Daughters*, Shanachie 79054 (1985).

31 For a longer discussion of Mary Kilcar, Lucy Farr and Julia Clifford, see Slominski, *Trad Nation*.

Conclusion: A New Road

In this chapter, I have begun to demonstrate how the enduring problem of heteropatriarchy – represented through discussions of compulsory heterosexuality and 'the traffic in women' – continues to oppress women, LGBTQ+, and nonbinary and gender nonconforming musicians. Because these problems reflect realities and anxieties around reproduction and the control of reproductive structures (and control of the meaning of reproductive structures!), addressing them is also vital in confronting exclusions based on race and ethnicity. The problem of oppression is overwhelming, and a commitment to intersectionality presents a challenge: how do we actively seek to understand how oppression and privilege operate on multiple axes while working towards improvement on only one or two of those axes? Foregrounding the intersectional nature of identity is vital for raising awareness and building meaningful coalitions in activist work, but grassroots groups often form with focused goals and limited resources. While some focus is necessary, a blinkered focus can dismiss or exclude – or perhaps worse, pay mere lip service to – broader but related needs and goals. Today's feminist activist movements in Irish music face the challenge of engaging with heterosexism, racism and classism in real ways in a larger social context that has not quite figured out how to do so, either. But until they engage across multiple axes of identity, they will remain incomplete and will do unwitting damage – even more so if they claim to be intersectional but their personnel and activities do not support this claim.

Fighting oppression should be everyone's job, and an important part of this work is examining the role of social norms in perpetuating oppressive systems. Compulsory heterosexuality, sexism and racism are not natural, inevitable or inflexible, but beginning to dismantle them takes considerable self-reflection, open conversations with people from a range of backgrounds, numerous missteps and false starts, and a tremendous amount of effort. As someone who has spent the past decade pointing out exclusions and inequities in the music I so dearly love, I am often asked how to begin this work. I do not have all the answers, of course, and look towards other liberation movements for cues on how to proceed. I have adapted the following practical recommendations from other queer and anti-racist liberation movements:[32]

32 Resources on social justice activism abound. See, for example, Peggy McIntosh's classic 'White Privilege: Unpacking the Invisible Knapsack', *Peace and Freedom* (1989), 10–12; the unattributed 'Unpacking the Invisible Knapsack II', which addresses straight and cisgender privilege; and Ibram X. Kendi's 'The Anti-Racist Reading List: 38 Books for Those Open to Changing Themselves, and Their World', *The Atlantic*, 12 February 2019. Though these movements and sources are US-based, many of their lessons are portable.

1. Ask queer musicians (or women, or musicians of colour) how you can help; do not just assume you know what will be most helpful. This is especially important with queer musicians, who may not be fully out in the trad scene or in other areas of their lives, including with their families of origin.
2. If you see something, say something. If you witness harassment or violence, do not just turn away. If you are worried about your own safety, join forces with another musician or ask a member of the bar or festival staff to intervene.
3. If a queer musician (or woman musician, or musician of colour) tells you about a negative experience, believe them. Do not try to explain it away with phrases like 'I'm sure he didn't mean it that way', or 'You're so sensitive – you need to be more thick-skinned', or 'She's really actually a very nice person'. Listen, acknowledge and ask how you can help.
4. Consider whether your efforts to include women, LGBTQ+ and BIPOC musicians reinforce exclusions through tokenisation. Ensure that you approach potential participants as musicians (or dancers or scholars) rather than as embodiments of difference. If your organisation or group only approaches women for input or gigs during Women's History Month or Nollaig na mBan, LGBTQ+ people during Pride Month (June), or people of colour during Kwanzaa, Chinese New Year or other such times, this is a signal that tokenisation is occurring. Instead, ask yourself and your colleagues what true representation might look like and then begin laying the groundwork for it.

Most important, seek to understand the community norms that exist in your local scene and consider them carefully. Work deliberately and collaboratively to eliminate the damaging ones, reinforce the ones you want to keep, and establish new ones. It takes discomfort, time, effort and community agreement to establish or change norms, but this is the only way to create lasting change. Strive to empower each other to speak out when your new, more inclusive norms are being violated, consider repercussions for repeat offenders and find ways to reinforce positive behaviours. As long as social norms reinforce the acceptability of sexism, heterosexism, racism and other exclusions, those exclusions will continue needlessly and in perpetuity. But they need not do so – after all, the goal of any good liberation movement is just that: liberation.

BIBLIOGRAPHY

Manuscript and archival collections

BBC Written Archives Centre C124:

John Reith, 30 April 1926. 'Women in the BBC'

A.C. to D.G. (full names unknown), November 1928

Bibliothek der MdW, Universität für Musik und darstellende Kunst Wien:

Nachlass Mary Dickinson-Auner. (Estate of Mary Dickinson-Auner, Library of the University of Music and Performing Arts, Vienna)

Cáirde na Cruite Archive:

Letter from Eibhlín Ní Chathailriabhaigh on behalf of Sheila Larchet Cuthbert to composers, 6 July 1966

Cambridge University Library, Joseph Needham Papers

Needham, Alicia Adelaide, 'A Daughter of Music' (unpublished autobiography), item A.97

Needham, Alicia Adelaide, diaries, item A.99

Irish Architectural Archive, Conolly Letters, 94/136/1:

Louisa Conolly to Thomas Conolly, 3 April 1772

Louisa Conolly to Sarah Bunbury, 29 January 1772

Irish Architectural Archive, Conolly Letters, 94/136/2:

Louisa Conolly to Sarah Napier, 2 February 1785

Louisa Conolly to Sarah Napier, 6 January 1785

National Library of Ireland, Feis Ceoil Association Records:

Feis Ceoil Syllabus (1945), p. 51, MS Collection List 92, MS 40228/6

Feis Ceoil Programmes, 1897–1917, NLI, IR 780941, f2

National Library of Ireland, Lennox/Fitzgerald/Campbell Papers:

Journal of Lady Sophia Fitzgerald, 19 February 1783 (MS 35,012/1)

Royal College of Music Library Collections, Society of Women Musicians Archive:

Annual Report, RCM, SWM/No. 175 Box 4

University of Limerick Special Collections, Glin Papers, P1/22:

Diary of William Massy Blennerhassett, 26 August and 7 September 1867

Printed primary sources

The Gentleman's and Citizen's Almanack (Dublin, 1777)
The Gentleman's Almanack (1806)
Freeman's Journal, 31 May 1811
Freeman's Journal, 13 January 1815
Dublin, 'The Ancient Concerts', *The Musical World*, 22 March 1838, p. 202
Dublin Almanac and General Register of Ireland (Dublin, 1838)
Saunders Newsletter, 11 May 1843
Freeman's Journal, 20 February 1849
Freeman's Journal, 17 October 1856
'Ferdinand Glover', *Leinster Express*, 25 October 1856, p. 3
'Ferdinand Glover', *Freeman's Journal*, 4 August 1857, p. 3
'Theatrical Chit Chat', *Reynold's Newspaper*, 1 May 1859, p. 9
Freeman's Journal, 20 May 1862
'Waterford Mechanics' Institute', *Munster Express*, 14 December 1867, p. 2
'Harp Music by Emilie Glover', *The Musical World*, 45, 12 October 1867, p. 704
'Harp Recital', *Freeman's Journal*, 17 March 1868, p. 3
'Exhibition Palace', *Freeman's Journal*, 23 June 1868, p. 1
'Music', *The Nation*, 17 July 1869, p. 12
'Harp and Vocal Concerts', *Freeman's Journal*, 3 December 1869, p. 1
'Fine Arts and Music', *The Tablet*, 18 February 1871, p. 212
'Professor Glover's New Cantata', *Morning Advertiser*, 16 March 1871, p. 3
'Musical Gossip', *The Athenaeum*, 25 March 1871, p. 377
'Public Amusements', *Freeman's Journal*, 16 May 1871, p. 1
'A Grand Musical Festival', *The Morning Post*, 8 February 1872, p. 4
'Tonight – Irish Ballad Programme', *The Standard*, 16 March 1872, p. 1
'Fashion and Varieties', *Freeman's Journal*, 23 July 1872, p. 2
'Philharmonic Society', *Irish Times*, 1 February 1873, p. 3
'Public Amusements', *Irish Times*, 21 July 1873, p. 1
'The Oratorio of St. Patrick at Tara', *Freeman's Journal*, 11 March 1874, p. 3
'New Music', *The Era*, 15 March 1874, p. 12
'New Music', *Irish Times*, 9 April 1874, p. 2
'The British Musical and Dramatic Institute', *The Era*, 19 April 1874, p. 9
'Gossip: Music and the Drama', *Irish Times*, 17 January 1876, p. 6
'Public Amusements', *Liverpool Mercury*, 28 September 1876, p. 1
Irish Times, 11 November 1876
'Morning Concert in the Ulster Hall', *Belfast News-Letter*, 9 March 1877, p. 3
'Notes on News', *Irish Times*, 21 May 1879, p. 4
'Mrs Mackey, Harpist', *Cork Examiner*, 17 February 1881, p. 1
'Public Amusements', *Irish Times*, 23 April 1881, p. 2
'Death of Mrs Mackey', *Irish Times*, 8 June 1883, p. 5
'School, Lesson, &c.', *Freeman's Journal*, 14 January 1886, p. 1

'The Opening of the New Leinster Hall', *Irish Times*, 1 November 1886, p. 5
Freeman's Journal, 9, 12, 25 March 1892, 23 February 1893
'Madame Emilie Grey', *Irish Times*, 29 November 1897, p. 6
Patterson, Annie, 'Alicia Adelaide Needham', *Weekly Irish Times*, 9 June 1900, p. 4
Weekly Irish Times, 17 November 1900
'St Patrick at Tara', *Irish Times*, 24 November 1902, p. 8
Patterson, Annie, 'Coronation Music A Triumph for Ireland', *Weekly Irish Times*, 21 June 1907, p. 7
Patterson, Annie, 'The Interpretation of Irish Music', *Journal of the Ivernian Society*, 2: 5 (1909), pp. 31–42
——, 'Alicia Adelaide Needham', *The Leader*, xxiii (1916) no. 14, pp. 227–8
——, 'Late Professor Glover', *Freeman's Journal*, 6 November 1917, p. 2
'Miss Coghill's Pianoforte Recital', *Irish Times*, 23 February 1920, p. 3
The Irish Times, 25 October 1922, p. 6
'Miss Rhoda Coghill's Recital', *Irish Times*, 20 March 1925, p. 3
'Pianoforte Recital: Miss Rhoda Coghill', *Irish Times*, 21 November 1925, p. 9
'Broadcasting Today', *Irish Times*, 4 April 1927, p. 3
'Obligato', 'Tchaikovsky's Piano Concerto: His Use of Russian Themes', *Irish Times*, 24 October 1927, p. 4
'An Irishman's Diary', *Irish Times*, 27 January 1928, p. 4
'Eminent Musician to Visit Dublin', *Irish Times*, 13 July 1929, p. 6
'Sir Thomas Beecham in Dublin: To-Day's Orchestral Concert', *Irish Times*, 14 September 1929, p. 5
'Fugato', 'A Vocal Interlude', *Sunday Independent*, 15 September 1929, p. 9
The Irish Times, 26 June 1933, p. 6
The British Medical Journal, 14 October 1933, p. 716
'King Edward's Coronation Song Prize-Winner', *Irish Times*, 21 December 1934, p. 8
Letter from E.M. Clark, *Irish Times*, 9 January 1939, p. 7
'New Music', *Musical Times*, 83 (1942), 114–15
'Symphony Concerts', *Irish Times*, 24 September 1942, p. 3
'Feis Ceoil Awards', *Irish Times*, 10 May 1944, p. 3
'Symphony Concert', *Irish Times*, 22 May 1944, p. 3
'Symphony Concert', *Irish Times*, 15 January 1945, p. 2
'Radio Éireann Orchestra', *Irish Times*, 9 December 1946, p. 5
'Concert', *Irish Press*, 4 August 1947, p. 10
'Ensemble's Fine Recital', *Irish Independent*, 24 January 1953, p. 7
'Enjoyable Concert', *Irish Examiner*, 14 February 1953, p. 8
'Quidnunc', 'An Irishman's Diary', *Irish Times*, 5 January 1955, p. 6
'Harpers' Festival in Israel', *Irish Press*, 17 February 1959, p. 10
'Students' Enjoyable Recital', *Irish Independent*, 28 June 1960, p. 7

'Intimate Occasion', *Irish Press*, 13 June 1961, p. 7
'Wigmore Hall Recital by Gráinne Yeats', *Irish Times*, 18 March 1966, p. 8
'Grainne Yeats in Sligo', *Irish Times*, 24 August 1968, p. 12
G.O. Simms, 'James Henthorn Todd', *Hermathena*, 109 (1969), 5–23
'Girls from Jacobs Picket Award Winners Banquet', *Irish Independent*, 11 December 1970, p. 13
Sheila Walsh and Noel Conway, 'Press Diary: Two Smashing Parties', *Irish Press*, 11 December 1970, p. 13
'An Irishman's Diary', *Irish Times*, 12 December 1970, p. 11
'The Irish Harp for Players', *Irish Times*, 3 December 1975, p. 8
'Traditional Fiddler Who Opposed the Purists', *Irish Times*, 2 April 2005, p. 12

Secondary sources

Adkins Chiti, Patricia (ed.), *European Key Changes for Women and the Performing Arts* (Brussels European Parliament, 2014)
Andrews, Maggie, *Domesticating the Airwaves: Broadcasting, Domesticity and Femininity* (London and New York, 2012)
Bardon, Jonathan, *Hallelujah: The Story of a Musical Genius and the City that Brought His Masterpiece to Life* (Dublin, 2015)
Barger, Judith, *Elizabeth Stirling and the Musical Life of Female Organists in Nineteenth-Century England* (Aldershot, 2007)
Barnard, Toby, *Brought to Book: Print in Ireland 1680–1784* (Dublin, 2017)
Beausang, Ita, 'Echoes of the Lied: Women's Vocal Repertoire in Nineteenth-Century Ireland', in Aisling Kenny and Susan Wollenberg (eds), *Women and the Nineteenth-Century Lied* (Farnham, 2015), pp. 251–8
——, 'Levey Family', in White and Boydell (eds), *Encyclopaedia* (Dublin, 2013), vol. 2, pp. 587–8
Beausang, Ita and Séamas de Barra, *Ina Boyle, 1889–1967: A Composer's Life* (Cork, 2018)
Berberova, Nina, trans. Marian Schwartz, *The Accompanist* (New York, 1988)
Biasutti, Michele, 'Pedagogical Applications of Cognitive Research on Musical Improvisation', *Frontiers in Psychology*, 6 (2015) <https://www.frontiersin.org/articles/10.3389/fpsyg.2015.00614/full> [accessed 22 August 2017]
Born, Georgina and Kyle Devine, 'Gender Creativity and Education in Digital Musics and Sound Art', *Contemporary Music Review*, 35 (2016), 1–20
Bowen, Elizabeth, *The Last September* (London, 1929)
Bowers, Jane and Judith Tick (eds) *Women Making Music: The Western Art Tradition 1150–1951* (London, 1986)

Boydell, Brian, 'Music 1700–1850', in T.W. Moody and W.E. Vaughan (eds), *A New History of Ireland vol.4: Eighteenth-Century Ireland 1691–1800* (Oxford, 1986), pp. 568–628
——, *Rotunda Music in Eighteenth-Century Dublin* (Dublin, 1992)
Breathnach, Breandán, *Folk Music and Dances of Ireland* (Dublin, 1971)
Buckley, Ann, 'Musical Instruments in Ireland from the Ninth to the Fourteenth Centuries', in Dáibhí Ó Cróinín (ed.), *A New History of Ireland I: Prehistoric and Early Ireland* (Oxford, 2005), pp. 760–2
——, 'Music in Ireland to *c*.1500', in Gerard Gillen and Harry White (eds), *Irish Musical Studies 1: Musicology in Ireland* (Dublin, 1990), pp. 13–57
Bunting, Edward, *A General Collection of the Ancient Irish Music* (Dublin, 1796)
——, *A General Collection of the Ancient Music of Ireland* (London, 1809)
——, *The Ancient Music of Ireland* (Dublin, 1840)
Burke, Joe, 'He Made Great Music ... He Made History!' *Honouring Sean McGuire and Kilcogy Musicians* (Dublin, 2012), pp. 8–9
Burke-Plunkett, Elizabeth, Lady Fingall, *Seventy Years Young: Memories of Elizabeth, Countess of Fingall* (Dublin, 1991)
Burn, Sarah M., 'Ina Boyle', in Stanley Sadie and John Tyrrell (eds), *New Grove Dictionary of Music and Musicians* (New York, 2001), vol. 4, p. 167
Burns, Debra Brubaker, Anita Jackson and Connie Arrau Sturm, 'Contributions of Selected British and American Women to Piano Pedagogy and Performance', *The International Alliance for Women in Music Journal*, 8 (2002), 1–9
Campbell, Mary, *Lady Morgan: The Life and Times of Sydney Owenson* (London, 1988)
Carson, Ciarán, *Pocket Guide to Irish Traditional Music* (Belfast, 1986)
Carter, Angela, *The Sadeian Woman: An Exercise in Cultural History* (London, 1979)
Casey, Karan, 'Truth is the Daughter of Time', *Ethnomusicology Ireland*, 7 (2021), 139–46
Cawley, Jessica, 'Musical Development in Irish Traditional Music: An Exploration of Family Influences', *Ethnomusicology Ireland*, 2 (2013), 95–111
Ceol Camlocha, *Aoibhneas na Bealtaine: The Sweets of May: The Céilí Band Era, Music & Dance of South Armagh* (Armagh, 2008)
Ceribašić, Naila, 'Social Canons Inherited from the Past: Women Players of Folk Music Instruments in Croatia', *Studia Musicologica Academiae Scientiarum Hungaricae*, T. 44, Fasc. 1/2 (2003), 147–57
Chadwick Simon, 'The Cloyne Harp', *Early Gaelic Harp* <http//wwwearlygaelicharp.info/harps/cloyne/htm> [accessed 11 July 2022]
——, 'The Early Irish Harp', in *Early Music*, 36 (2008), 521–31

Chiff and Fipple, 'O'Farrell's Welcome to Limerick' <http://forums.chiffandfipple.com/viewtopic.php?t=14026> [accessed 29 August 2021]

Citron, Marcia, *Gender and the Musical Canon* (Cambridge, New York and Melbourne, 1993)

——, *Gender and the Musical Canon*, 2nd edn (Chicago, 2000)

——, 'Gender, Professionalism and the Musical Canon', *The Journal of Musicology*, 8

(1990), 102–17

——, *The Letters of Fanny Hensel to Felix Mendelssohn* (New York, 1987)

Collins, Derek, 'Music in Dublin', in Richard Pine and Charles Acton (eds), *To Talent Alone: The Royal Irish Academy of Music, 1848–1998* (Dublin, 1998)

Collins, Nick and Julio d'Escriván (eds), *The Cambridge Companion to Electronic Music*, 2nd edn (Cambridge, 2017)

Collins, Paul, 'John William Glover', in White and Boydell (eds), *Encyclopaedia*, vol. 1, p. 435

Commins, Adèle, 'Royal Choral Institute', in White and Boydell (eds) *Encyclopaedia*, vol. 2, p. 897

Colum, Padraic, *A Treasury of Irish Folklore* (New York, 1967)

Commins, Verena, Síle Denver, Úna Monaghan and Méabh Ní Fhuartháin, 'Editors' Preface', *Ethnomusicology Ireland*, 7 (2021), 1–2

Conrad, Ryan (ed.) *Against Marriage: Queer Revolution, Not Mere Inclusion* (Oakland, CA, 2014)

Crawford, Elizabeth, *The Women's Suffrage Movement, A Reference Guide 1866–1928* (London, 1999)

Crenshaw, Kimberlé, 'Demarginalizing the Intersection of Race and Sex: A Black Feminist Critique of Antidiscrimination Doctrine, Feminist Theory and Antiracist Politics', *University of Chicago Legal Forum*, 1 (1989), 139–67

Cullen, Emily, 'Tempering the Stereotypes of Irishness Abroad: The Irish Harp as Golden Lever of Temperance and Respectability', in Joyce and Lawlor (eds), *Harp Studies*, pp. 105–20

Cunningham, John '"Irish Harpers are Excellent, and their Solemn Music is Much Liked of Strangers": The Irish Harp in Non-Irish Contexts in the Seventeenth Century', in Barra Boydell and Kerry Houston (eds), *Irish Musical Studies 10: Music, Ireland and the Seventeenth Century* (Dublin, 2009), pp. 62–81

Curtis, Bernard, *Centenary of the Cork School of Music: Progress of the School, 1878–1978* (Cork, 1978)

Curtis, P.J., *Notes from the Heart: A Celebration of Traditional Irish Music* (Dublin, 1994)

Curwen, John, *Musical Theory*, 10th edn (London, 1879)

Curwen, Mrs A.J., *The Teacher's Guide to Mrs Curwen's Pianoforte Method*, 16th edn (London, 1913)

Cusack, Joanne, 'Commercialisation, Celtic and Women in Irish Traditional Music', *Ethnomusicology Ireland*, 7 (2021), 94–109

De Paor, Paschall, 'The Development of Electroacoustic Music in Ireland', in Gareth Cox and Axel Klein (eds), *Irish Musical Studies 7: Irish Music in the Twentieth Century* (Dublin, 2003), pp. 29–38

Delany Mrs, *The Autobiography and Correspondence of Mary Granville, Mrs Delany*, ed. Lady Llanover (London, 1861)

Dervan, Michael, 'Gender Balance Not Being Taken Seriously by Irish Music Organisations', *Irish Times*, 18 July 2018 <https://www.irishtimes.com/culture/music/gender-balance-not-being-taken-seriously-by-irish-music-organisations-1.3567760> [accessed 11 July 2022]

——, (ed.), *The Invisible Art: A Century of Music in Ireland, 1916–2016* (Dublin, 2016)

Dignam, Barbara Jillian, 'Chasing Sonic Threads: Disentangling the Electroacoustic Tapestry of Ireland', *TEMPO*, 71: 281 (2017), 5–26

——, 'Electro-acoustic Music', in White and Boydell (eds), *Encyclopaedia*, vol. 1, pp. 348–50

Dillane, Aileen, 'Raging Mother Ireland: Faith, Fury and Feminism in the Voice and Songs of Sinéad O'Connor', in Áine Mangaoang, John O'Flynn and Lonán Ó Briain (eds), *Made in Ireland: Studies in Popular Music* (New York and Abingdon, 2021), pp. 54–66

Dillane, Aileen and Nic Gareiss, 'The Lion, the Witch, and the Closet: Heteronormative Institutional Research and the Queering of "Traditions"', in Gregory Barz and William Cheng (eds), *Queering the Field* (New York, 2020), pp. 235–56

Dixon, W.H. (ed.), *Lady Morgan's Memoirs: Autobiography Diaries and Correspondence*, 3 vols (London: 1862)

Doctor, Jennifer, *The BBC and Ultra-Modern Music, 1922–1936: Shaping a Nation's Tastes* (Cambridge, 1999)

——, 'Intersecting Circles: The Early Years of Elizabeth Maconchy, Elizabeth Lutyens and Grace Williams', *Women and Music: A Journal of Gender and Culture*, 2 (1998), 90–109

——, '"Working for her Own Salvation"; Vaughan Williams as Teacher of Elizabeth Maconchy, Grace Williams and Ina Boyle', in Lewis Foreman (ed.), *Vaughan Williams In Perspective* (London, 1998)

Dooley, Paul, 'The Harp in the Time of Giraldus', in Joyce and Lawlor (eds), *Harp Studies*, pp. 21–58

Dooley, Terence, *The Big Houses and Landed Estates of Ireland: A Research Guide* (Dublin, 2007)

Dooley, Terence and Christopher Ridgway (eds), *The Country House and the Great War: Irish and British Experience* (Dublin, 2016)

——, *The Irish Country House: Its Past, Present and Future* (Dublin, 2011)

Dooley, Terence, Maeve O'Riordan and Christopher Ridgway (eds), *Women and the Country House in Ireland and Britain* (Dublin, 2018)

Dowling, Martin, 'Ways of Talking and Thinking About Irish Traditional Music', *The Journal of Music*, 10 August 2021 <https://journalofmusic.com/focus/ways-talking-and-thinking-about-irish-traditional-music> [accessed 9 September 2021]

Dreyfus, Kay, Margarethe Engelhardt-Krajanek and Barbara Kühnen, *Die Geige war ihr Leben. Drei Frauen im Portrait* (Strasshof, 2000)

Dwyer, Benjamin, *Different Voices: Irish Music and Music in Ireland* (Hofheim, 2014)

Ellis, Katharine, 'Female Pianists and Their Male Critics in Nineteenth-Century Paris', *Journal of the American Musicological Society*, 50 (1997), 353–85

Elson, Arthur and Everett E. Truette, *Woman's Work in Music* (Boston, 1903)

Emmerson, Simon, *The Language of Electroacoustic Music* (New York, 1986)

Emmerson, Simon and Denis Smalley, 'Electronic-Acoustic Music', *Grove Music Online* <http://www.oxfordmusiconline.com> [accessed 16 March 2021]

Emmerson, Simon and Leigh Landy (eds), *Expanding the Horizon of Electroacoustic Music Analysis* (Cambridge, 2016)

Erwin, Max, 'Wet Hot Kranichstein Summer: Darmstadt 2016', *TEMPO*, 71 (2017), 87–91

Essex, John, *The Young Ladies' Conduct, or, Rules for Education* (London, 1722), p. 8

Evene, Christine Eyene (ed.), *Sounds Like Her: Gender, Sound Art & Sonic Cultures* (Nottingham, 2019)

Every Woman's Encyclopaedia (London, n.d.) [1910]

Fairchild, Augie, LGBTQ+ Panel Discussion, Celtic Junction Arts Centre, St Paul, MN, 18 June 2021

Fegan, Tommy, 'Josephine Keegan', in Fintan Vallely (ed), *Companion to Irish Traditional Music* (Cork, 2011)

Fitzgerald, Mark, 'Composing Equality', *Enclave Review*, 16 (2018) <http://enclavereview.org/composing-equality/> [accessed 16 March 2021]

Fitzgerald, Elizabeth, *Lord Kildare's Grand Tour: The Letters of William Fitzgerald, 1766–1769* (Cork, 2000)

Fitzgibbon, Gerald, '"College Choral" 1837–1987', *Hermathema: A Trinity College Dublin Review* (1988)

Fleischmann, Aloys (ed.), *Music in Ireland: A Symposium* (Oxford, 1952)

——, 'Music and Society 1850–1921' in W.E. Vaughan (ed.), *A New History of Ireland under the Union VI; Ireland under the Union II, 1870–1921* (Oxford, 2010)

Flood, W.H. Grattan, *A History of Irish Music* (Dublin, 1906; Shannon, 1970 [1913])

Ford, Thomas E., 'Psychology Behind the Unfunny Consequences of Jokes that Denigrate', *The Conversation*, 6 September 2016 <https://

theconversation.com/psychology-behind-the-unfunny-consequences-of-jokes-that-denigrate-63855> [accessed 28 August 2021]

Ford, Thomas E., Erin R. Wentzel and Joli Lorion, 'Effects of Exposure to Sexist Humor on Perceptions of Normative Tolerance of Sexism', *European Journal of Social Psychology*, 31 (2001) 677–91

Friedan, Betty, *The Feminine Mystique* (London, 2010)

Gareiss, Nic, 'Light in My Loafers: Thoughts on Queer Irish Dancestry', *Our Steps* (2020) <https://www.our-steps.com/dialogue/light-in-my-loafers-thoughts-on-queer-irish-dancestry> [accessed 31 August 2021]

Gilbert, John T., *A History of the City of Dublin*, 3 vols (1854–59) (Shannon,1972)

Gillett, Paula, *Musical Women in England, 1870–1914: Encroaching on All Man's Privileges* (London, 2000)

Gleeson, Sinéad (ed.), *The Long Gaze Back* (Dublin, 2016)

Glover, James Mackey, *Hims Ancient and Modern* (London, 1926)

——, *Jimmy Glover and his Friends* (London, 1913)

——, *Jimmy Glover, His Book* (London, 1911)

Granville, Aoife, 'Pioneering Women Flute Players', *Drawing from the Well* video series, Irish Traditional Music Archive, 2021 <https://youtu.be/LaGg30oBJQY> [accessed 31 August 2021]

Gregory, Lady Augusta, *Complete Irish Mythology* (London, 1994)

Greer, Germaine, *The Obstacle Race: The Fortunes of Women Painters and Their Works* (New York, 1979)

Hall, Reg, *A Few Good Tunes: A History of Irish Music and Dance in London, 1800–1980 and Beyond* (London, 2016)

Halstead, Jill, *The Woman Composer: Creativity and the Gendered Politics of Musical Composition* (Aldershot, 1997)

Hamer, Laura (ed.), *The Cambridge Companion to Women in Music since 1900* (Cambridge, 2021)

Hammond, Philip, 'Woman of Parts, Joan Trimble', *Sound Post*, 5 (1984–5), 24–7

Hanlon, Ann-Marie, '"Missing from the Record": Zrazy and Women's Music in Ireland', in Áine Mangaoang, John O'Flynn and Lonán Ó Briain (eds), *Made in Ireland: Studies in Popular Music* (New York and Abingdon, 2021), pp. 67–78

Harden, Geoff, 'The Passing of the Fiddler', *Fortnight*, 436 (2005), 10–11

Heymann, Ann, 'Harp', in Fintan Vallely (ed.), *The Companion to Irish Traditional Music* (Cork, 1999), pp. 175–81

——, 'Three Iconic Gaelic Harp Pieces', in Joyce and Lawlor (eds), *Harp Studies*, pp. 184–208

Hildebrandt, Dieter, *Pianoforte: A Social History of the Piano*, trans. Harriet Goodman (New York, 1988)

Hinkle-Turner, Elizabeth, *Women Composers and Music Technology in the United States Crossing the Line* (Abingdon, 2006)

Hoffmann, Freiea, 'Dickenson-Auner, Auner, Mary (Frances Dorothée), geb. Dickenson' (2012) <https://www.sophie-drinker-institut.de/dickenson-auner-mary> [accessed 11 July 2022]

Hogan, Ita, *Anglo-Irish Music, 1780–1830* (Cork, 1966)

Holmes, Thom, *Electronic and Experimental Music: Pioneers in Technology and Composition* (London, 2002)

Horton, Peter, 'William Sterndale Bennett, Composer and Pianist', in Therese Ellsworth and Susan Wollenberg (eds), *The Piano in Nineteenth-Century British Culture: Instruments, Performers and Repertoire* (Aldershot, 2007), pp. 119–48

Humphries, Charles and William Smith, *Music Publishing in the British Isles* (Oxford, 1970)

Hunt, Edmund Hunt, '"A National School of Music Such as the World has Never Seen": Re-appropriating the Early Twentieth Century into a Chronology of Irish Composition', in Mark Fitzgerald and John O'Flynn (eds), *Music and Identity in Ireland and Beyond* (Aldershot, 2014), pp. 53–68

Hurrell, Nancy, *The Egan Irish Harps: Tradition, Patrons and Players* (Dublin, 2019)

——, 'The Royal Portable Harp by John Egan', *Journal of the Historical Harp Society*, Spring (2003) <https://citeseerx.ist.psu.edu/viewdoc/download?doi=10.1.1.518.6536&rep=rep1&type=pdf> [accessed 9 August 2013]

Jamieson, Alasdair, *Music in Northern Ireland: Two Major Figures: Havelock Nelson (1917–1996) and Joan Trimble (1915–2000)* (Claygate, 2017)

Johnstone, H. Diack and Roger Fiske (eds), *The Blackwell History of Music in Britain vol.4: The Eighteenth Century* (Oxford, 1990)

Joyce, James, 'The Dead', *Dubliners* (London, 1956)

Joyce, Sandra and Helen Lawlor (eds), *Harp Studies* (Dublin, 2016)

Keegan, Josephine, *The Keegan Tunes, Cuid a Dó* (Mullaghbawn, 2006)

——, 'There Will Never Be Another One!', in *Honouring Seán McGuire and Kilcogy Musicians* (Dublin, 2012), p. 7

Kelly, Linda, *Ireland's Minstrel: A Life of Tom Moore: Poet, Patriot and Byron's Friend* (London, 2006)

Kendi, Ibram X., 'The Anti-Racist Reading List: 38 Books for Those Open to Changing Themselves, and Their World', *The Atlantic*, 12 February 2019 <https://www.theatlantic.com/ideas/archive/2019/02/antiracist-syllabus-governor-ralph-northam/582580/> [accessed 31 August 2021]

Klein, Axel, 'Irish Composers and Foreign Education: A Study of Influence', in Patrick F. Devine and Harry White (eds), *Irish Musical Studies 4: The Maynooth International Musicology Conference 1995* (Dublin, 1996), pp. 271–84

Klein, Axel, 'Dickenson-Auner, Mary', in White and Boydell (eds), *Encyclopaedia* (Dublin, 2013), vol. 1, p. 297

——, 'Roots and Directions in Twentieth-Century Irish Art Music', in

Gareth Cox and Axel Klein (eds), *Irish Musical Studies 7: Irish Music in the Twentieth Century* (Dublin, 2003), pp. 168–82
——, 'Stage-Irish, or the National in Irish Opera, 1780–1925', *The Opera Quarterly*, 21 (2005), 27–67
Kloos, Franziska Kloos, *Jennifer Walshe. Spiel mit Indentitäten* (Hofheim, 2017)
Koskoff, Ellen, *A Feminist Ethnomusicology: Writings on Music and Gender* (Urbana, Chicago and Springfield, 2014)
Krassen, Miles Krassen, 'An Analysis of a Jean Carignan Record', *Canadian Journal for Traditional Music* (1974), 40–4
Lady Granville (ed.), *The Autobiography and Correspondence of Mary Granville (Mrs Delany)*, 3 vols (London, 1861)
Laffey, Seán Laffey, 'Review: Josephine Keegan, *The Fairy Bridges*', *Irish Music Magazine*, 13: 5 (2007), 65
Landy, Leigh, *Understanding the Art of Sound Organisation* (Cambridge, 2007)
Larchet Cuthbert, Sheila, *The Irish Harp Book: A Tutor and Companion* (Cork and Dublin, 1975)
Lawlor, Helen, *Irish Harping, 1900–2010* (Dublin, 2012)
Leppert, Richard, *Music and Image: Domesticity, Ideology, and Socio-Cultural Formation in Music Eighteenth-Century England* (Cambridge, 1993)
Levey [O'Shaughnessy], Richard Michael, *Collection of the Dance Music of Ireland* (Part I, Dublin, 1858; Part II, Dublin, 1868)
Licata Thomas (ed.) *Electroacoustic Music: Analytical Perspectives* (London, 2007)
Long, Siobhán, 'The Best of Seamus Tansey: Traditional Irish Flute', *Irish Times*, 5 February 2010
Luddy, Maria, *Women and Philanthropy in Nineteenth-Century Ireland* (Cambridge, 1995)
——, *Women in Ireland, 1800–1918: A Documentary History* (Cork, 1995)
Lynch, Charles, 'The Concert Pianist in Ireland', in Aloys Fleischmann (ed.), *Music in Ireland: A Symposium* (Cork, 1952)
MacConnell, Seán, 'Death of Fiddler Sean McGuire', *Irish Times*, 25 March 2005, p. 8
MacGabhann, Antóin, 'Seán McGuire', in *Honouring Seán McGuire and Kilcogy Musicians* (Dublin, 2012), pp. 13–16
Mackey, James [Jimmy Glover], *Hims Ancient and Modern* (London, 1926)
——, *Jimmy Glover and his Friends* (London, 1913)
——, *Jimmy Glover, His Book* (London, 1911)
Maconchy, Elizabeth, *Ina Boyle: An Appreciation, with a Select List of her Music* (Dublin, 1974)
MacPherson, D.A.J., *Women of the Irish Nation: Gender, Culture, and Irish Identity, 1890–1914* (London, 2012)
Manning, Peter, *Electronic and Computer Music*, 4th edn (Oxford, 2013)

Mathias, Rhiannon (ed.), *The Routledge Handbook of Women's Work in Music* (Abingdon, 2021)

McCarthy, Patricia, *Life in the Country House in Georgian Ireland* (Yale, 2016)

McCartney, Andra, 'Gender, Genre and Electroacoustic Soundmaking Practices', *Intersections Canadian Journal of Music*, 26 (2006), 20–48

——, 'Inventing Images and Contesting Gender in Thinking about Electroacoustic Music', *Leonardo Music Journal*, 5 (1995) 57–66

McClary, Susan, *Feminine Endings*, 2nd edn (Minneapolis, 2002)

McClean, Paul, *Culture from the Networks: The Network Genesis of Culture* (Cambridge, 1917)

McCrann, Aibhlín, 'Mercedes Garvey – A Tribute', *An Cruitire*, 12 (2013), 4–5

McGinley, Martin, 'A Presence Wherever Folk Music is Played on the Fiddle', *Treoir*, 2005

McGuire, Seán and Josephine Keegan, *Irish Tunes by the 100* (Lincolnshire, 1975)

McIntosh, Peggy, 'White Privilege: Unpacking the Invisible Knapsack', *Peace and Freedom* (1989), 10–12

McLaughlin, Noel and Joanna Braniff, 'Irish Lady Sings the Blues: History, Identity, and Ottilie Patterson', in Áine Mangaoang, John O'Flynn and Lonán Ó Briain (eds), *Made in Ireland: Studies in Popular Music* (New York and Abingdon, 2021), pp. 97–108

Metzelaar, Helen, 'Women and "Kraakgeluiden": The Participation of Women Improvisers in the Dutch Electronic Music Scene', *Organised Sound*, 9 (2004), 199–206

Moloney, Colette, *The Irish Music Manuscripts of Edward Bunting* (Dublin, 2000)

Monaghan, Úna, '121 Stories: The Impact of Gender on Participation in Irish Traditional Music', *Ethnomusicology Ireland*, 7 (2021), 17–32

Mullaney-Dignam, Karol, 'Expanding the Narrative: Public History, Music, and the Irish Country House', in Jeanice Brooks, Matthew Stephens and Wiebke Thormählen (eds), *Sound Heritage: Making Music Matter in Historic Houses* (London, 2022)

——, '"French Horns Playing at Every Meal" Music at Carton', in Patrick Cosgrove, Terence Dooley and Karol Mullaney-Dignam (eds), *Aspects of Irish Aristocratic Life: Essays on the Fitzgeralds and Carton House* (Dublin, 2014), pp. 92–105

——, 'Irish Country House Collections: Birr Castle Co. Offaly', *Brio: Journal of the International Association of Music Libraries UK and Ireland*, 49 (2012), 23–36

——, *Music and Dancing at Castletown, Co. Kildare, 1759–1821* (Dublin, 2011)

——, '"Spacious and Splendid" Music, Dancing and Social Life at Glin

Castle 1781–1854', *Irish Architectural and Decorative Studies*, 14 (2012), 16–37

——, 'Useless and Extravagant? The Consumption of Music in the Irish Country House', in Andrew Hann and Jon Stobart (eds), *The Country House: Material Culture and Consumption* (English Heritage, 2016), pp. 156–65

Murphy, Gerard, *Saga and Myth in Ancient Ireland* (Cork, 1971)

Murphy, Michael 'The Musical Press in Nineteenth-Century Ireland', in Michael Murphy and Jan Smaczny (eds), *Irish Musical Studies 9: Music in Nineteenth-Century Ireland* (Dublin, 2007), pp. 257–60

Myers, Kevin, 'An Irishman's Diary', *The Irish Times*, 12 October 2000 <https://www.irishtimes.com/opinion/an-irishman-s-diary-1.1108484> [accessed 11 July 2022]

Nachmanovich, Stephen, *Fair Play: Improvisation in Life and Arts* (New York, 1990)

Nettl, Bruno, *The Study of Ethnomusicology: Thirty-One Issues and Concepts* (Illinois, 2005)

Neul-Bates, Carol, *Women in Music: An Anthology of Source Readings from the Middle Ages to the Present* (New York, 1982)

Ng, Alan, 'Irish Traditional Music Tune Index' <www.irishtune.info> [accessed 14 August 2021]

Ní Ghríofa, Doireann, *A Ghost in the Throat* (Dublin, 2020)

Ní Shíocháin, Tríona, 'Mother Music: Socially Embedded Creative Practice and the Marketisation of Irish Traditional Music', *Ethnomusicology Ireland*, 7 (2021), 110–22

Nic Chartaigh, Deirdre, 'Cia an Saoi le Seinntear an Chruit: A Bardic Poem to a Harper', in Helen Lawlor and Sandra Joyce (eds), *Harp Studies II: World Harp Traditions* (Dublin, forthcoming)

Ó Canainn, Tomás, *Traditional Music in Ireland* (Cork, 1993)

Ó Cathaoir, Eva, *Soldiers of Liberty: A Study of Fenianism 1858–1908* (Dublin, 2018)

O'Céirín, Kit and Cyril, *Women of Ireland: A Biographic Dictionary* (Galway, 1996)

O'Connor, Jennifer, 'Robinson [née Arthur], Fanny', in White and Boydell (eds), *Encyclopaedia*, vol. 2, p. 888

——, *Robinson, Fanny* < www.sophie-drinker-institut.de> [accessed 9 July 2021]

Ó Cróinín, Dáibhí (ed.) *A New History of Ireland I: Prehistoric and Early Ireland* (Oxford, 2005)

O'Curry, Eugene, *On the Manners and Customs of the Ancient Irish* (Dublin, 1873)

O'Donnell, Mary Louise, 'The Bengal Subscription: Patriotism, Patronage and the Perpetuation of the Irish Harp Tradition in the Early Nineteenth Century', in Joyce and Lawlor (eds), *Harp Studies*, pp. 75–89

——, 'Heavenly Harps, Heavenly Cloths', in Barra Boydell and Barbara Dignam (eds), *Brian Boydell Centenary Essays* (Dublin, 2021), pp. 121–36

——, 'In the Shadow of Bochsa: A Study of Three Foreign Virtuoso Pedal Harpists in Dublin (*c.*1850–1900)', in Helen Lawlor and Sandra Joyce (eds), *Harp Studies II: World Harp Traditions* (Dublin, forthcoming)

——, *Ireland's Harp: The Shaping of Ireland's Identity, c.1770–1880* (Dublin, 2014)

——, 'Owen Lloyd and the De-Anglicization of the Irish Harp', *Éire-Ireland*, 48 (Fall/Winter 2013), 155–75

O'Donnell, Teresa, 'Gráinne Yeats: A Modern-Day Bard Remembered', *The American Harp Journal* (Summer, 2014), 15–21

O'Farrell, Anne-Marie, 'The Chromatic Development of the Lever Harp: Mechanism, Resulting Technique and Repertoire', in Joyce and Lawlor (eds), *Harp Studies*, pp. 209–38

Ó hAlmhuráin, Gearóid, *Pocket History of Irish Traditional Music* (Dublin, 1997)

——, *A Short History of Irish Traditional Music* (Dublin, 1994)

Ó hÓgáin, Dáithí *The Lore of Ireland, An Encyclopaedia of Myth, Legend and Romance* (Cork, 2006)

O'Leary, Jane, '25 Years of Concorde', *Journal of Music in Ireland*, 1 September 2001, <https://journalofmusic.com/focus/25-years-concorde> [accessed 11 July 2022]

——, 'Contemporary Music in Ireland: Developments in the Past Twenty Years', in Devine and White (eds), *Irish Musical Studies 4*, pp. 285–95

——, 'Outside the Pale of Musical Civilisation', *The Irish Composer* (1988), 24–6 <https://www.aicnewmusicjournal.com/articles/archives-women-composers-outside-pale-musical-civilisation> [accessed 11 July 2022]

——, 'Women Composers in Ireland: A Changing Profile', *International Alliance for Women in Music Journal* (October 1996), 16–17

O'Neill, Francis, *Irish Minstrels and Musicians* (Cork, 1987)

O'Neill, Francis, and James O'Neill, *O'Neill's Music of Ireland: Eighteen Hundred and Fifty Melodies* (Pacific, MO, 1996)

Ó Riada, Seán, *Our Musical Heritage* (Portlaoise, 1982)

O'Riordan, Maeve, *Women of the Country House in Ireland, 1860–1914* (Liverpool, 2018)

O'Shea, Helen, '"Good man, Mary!" Women Musicians and the Fraternity of Irish Traditional Music, *Journal of Gender Studies*, 17 (2008), 55–70

——, *The Making of Irish Traditional Music* (Cork, 2008)

Owenson, Sydney [Lady Morgan], *The Wild Irish Girl: A National Tale* (London, 1806)

Parakilas, James et al., 'The Piano Lesson', in Parakilas (ed.), *Piano Roles: A New History of the Piano* (New Haven and London, 2002), pp. 110–49

Parakilas James, Mark Tucker and Michael Chanan, '1920s to 2000: New

Voices from an Old Impersonator', in Parakilas (ed.), *Piano Roles: A New History of the Piano* (New Haven and London, 2002), pp. 288–320

Patterson, Annie W., Preface, *Six Gaelic Songs* (London, 1896)

Pine, Richard, *Music and Broadcasting in Ireland* (Dublin, 2005)

Pine, Richard and Charles Acton (eds) *To Talent Alone: The Royal Irish Academy of Music 1848–1998* (Dublin, 1998)

Quinn, Toner, *Report on the Harping Tradition in Ireland* (Dublin, 2015)

Ramón, Marta, *A Provisional Dictator: James Stephens and the Fenian Movement* (Dublin, 2007)

Redhead, Lauren, '"New Music" as Patriarchal Category', in Catherine Haworth and Lisa Colton (eds), *Gender, Age and Musical Creativity* (Abingdon, 2015), pp. 171–84

Reich, Nancy B., *Clara Schumann: The Artist and the Woman*, rev. edn (London, 2001)

——, 'European Composers and Musicians ca1800–1900', in Karin Pendle (ed.), *Women and Music* (Indiana, 1991), pp. 97–122

Rempel, Ursula M., 'The Complete Female: Musical "Accomplishment" in the Late Eighteenth Century', *Man and Nature/L'homme et la Nature*, 8 (1989), 39–48

Rensch, Roslyn, *Harps and Harpists*, 2nd edn (Bloomington and Indianapolis, 2007)

Rich, Adrienne, 'Compulsory Heterosexuality and Lesbian Experience', *Signs*, 5 (1980), 631–60

Rimmer, Joan, *The Irish Harp*, 3rd edn (Dublin, 1984)

Rodgers, Tara, *Pink Noises: Women on Electronic Music and Sound* (London, 2010)

Rodmell, Paul, 'MacDonnell, Hercules Henry Graves', in White and Boydell (eds), *Encyclopaedia* (Dublin, 2013), vol. 2, p. 613

Rohr, Deborah, *The Careers of British Musicians 1750–1850* (Cambridge, 2001)

Rubin, Gayle, 'The Traffic in Women: Notes on the "Political Economy" of Sex', in Joan Wallach Scott (ed.) *Feminism and History* (New York, 1996)

Rupprecht, Carol Schreier, 'Third International Congress on Women', *Signs*, 104 (1988), 235–42

Saunders, James, 'Interview with Jennifer Walshe', in James Saunders (ed), *The Ashgate Research Companion to Experimental Music* (Abingdon, 2017), pp. 343–51

Schiller, Rena, 'Gender and Traditional Irish Music', in Fintan Vallely et al. (eds), *Crosbhealach an Cheoil: The Crossroads Conference* (Dublin, 1996), pp. 200–5

Sherlock, Roger, 'My Memories of Seán McGuire', in *Honouring Sean McGuire and Kilcogy Musicians* (Dublin, 2012), p. 18

Slominski, Tes, 'Queer as Trad: LGBTQ Performers and Irish Traditional

Music in the United States', in, Fred Maus and Sheila Whiteley (eds), *The Oxford Handbook of Music and Queerness* (New York, 2021)
——, 'Taming "the Tradition Bear": Reflections on Gender, Sexuality, and Race in the Transmission of Irish Traditional Music', *Ethnomusicology Ireland*, 7 (2021), 8–16
——, *Trad Nation: Gender, Sexuality, and Race in Irish Traditional Music* (Middletown, 2020)
Smith, Gillian, *Olive Smith: A Musical Visionary* (Bantry, 2019)
Smither, Howard E., *A History of the Oratorio, vol. 4: The Oratorio in the Nineteenth and Twentieth Centuries* (Chapel Hill and London, 2000), pp. 255–6
Solie, Ruth A., 'Feminism', *Grove Dictionary of Music and Musicians Online* <www.oxfordmusiconline> [accessed 6 January 2021]
Stanley, Roy, *In Tune: A Millennium of Music in Trinity College Library* (Dublin, 2013)
Strunk, Oliver, *Source Readings in Music History* (London, 1952)
Sullivan, Mairéid, *Celtic Women in Music: A Celebration of Beauty and Sovereignty* (Ontario, 1999)
Taylor, Timothy D., *Strange Sounds Music Technology and Culture* (New York, 2001)
Thomas, John (Aptommas), *Harp Journal* (New York, 1856–60)
——, *History of the Harp* (New York, 1856–60)
Thuente, Mary Helen, 'The Origin and Significance of the Angel Harp', in Patricia A. Lynch, Joachim Fischer and Brian Coates (eds), *Back to the Present, Forward to the Past: Irish Writing and History since 1798* (Amsterdam and New York, 2006), pp. 181–208
Tick, Judith, *Ruth Crawford Seeger: A Composer's Search for American Music* (New York and London, 1997)
Tick, Judith, Margaret Ericson and Ellen Koskoff, 'Women in Music', *Oxford Music Online* <www.oxfordmusiconline> [accessed 6 January 2021]
Thorpe, Ruth, *Women, Architecture and Building in the East of Ireland, c.1790–1840* (Dublin, 2013)
Torczyner, Harry, *Magritte: Ideas and Images*, trans. Richard Millen (New York, 1979)
Trimble, Joan, 'Intermezzo, Joan Trimble', in Richard Pine and Charles Acton (eds), *To Talent Alone: The Royal Irish Academy of Music, 1848–1998* (Dublin, 1998), pp. 396–9
——, 'Joan Trimble', *Contemporary Music Review*, 11 (1994), 277–84
Vallely, Fintan and Charlie Piggott, *Blooming Meadows: The World of Irish Traditional Musicians* (Dublin, 1998)
Veblen, Thorstein, *The Theory of the Leisure Class: An Economic Study in the Evolution of Institutions* (London, 1899)

Vickery, Amanda, *The Gentleman's Daughter: Women's Lives in Georgian England* (New Haven and London, 2003)
Vignoles. Olinthus J., *Memoir of Sir Robert P. Stewart* (Dublin, 1898)
Walsh, Basil, *Catherine Hayes: The Hibernian Prima Donna* (Dublin, 2000)
Walsh, Patrick, *Castletown, Co. Kildare* (Dublin, 2007)
Ward, Margaret, *In Their Own Voice: Women and Irish Nationalism* (Cork, 2001)
Watson, Laura, 'Epitaph for a Musician: Rhoda Coghill as Pianist, Composer, and Poet', *Journal for the Society for Musicology in Ireland*, 11 (2016), 3–23
——, 'Feminist Musical Activism in Ireland (2016–21) and Feminist Musicology', *Ethnomusicology Ireland*, 8 (2022)
——, 'Sexism and the Leaving Certificate Music Syllabus', *The Journal of Music*, 25 August 2015 <https://journalofmusic.com/focus/sexism-and-leaving-cert-music-syllabus> [accessed 11 July 2022]
——, 'Sounding the Feminists: Campaigning for Institutional Change to Support Women in Music in Contemporary Ireland', in Laura Hamer and Helen J Minors (eds), *The Routledge Companion to Women and Musical Leadership: The Nineteenth Century and Beyond* (New York, 2023)
Weisner, Merry E., *Women and Gender in Early Modern Europe* (Cambridge, 2000)
White, Harry, 'The Lyre of Apollo: Thomas Moore and the Irish Harp', in Joyce and Lawlor (eds), *Harp Studies*, pp. 90–104
White, Harry and Barra Boydell (eds), *The Encyclopaedia of Music in Ireland*, 2 vols (Dublin, 2013)
Williams, Seán, *Focus: Irish Traditional Music* (London, 2010)
——, *Musics of the World* (New York, 2021)
Williams, Sean and Lillis Ó Laoire, *Bright Star of the West: Joe Heaney, Irish Song-Man* (New York, 2016)
Wingfield, Sheila, *Sun Too Fast* (London, 1974)
Woolf, Virginia, *A Room of One's Own* (London, 1945)
Wright, Christopher, *George III* (London, 2005)
Wright, David C.H., *The Associated Board of the Royal Schools of Music: A Social and Cultural History* (Woodbridge, 2013)
Yeats, Gráinne, *The Harp of Ireland: The Belfast Harpers' Festival, 1792, and the Saving of Ireland's Music by Edward Bunting* (Dublin, 1980)
——, 'The Rediscovery of Carolan', in Bernard Harris and Grattan Freyer (eds), *Integrating Tradition: The Achievement of Seán Ó Riada* (Ballina, 1981)
——, 'Some Thoughts on Irish Music', *Ceol*, 4:2 (1973), 37–50
Young, Percy M., *George Grove 1820–1900: A Biography* (London, 1980)
Zingel, Hans Joachim, *Harp Music in the Nineteenth Century* (Bloomington, 1992)

Unpublished theses

Dillane, Aileen, 'The Ivory Bridge: Piano Accompaniment on 78rpm Recorded Sources of Irish Traditional Dance Music in America *c.*1910–1945' (Unpublished MA dissertation, University of Limerick, 2000)

Doherty, Liz, 'The Paradox of the Periphery: Evolution of the Cape Breton Fiddle Tradition *c.*1928–1995' (Unpublished PhD dissertation, University of Limerick, 1996)

Dolphin, Christina, 'Reels, Heels and Glass Ceilings: Women Musicians in the Professional Sphere of Irish Traditional Music' (Unpublished MA dissertation, University of Limerick, 2013)

Doran, Caitriona, 'The Robinsons: A Nineteenth-Century Dublin Family of Musicians and their Contribution Towards Musical Life in Dublin' (Unpublished MA dissertation, Maynooth University, 1998)

Engelhardt-Krajanek, Margarethe, 'Mary Dickenson-Auner, Violinistin-Pädagogin-Komponistin, Leben und Werk' (Unpublished PhD thesis, Bergische Universität Wuppertal, 1995)

Ferris, Catherine, 'The Use of Newspapers as a Source for Musicological Research: A Case Study of Dublin Musical Life 1840–1844' (Unpublished PhD dissertation, Maynooth University, 2011)

Hall, Reg, 'Irish Music and Dance in London, 1890–1970: A Socio-Cultural History, Parts I and II' (Unpublished PhD dissertation, University of Sussex, 1994)

Kearney, Daithí, 'Towards a Regional Understanding of Irish Traditional Music' (Unpublished PhD dissertation, University College Cork, 2009)

Kehoe, Patrick Joseph, The Evolution of the Radio Eireann Symphony Orchestra 1926–41 (Unpublished PhD dissertation, TU Dublin, 2017)

McCarroll, Lisa, 'The Celtic Twilight as Reflected in the Two-Piano Works of Joan Trimble (1915–2000)' (Unpublished DMA thesis, University of Houston, 2013)

O'Connor, Jennifer, 'The Role of Women in Music in Nineteenth-Century Dublin' (Unpublished PhD dissertation, Maynooth University, 2010)

Parker, Lisa, 'Robert Prescott Stewart (1825–94): A Victorian Musician in Dublin' (Unpublished PhD dissertation, Maynooth University, 2009)

Schulte,M., 'A Study of the Piano Pedagogy of Annie Curwen: Its Correlation and Adaption with the Hungarian Method for the Instruction of Beginning Pianists and Its Implications for Modern Piano Teaching' (Unpublished MA dissertation, Catholic University of America, 1971)

Slominski, Tes, 'Music, Gender, and the Public Sphere: in Twentieth-Century Ireland' (Unpublished PhD dissertation, New York University, 2010)

Stanley, Ruth, 'Joan Trimble (1915–2000) and the Issue of her Irish Identity' (Unpublished MA dissertation, University of Limerick, 2003)

Web-based sources

Angus, Gussie, 'Violet Tulloch "The Star"' <https://boxandfiddlearchive.weebly.com/violet-tulloch.html> [accessed 1 March 2021]

Aosdána <http://aosdana.artscouncil.ie/members/> [accessed 18 June 2021]

Association of Irish Composers see <http://www.composers.ie/about> [accessed 18 June 2021]

Blue, Gregory, 'Needham, (Noël) Joseph Terence Montgomery (1900–1995)', in *Oxford Dictionary of National Biography* <https://www.oxforddnb.com/> [accessed 16 June 2021]

Composing the Island festival brochure (2016) <https://issuu.com/rtenationalsymphonyorchestra/docs/composing_island_brochure_final_pri> [accessed 11 July 2022]

Contemporary Music Centre <https://www.cmc.ie/composers> [accessed 18 June 2021]

Crowdfunder campaign for Ina Boyle < https://www.crowdfunder.co.uk/discovering-ina-boyle> [accessed 2 July 2021]

Fund:It campaign for 2nd Women and Music in Ireland Conference <https://fundit.ie/project/women-and-music-in-ireland-conference> [accessed 11 July 2022]

Internet Broadway Database <https://www.ibdb.com/broadway-show/peggy-machree-7014> [accessed 11 July 2022]

Irish National Opera schedule <https://www.irishnationalopera.ie/whats-on/current-upcoming-productions> [accessed 2 July 2021]

McCann, Kevin, 'Scottish Fiddle Playing and Its Irish Connections', *Box and Fiddle*, 19: 3 (1995) <https://boxandfiddlearchive.weebly.com/scottish-fiddle-playing-and-its-irish-connections.html> [accessed 11 July 2022]

McLaren, Nicol, 'Ronnie Cooper' <https://boxandfiddlearchive.weebly.com/ronnie-cooper-1982.html> [accessed 1 March 2021]

Musica <http://www.musicanet.org/robokopp/moore.html> [accessed 11 July 2022]

Prix Italia Archive <http://www.archive.prixitalia.rai.it/> [accessed 18 June 2021]

Sexton, Rowan, 'tête-à-tête' < https://www.mariehanlon.com/words/tete-a-tete/> [accessed 11 July 2022]

Sonic Vigil <https://www.facebook.com/SonicVigil8/?ref=page_internal> and <https:/facebook.com/Sonic-Arts-Waterford-827639897318042/> [accessed 18 June 2021]

Sounding the Feminists <https://www.soundingthefeminists.com/> [accessed 27 May 2021]

Women in Music (WiM) <http://www.womeninmusic.org.uk/history.htm> [accessed 1 July 2021]

Women in Music Proms statistics <http://www.womeninmusic.org.uk/proms10.htm> [accessed 1 July 2021]

Recordings and broadcast media

'A Piano Portrait: Fanny Robinson' presented by Una Hunt on *The Lyric Feature*, RTÉ Lyric Fm, 22 February 2013
'A Tale of Two Siblings', *The Lyric Feature*, presented by Claire Cunningham, RTÉ Lyric Fm, 8 March 2013
At Their Best: Sean McGuire and Roger Sherlock, Outlet SOLP 1008 (1971)
Ina Boyle: Orchestral Works, Dutton Vocalion, CDLX&352 (2018)
Ina Boyle Songs, Delphian, DCD34264 (2021)
Cherish the Ladies, RTÉ Radio 1, July 2006
Rhoda Coghill Talks to Ray Lynott About Her Career, RTÉ FM3, 14 October 1993
Finbarr Dwyer with Teresa McMahon, *Pure Traditional Irish Accordion Music* (also issued as *Irish Traditional Accordionist*), Outlet Label PTICD 1004 (1994)
Deborah Grimmett, *Lineage: Tracing Influence* New Classics Records (2021)
Josephine Keegan *Irish Traditional Music*, LP, Outlet SOLP1033 (1977)
——, *Irish Traditional Music: Reels, Jigs, Hornpipes, Airs*, LP, Outlet, OAS 3030 (1980)
——, *Traditional Irish Music: Reels, Jigs, Hornpipes, Airs*, LP, Outlet SOLP1040 (1980)
——, *Irish Traditional Music: Reels, Jigs, and Hornpipes*, LP, Outlet OAS 3037 (1982)
——, *Josephine Keegan*, LP, Outlet SOLP1044 (1983)
——, *The Keegan Tunes: A Selection of Traditional Irish Music Composed by Josephine Keegan* [audio recording] (Armagh, 2002)
Grainne Mulvey, *Akanos and Other Works*, Navona Records, NV5943 (2014)
Jane O'Leary, *In the Stillness of Time*, Capstone Records, CPS-8789 (2008)
Judith Ring, *Within an egg of space*, on *Contemporary Music from Ireland*, vol. 9, CMC CD09 (2009)
Lisa Rovner, *Sisters with Transistors*, narrated by Laurie Anderson (Modern Films UK, 2020)
Various artists, *Fathers and Daughters*, Shanachie Records 79054 (1985)
'Women of Note' episode on Augusta Holmès, *The Lyric Feature*, Lyric Fm, 7 September 2012

INDEX

Irish Musical Studies
Previous volumes

Titles published by Irish Academic Press

1
Musicology in Ireland
Gerard Gillen and Harry White

2
Music and the Church
Gerard Gillen and Harry White

3
Music and Irish Cultural History
Gerard Gillen and Harry White

Titles published by Four Courts Press

4
The Maynooth International Musicological Conference 1995: Selected Proceedings, Part One
Patrick F. Devine and Harry White

5
The Maynooth International Musicological Conference 1995: Selected Proceedings, Part Two
Patrick F. Devine and Harry White

6
A Historical Anthology of Irish Church Music
Gerard Gillen and Andrew Johnstone

7
Irish Music in the Twentieth Century
Gareth Cox and Axel Klein

8
Bach Studies from Dublin
Anne Leahy and Yo Tomita

9
Music in Nineteenth-Century Ireland
Michael Murphy and Jan Smaczny

10
Music, Ireland and the Seventeenth Century
Barra Boydell and Kerry Houston

11
Irish Musical Analysis
Gareth Cox and Julian Horton

12
Documents of Irish Musical History
Kerry Houston, Maria McHale and Michael Murphy

Titles Published by The Boydell Press

13
Women and Music in Ireland
Jennifer O'Connor-Madsen, Laura Watson, Ita Beausang

Lightning Source UK Ltd.
Milton Keynes UK
UKHW022009021122
411531UK00001B/2